BIBLICAL POETRY THROUGH MEDIEVAL JEWISH EYES

ADELE
BERLIN

INDIANA UNIVERSITY PRESS
BLOOMINGTON & INDIANAPOLIS

The paper used in this publication meets the minimum requirements of American National Standard for Information Sciences—Permanence of Paper for Printed Library Materials, ANSI Z39.48–1984.

∞™

Manufactured in the United States of America

Library of Congress Cataloging-in-Publication Data

Biblical poetry through medieval Jewish eyes / [translated and edited by] Adele Berlin.
p. cm. — (Indiana studies in biblical literature)
Translated from Hebrew and Judeo-Arabic.
Includes bibliographical references and index.
ISBN 0-253-31176-4 (alk. paper)
1. Hebrew poetry, Biblical—History and criticism. 2. Bible. O.T. Psalms—Criticism, interpretation, etc., Jewish—History. 3. Bible. O.T. Psalms—Criticism, interpretation, etc.—History—Middle Ages, 600–1500. I. Berlin, Adele. II. Series.
BS1430.2.B515 1991
221.6′6′0902—dc20 90-26773

1 2 3 4 5 95 94 93 92 91

For the Grandparents of Our Children

Phil Feigenbaum ז"ל
Sadie Feigenbaum ז"ל
Joseph Berlin ז"ל
ותבדל לחיים ארוכים
Etta Berlin

CONTENTS

PREFACE

At no time in *recent* history has literary theory been taken more seriously by biblical scholars or has the Bible been given more attention by literary scholars. As a result, there is now much common ground between these two disciplines. It is at the juncture of biblical and literary studies that this book has its place, for it seeks to present to members of these disciplines material that, for different reasons, should be of interest to both—namely, medieval and Renaissance Jewish writings on biblical poetry and poetic theory.

The influences on the reading of the Bible are manifold and complex, but in general they can be grouped around two poles: the pull of tradition and the attraction of contemporary ideas. Nowhere is this more evident than in the writings examined in this book. On the one hand, they form a link in the chain of traditional Jewish Bible study, and on the other hand, they are informed by and engaged with the dominant literary theories of their own times. Furthermore, certain literary theories themselves acquired a tradition within Jewish circles, and it is interesting to see both how they were preserved and how they were altered in the hands of various authors.

The writings presented here are culled from different times and places and different genres. They date from the Middle Ages and the Renaissance and were produced in three of the main centers of Jewish culture: Spain, Provence, and Italy. Some are excerpts from biblical commentaries, while others are found in historical, philosophical, grammatical, and literary treatises. They have been neglected, by and large, even by scholars of Jewish Studies; and, because most have not been translated into modern European languages, they are unknown to those who do not read Hebrew. My main purpose here is to call attention to the existence of this body of work, and to make it available in English translation. (I have relied on printed editions since I present only small excerpts of longer works and my goal is not critical editions of these works.)

My second purpose is to understand these writings—to enter their world and see biblical poetry through their eyes. Of course, to do so is not quite possible, since we can never free ourselves of our own worldview. So this book, like the texts it studies, is a refraction of earlier visions through later lenses. This, it turns out, is not cause for despair. If anything, our own preoccupation with literary theory and its application to the Bible should make us more appreciative of earlier attempts along the same lines, and should put us in a position to understand them better. They, on their part, also have something to teach us, for while we may not always agree with their interpretations, their literary insights are no less perceptive than our own. Above all, through reading these earlier texts we become aware that we are not the first to apply poetic theory to the Bible. It is both humbling and exciting to see how previous generations pursued this effort.

The book is divided into two parts. Part I contains a discussion of medieval and Renaissance views of biblical poetry and rhetoric in the context of the history of the study of biblical poetry and in the context of medieval views of poetic language and the place of the Bible in it. Part II presents translations of individual excerpts. Each is preceded by a brief biographical note on the author, the general contents of the work from which the excerpt is taken, and a summary of the excerpt. Bibliographical references are given for each text, and a complete bibliography of primary and secondary sources can be found at the end of the book. A glossary of important recurring terms and concepts is provided.

I have learned much from my reading of the secondary sources in the fields of medieval Hebrew literature and Jewish thought. For the most part, I do not depart from the current consensus, and I have tried to acknowledge previous discussions and discoveries to the extent that it seemed appropriate and practical. In some particulars, however, I have made my own small discoveries or ventured my own interpretations. In these cases I do not call attention to differing opinions, for I have no desire to appear polemical—that trait already being sufficiently pervasive in this field of scholarship. Those who are familiar with the texts presented here will know if and where I have advanced our understanding of them.

In the course of my research I have benefited from the expertise of many scholars whom I acknowledge here with pleasure and gratitude. First among them is Ross Brann, who served as my consultant on Judeo-Arabic and on Hebrew poetry, and who made available to me his unpublished work. I also thank Raymond Scheindlin for his apt comments on portions of the manuscript. I am, in addition, indebted to Bernard D. Cooperman, Yehudit Dishon, Benjamin Gampel, Regina Igel, Arthur Lesley, Jesse Mashbaum, and David Ruderman. Last and most dear, my husband, George Berlin, who not only gave me support and encouragement but shared with me unstintingly, as he does in all things, his knowledge of Jewish history and texts.

This project arose out of my work on linguistic approaches to biblical poetry, supported by the John Simon Guggenheim Memorial Foundation and the American Council of Learned Societies. The initial research was conducted at the Hebrew University, Jerusalem, Israel. The later stages of research were supported by grants from the National Endowment for the Humanities, an independent federal agency, and the General Research Board of the University of Maryland. The publication of this volume was supported in part by the Littauer Judaica Publication Fund through the Joseph and Rebecca Meyerhoff Center for Jewish Studies, University of Maryland, College Park.

NOTE ON THE TRANSLATIONS AND TRANSLITERATIONS

The translations are based on printed editions of varying degrees of accuracy. I have not attempted to prepare critical editions of the excerpts, and so I did not consult manuscripts or original printings. In cases of multiple printed editions, I chose what seemed to me to be the most authoritative. In some cases I note variants, but not in all—the criterion being the significance of the variant. Words contained in brackets [ ] are references or my explanations. Although I have rendered the texts as literally as I could without sacrificing clarity, and have tried to convey their tone and flavor, perhaps their most distinctive characteristic has been lost in translation—that is their constant allusion to biblical and rabbinic expressions, not only when citing verses but for all manner of statements.

Transliterations of Hebrew and Arabic follow the tables below. Exceptions are the conventional spellings of proper names and quotations.

TRANSLITERATION OF HEBREW

'	א	l	ל
b	ב	m	מ
g	ג	n	נ
d	ד	s	ס
h	ה	'	ע
w	ו	p	פ
z	ז	ṣ	צ
ḥ	ח	q	ק
ṭ	ט	r	ר
y	י	s	שׂ, š שׁ
k	כ	t	ת

i	xִי, xִ
e	xֶ, xֵ
ê	xֵי
a	xַ, xָ, final *qameṣ he*
ay	xַי
ayw	xָיו
o	xוֹ, xֹ, *qameṣ qaṭan*
u	xוּ, xֻ
e	(mobile *shwa*) xְ

TRANSLITERATION OF ARABIC

'	ء، ا
b	ب
t	ت
th	ث
j	ج
ḥ	ح
kh	خ
d	د
dh	ذ
r	ر
z	ز
s	س
sh	ش
ṣ	ص
ḍ	ض
ṭ	ط
ẓ	ظ
'	ع
gh	غ
f	ف
q	ق
k	ك
l	ل
m	م
n	ن
h	ه
w	و
y	ي

ABBREVIATIONS

Am	Amos
b.	Babylonian Talmud
BHK	*Biblia Hebraica Kittel*
BHS	*Biblia Hebraica Stuttgartensia*
Chr	Chronicles
Dan	Daniel
Deut	Deuteronomy
Ecc	Ecclesiastes
EJ	*Encyclopedia Judaica*
Esth	Esther
Exod	Exodus
Ezek	Ezekiel
Gen	Genesis
Hab	Habakkuk
Hag	Haggai
Hos	Hosea
HUCA	*Hebrew Union College Annual*
Isa	Isaiah
JAOS	*Journal of the American Oriental Society*
Jer	Jeremiah
Jon	Jonah
Josh	Joshua
JQR	*Jewish Quarterly Review*
Jud	Judges
Kgs	Kings
Lam	Lamentations
Lev	Leviticus
m.	Mishna
Mal	Malachi
Mic	Micah
Nah	Nahum
NEB	*New English Bible*
Neh	Nehemiah

NJPS	New Jewish Publication Society
Num	Numbers
Obad	Obadiah
Prov	Proverbs
Ps	Psalms
RSV	*Revised Standard Version*
Sam	Samuel
Song	Song of Songs
UF	*Ugarit Forschungen*
Zech	Zechariah
Zeph	Zephaniah

·I·

BIBLICAL POETRY THROUGH MEDIEVAL EYES

•1•

INTRODUCTION

Modern biblical and literary scholars sometimes give the impression that they are the first to approach the Bible from a literary perspective, but in reality the literary study of the Bible is one of the most ancient methods of understanding the biblical text.[1] To be sure, the literary approach was eclipsed during the last century by the historical approach, and has only recently come back into its own. But this is all the more reason to be aware of its antecedents. Although it is true that modern literary and linguistic theories are a far cry from their medieval counterparts, nevertheless, many a modern observation about biblical language and style can be found, in different guise, in earlier works. This is not so surprising for, after all, the biblical text has not changed; only the models and theories used to explain it have changed. As we come to understand these earlier models and theories, we come to see our own work as part of a long tradition which had as its goal *the analysis of the form and style of the Hebrew Bible in terms of the highest poetic standards and the most advanced linguistic knowledge available.*

A worthwhile effort in its own right, this goal was not always, nor is it today, an end in itself. Like any mode of interpretation, it can be used to further religious, nationalistic, or humanistic needs. Therefore, when we engage in a study of the history of the literary interpretation of the Bible, we are entering the realm of intellectual and cultural history. We learn about the role of literature in society, and about earlier stances to the Bible. We glimpse the way in which certain authors synthesized traditional religious teachings and contemporary secular learning and values.[2] The writings to be presented here not only offer insights into biblical poetics, they also relate to the broader question of cultural interactions and tensions; for the study of the Bible's literary form, especially of poetry, involved medieval and Renaissance Jewish scholars in a struggle between their religious conviction that the Bible was superior to all other literatures and their contemporary aesthetic judgment that its poetry fell short of the standards achieved in medieval Arabic and Hebrew poetry.

No genre lends itself to literary analysis more than poetry. But what constitutes poetry in the Bible? How can it be identified? What are its properties? These and other questions about rhetoric and poetics are debated in a number of Jewish writings in Hebrew and Judeo-Arabic from the twelfth to the seventeenth centuries. With few exceptions, these works are not devoted to the study of literature per se. The literary matters with which they deal occupy but a small part of the total composition, and emerge from other concerns; the compositions themselves are exegetical works, philosophical treatises, historical writings, or grammatical and lexicographical texts.

Because they do not all come from one genre, the excerpts that I will present are rarely treated together under one rubric. Yet they form a discrete category and demonstrate a continuity of thought, with some innovations along the way, relating to the identification and analysis of biblical poetry. I am, however, not the first to gather them together. As early as 1660 Johannes Buxtorf II included five excerpts on the subject of biblical poetry[3] in Latin translation as an appendix to his *Liber Cosri,* a translation of Judah Halevi's *Kuzari.* Much more recently, Alan M. Cooper included an appendix describing (but not translating) most of these works in his unpublished dissertation "Biblical Poetics: A Linguistic Approach." The most thorough presentation of the topic is found in James L. Kugel's *The Idea of Biblical Poetry: Parallelism and Its History.* In the second part of his book, Kugel provides a sweeping survey of the history of the study of biblical poetry from postbiblical times until the eighteenth century, concentrating mainly on the question of parallelism. He whets the appetite for a more intensive study of these compositions and a better grasp of the context and issues surrounding them.

In a sense, these Latin and English collections continue the tradition of the texts themselves, in which earlier ones are cited by successive ones in an ever-growing chain. The earliest, and most often cited, is *The Kuzari.*[4] By the time one reaches Azariah de' Rossi's *Me'or 'Ênayim,* one finds a mini-history of the subject, including not only some of the major Jewish sources but the most influential Greco-Roman sources as well. Yet there is not unanimous agreement on the issues raised. Don Isaac Abravanel, for example, is generally looked upon favorably, but Immanuel Frances criticizes his attempts to find meter in Exodus 15. So the debate continues, and the corpus grows. The question of meter in biblical poetry is no closer to being resolved in our day than it was in medieval Spain or Renaissance Italy.

When we first read the medieval and Renaissance Jewish writings which this book will present, they seem strange and distant. We do not share some of their basic assumptions about the nature of the Hebrew Bible, nor do we understand their frame of reference, especially their philosophical frame of reference. Yet it is possible to enter their world, and to relate their views to some of our own. It becomes intriguing to watch the interplay between issues and views which seem modern and those which seem hopelessly outmoded. Take, for example, the following comments by Joseph ibn Kaspi (thirteenth century) in his commentary on the Song of Songs:

> Solomon, peace be upon him, composed three books which we possess, corresponding to the three types of discourse which the prophets, peace be upon them, used. The first is entirely open and literal, with nothing beyond this. . . . The second is entirely hidden, with nothing revealed, having only metaphors and imagery. . . . The third has both hidden and revealed [i.e., literal and figurative meanings]. . . . So Solomon, peace be upon him, composed the three books: Ecclesiastes is of the first type, Song of Songs is of the second type, and Proverbs is of the third type. Remember this and apply it to the Torah, the Writings, and the Prophets. Indeed, in every passage we are in danger of exchanging one type for another, until we exchange the living for the dead. For this leads us to one of two errors: [either we mistake the literal for the figurative or the figurative for the literal]. If we put into the composition something false and lying, something not intended by the author, this, then, is not an interpretation. It is a new and original work. I call an "interpretation" only that which calls forth the intent of the author. Each type [of discourse] is indicated to a person of clear mind and sound judgment; we cannot give complete proof for this. It suffices to say that the truth is self-evident.[5]

Ibn Kaspi is concerned with differentiating genres,[6] for, as he explains, and as literary scholars and biblical Form Critics know, one cannot understand the meaning of a passage if one does not know its genre and the conventions of that genre. One runs the risk of taking literally what should be taken figuratively, and so forth. Ibn Kaspi is also concerned with the original intention of the author, something rejected by New Criticism as the intentional fallacy yet not entirely dispensable to most biblical scholars. His characterization of an interpretation or commentary that is not true to the original intent of the work approaches the very modern notion, which goes a step beyond ibn Kaspi, which holds that, since no one can really know the original sense or intention, all interpretations create new texts. Yet despite the importance of genre identification, ibn Kaspi offers no concrete help in recognizing the three types of discourse he describes. To him the distinction is obvious. It is likewise obvious to him (because it was a commonplace in the Middle Ages) that Song of Songs is a philosophical allegory of the union of the receptive intellect with the active intellect. This would hardly be obvious to a modern biblical scholar, who not only would reject the philosophical interpretation but is more than likely to reject the allegorical interpretation as well.

In the end, we may reject the main thrust of ibn Kaspi's commentary, and declare that he has failed in his purpose, but we cannot help being fascinated by his use of the literary theory of his time, which, in principle if not in practice, is not so different from our own.

The following chapters will set the stage for understanding the medieval and Renaissance works, and will present translations of excerpts of the works themselves. Chapter 2 offers a survey of the history of the study of biblical poetry, a context in which to place the medieval Jewish writings on this subject. Chapter 3 discusses medieval Jewish attitudes toward the Hebrew language, the Bible, and poetry. Chapter 4 draws on the translated excerpts and on others, and presents an overview of the main concepts in the discussions of biblical poetry.

·2·

TRENDS IN THE HISTORY OF THE STUDY OF BIBLICAL POETRY

Poetry is notoriously difficult to define, but that has not deterred generation after generation from attempting to do so. The medieval and Renaissance authors with whom we are concerned come at about the midpoint in the long search for the definition and identification of biblical poetry. In order to fully appreciate their efforts and results, it is helpful to know what ideas about poetry preceded them, what ideas were current at their time, and what followed in later periods. This chapter will address the before and after, and chapter 3 will provide the contemporary background. It is not intended as a proper history of the study of biblical poetry,[1] but rather as a survey of the major turning points along the path of intellectual history as it pertains to the perception and evaluation of biblical poetry.

Unlike classical Greece, ancient Israel left us no theoretical discussions of its literature. We have only the Bible—no contemporaneous works about the Bible; and the Bible does not reflect on its own literary forms. Therefore, most of what has been said about the Bible is extrinsic to it, is supplied from knowledge outside the Bible. However, there are several textual phenomena which have, at least in the Jewish tradition, provided a starting point for discussions of biblical poetry. The Bible employs some terms, such as *šir, mizmor, qina*, and numerous technical terms in the Book of Psalms, that seem to indicate types of poetry or song. There is also the term *mašal*, with a range of meanings including "parable," "allegory," "proverb," and, as it was often understood by the medievals, "figurative language." Such terms are ancient, part of the wording of the biblical text, and have long been taken as at least the suggestion of literary terminology, though it is not clear exactly which generic distinctions they may represent. One step removed from this, though still a textual phenomenon, is the scribal tradition, witnessed in manuscripts from Qumran, in talmudic references, and in medieval masoretic manuscripts, of setting off certain passages from the surrounding discourse by means of special stichography. Two visual patterns were used to do this. One is, in rabbinic terminology, "log over brick, brick over log." It is an interlocking construction which looks like

```
— — — — — — — — — —                 — — — — — — — — — —
            — — — — — — — — — — — — — — — —
— — — — — — — — — —                 — — — — — — — — — —
```

or, an alternate form:

```
— — — — — — — — — —                 — — — — — — — — — —
— — — —      — — — — — — — — — — — —      — — — — —
— — — — — — — — — —                 — — — — — — — — — —
```

The other is "log over log, brick over brick." This pattern yields two columns with space between them:

```
— — — — — — — — — —                 — — — — — — — — — —
— — — — — — — — — —                 — — — — — — — — — —
— — — — — — — — — —                 — — — — — — — — — —
```

These patterns are most often used for poetic sections, but not all poetry (by modern standards) is written this way, and in two cases (Josh 12:9–24 and Esth 9:7–9) the "brick" pattern sets off lists of names. The poems most consistently written in one or the other of these stichographic forms are Exod 15:1–18 (the Song of the Sea), Deuteronomy 32 (Ha'azinu), Judges 5 (the Song of Deborah), and 2 Samuel 22 (the Song of David). Some manuscripts use these forms much more extensively—for the books of Psalms, Proverbs, Job, and occasionally Lamentations.

With the advent of printing, this convention changed. Most printed masoretic Bibles abandoned the stichographic presentation of Psalms, Proverbs, and Job and preserved only those passages required by the Talmud to be written stichographically: the Song of the Sea, the Song of Deborah, and the lists in Joshua 12 and Esther 9. Modern scholarly editions of the Bible have reversed this trend. In BHK and BHS not only are the traditionally stichographic sections so printed, but, in addition, everything considered poetic by modern standards, including the speeches of the classical prophets and small "poems" within narratives (such as 1 Sam 15:22–23), are printed stichographically.

Early medieval discussions of poetry predate printing and are influenced by the use of the word *šir,* "song," in connection with certain passages, and by the stichographic writing of some of these "songs" (and also by the talmudic reference to ten "songs"). They were also influenced by another textual factor, which moderns are more apt to ignore: the system of masoretic accents. The books of Psalms, Proverbs, and Job[2] utilize a slightly different set of accents from those used in the other twenty-one books. (Notice that these books are written stichographically in some manuscripts.)

To the medieval scholars, then, the accents, the traditional scribal stichography, and terminology such as *šir* were all intrinsic features of the biblical text. These were taken as indicators of poetry, or at least as the starting point for many discussions on the subject. But views of poetry are never based solely on intrinsic criteria. They are heavily influenced by current perceptions of what constitutes poetry. This, of course, varies from time to time and place to place. Let us briefly chart several of the major forces whose impact on the perception of biblical poetry was great.

The Influence of Classical Poetry and Rhetoric

The spread of Greek culture into the Jewish world (and the spread of Jews into the Greek world) inevitably brought readers of the Bible into contact with the Greek idea of *poiesis*. The Greek notion of poetry was then superimposed onto the Bible. Themes and subjects considered proper to Greek poetry were found to be poetic in the Bible as well, and meter, well defined and developed by the Greeks, was ascribed to biblical poems. The leading exponents of this approach were Philo and Josephus, who sought to interpret the Bible as a whole in a way meaningful to a Hellenistic audience.

The early Church, which adopted the allegorical method of interpretation prevalent in the Greek world, also adopted much of the appreciation of Greek poetic forms. Church Fathers (Origen, Eusebius, and others) spoke of poetic meter and tropes in connection with the psalms and pericopes such as Deuteronomy 32. Jerome, schooled in Latin poetry and an admirer of it, found its features, especially meters, to be present in, and indeed surpassed by, the poetry of the Bible. Theodore of Mopsuestia noted the rhetorical use of certain types of repetition or parallelism. Augustine spoke of meter and poetic figures in the Bible. To be sure, much of the Church Fathers' discussion of biblical poetry was designed to neutralize the tension between the attraction to and the rejection of secular (that is, pagan) literature, and to overcome the perceived lack of aesthetic appeal of the Bible (judged by classical standards). Nevertheless, this early focus on meter and certain tropes represents a sustained effort at poetic analysis and left its mark, even among Jews, in later times.

Early Jewish Interpretations

Although "Hellenized" Jews and early Christian interpreters had no difficulty in seeing rhetorical tropes and figures in the Bible, their rabbinic contemporaries largely ignored the Bible's stylistic aspect. This silence continued, for the most part, in the medieval Jewish commentaries. This was not due so much to literary ignorance as to different hermeneutic principles. For Jewish exegetes, every word of Scripture had its own significance. This meant that words and phrases were never just "decorative" stylistic devices, but always bore some specific meaning. This approach had the effect of limiting the recognition of literary features, including poetic forms. Occasionally we do find commentators who are sensitive to stylistic and poetic matters. For example, Abraham ibn Ezra and Rashbam (R. Samuel ben Meir, the grandson of Rashi and a leading Ashkenazic authority) noted that a certain amount of repetition and/or parallelism was stylistic and did not necessarily add new information. Don Isaac Abravanel, whose commentary on Exodus 15 and Isaiah 5 opens with a discussion of poetry (presented in part II), is something of an exception, for discussions of poetry were not apt to be found in commentaries; they were more likely to occur in the context of philosophical essays or grammatical works, where they grew out of a concern with current knowledge in those areas.

The Influence of Arabic and Medieval Hebrew Poetry

In the period upon which this book focuses, the greatest influence on perceptions of biblical poetry came from Arabic and medieval Hebrew poetry and poetic theory. The early Jewish discussions of biblical poetry were written by men of the Golden Age of Jewish culture in Spain, poets themselves, such as Judah Halevi and Moshe ibn Ezra, thoroughly versed in the Arabic literary culture in which they lived. (In fact, while their poems are in Hebrew, their writings about poetry are in Arabic.) Poetry and rhetoric were highly esteemed in the culture of al-Andalus (Muslim Spain), by Jews as well as by Muslims. The standards by which poetry was judged were Arabic standards. "Poem" meant *qaṣīda,* a composition (often translated as "ode") with quantitative meter and unified end rhyme. The Jews imitated Arabic poetic style and adapted it to the Hebrew language, with the result that Hebrew poetry entered a new stage. This model of what a poem should look and sound like affected the perception of biblical poetry in a number of complex ways, which will be discussed in greater detail in the following chapter. Suffice it to say that it was difficult, if not impossible, to find *qaṣīdas* in the Bible.

Yet there was a tradition, based on the intrinsic textual factors mentioned above, that the Bible contained poetry. Moreover, it became important for nationalistic reasons to demonstrate that the Hebrew scriptures were as good as, if not better than, the Qur'an in matters of literary elegance. All this led to interesting attempts to define biblical poetry and to compare it with its medieval Hebrew and Arabic counterparts. Many of these attempts were transmitted to Christian Spain, Provence, and Italy, so that even when Jews ceased to live under Islamic rule, their Hebrew poetry and poetic theory bore some of the marks of Andalusian influence. But there were innovations, too. Jews in Renaissance Italy met new poetic ideas, influenced by the rediscovery of classical rhetoric and the development of Italian poetry.

Influences on the Modern Study of Biblical Poetry

It is easier to see the influence of the vernacular culture on discussions of the Bible when that culture is different from our own. But too often we forget that we, too, are subject to the same influence. Take the example of meter. When modern English-speaking biblical scholars search for meter in the Bible, it is accentual meter that they have in mind, for that is the kind they are familiar with in their vernacular poetry. When confronted with a poem written in quantitative meter (as in Greek, medieval Arabic, and medieval Hebrew) they would not automatically perceive any meter at all. With only the text, and no information about its formal requirements, those requirements are anything but obvious. The history of the study of biblical poetry shows that each age has sought to discover its own poetic conventions in the Bible.

The same is true of more general trends in the evaluation of the Bible and its poetry. Each age has its own opinion of the relative merits of biblical poetry and its place in the history of literature. For the medievals, antiquity conferred honor. Hebrew was thought to be the first, most original language, and the Bible the earliest literature. The notion that later literature surpassed it in stylistic elegance was difficult to accept, for philosophical as well as for chauvinistic reasons. Jewish tradition perpetuates the idea that the former generations were superior to the later. How, then, could Judah Halevi have written better poetry than King David? Moderns have no such problem, for their view is just the opposite. The earlier is the more primitive. It remains only to decide whether the primitive is preferable to the sophisticated.

The modern study of biblical poetry is generally said to commence with Robert Lowth. Lowth's major contribution lies in his recognition of the phenomenon of parallelism, and in his shift of emphasis from meter to parallelism.[3] This was to change the agenda of poetic analysis in the Bible for the next two centuries. In addition, Lowth included in his definition of the poetic all texts which contained a sustained amount of parallelism, which meant that prophetic speech was now considered poetry. The body of poetic writing in the Bible thereby increased significantly. Lowth's contribution is important, and it is amply documented elsewhere. But his *weltanschauung*, and its effect on his stance to biblical poetry, is often forgotten.

Lowth was a Romantic. His historical research and critical examination did not prevent him from elevating the imaginative and emotional side of literary expression. For Lowth, Hebrew poetry was "sublime" —a term he used over and over and defined as "that force of composition . . . which strikes and overpowers the mind, which excites the passions and which expresses ideas at once with perspicuity and elevation" (*Lectures on the Sacred Poetry of the Hebrews*, Lecture XIV). The authors of this poetry led a simple pastoral life, unencumbered by the "studies and pursuits" of later civilizations (Lecture VII), and thus epitomized the "natural man" idealized in the Romantic period. As for the place of biblical poetry in the study of the history of literature, "the sacred Poetry is undoubtedly entitled to the first rank in this school since from it we are to learn both the origin of the art and how to estimate its excellence" (Lecture II). Similar thoughts were expressed by Lowth's more influential German contemporary Johann Gottfried Herder, in his *Vom Geist der ebraïschen Poesie*. Lowth's lectures, which had inspired Herder, were published in a German translation together with Herder's book in 1793. This Romantic attitude toward biblical poetry continued in the work of early nineteenth-century scholars and is evident in numerous commentaries on Psalms from this period.

Toward the end of the nineteenth century the trend shifted. Interest in evolutionary development quickened in this post-Darwinian age, and earlier stages were viewed as more "primitive" than later ones. Since most biblical scholars were also Orientalists—that is, knowledgeable in Arabic and often travelers to the Middle East—and, in addition, were influenced by the newly emerging disciplines of linguistics and folklore, they could not resist comparisons between "primitive Hebrews" and the Arab culture which they witnessed. (How different this was from the comparisons between these two cultures in medieval Spain!) The comparisons pertained to philology as well as to what T. K. Cheyne called "comparative ethnic-psychology." As Julius Wellhausen put it, "I have no doubt that the original gifts and ideas of the Primitive Hebrews can most readily be understood by comparing Arabian antiquity."[4] The Late

Victorian view of biblical poetry is perhaps best summed up by George Adam Smith in the 1910 Schweich Lectures (p. 10):

> All these facts of the language and syntax warn us not to expect in Hebrew poetry the regular, intricate and delicate metres of the Aryan styles. We are dealing with a people originally nomadic and to the end unskilled in architecture or any elaborate art. The essential looseness of their life, visible in their language, was bound to affect the highest achievements of their literature. When they did concentrate their minds on utterance, their earnestness would appear less in a passion for beauty than in a sense of urgency and responsibility. Israel was a people of prophets rather than poets.

Gone, here, is the Romantic celebration of the simple life and the Hebrew poetic genius. In its place is the negative valence of the nomadic, artistically unskilled Israelites who could not be expected to have produced poetry.

Closer to our own day we find other trends and the influence of other literary approaches. Hermann Gunkel's Form Critical approach had a great impact, especially his replacement of the traditional Greek categories used previously—lyric, didactic, elegiac, etc.—by a system of classification of the psalms based on their content and formulaic phraseology: hymn, community lament, individual lament, individual thanksgiving song, royal psalm. Form Criticism aims to understand a work in relation to its original life setting, and so this approach stimulated studies of the place of the psalms in Israel's worship, along with continued interest in the dating of the psalms and other poetry.[5] In addition, because it was intent on finding generic patterns and formulas, Form Criticism promoted the discovery of recurring phrases and stylistic usages, and the analysis of the structure of poems. It is but a small step from this aspect of Form Criticism to its cousin, the oral-formulaic theory of composition, borrowed from the work of M. Parry and A. Lord on ancient Greek and modern Serbian poetry. According to this theory, fixed word pairs in parallel lines (not the metrical formulas of Parry and Lord) were the building blocks of biblical poetry which enabled the poet to compose orally. The theory of oral composition drew on views of parallelism current in biblical studies at the time (see below) and on certain assumptions held by folklorists and scholars of comparative literature.

While Form Criticism sought the common elements in various poems, Rhetorical Criticism shifted the emphasis to the distinctive usages in each poem. In a separate but similar move, those more familiar with literary criticism applied the methods of New Criticism and Werkinterpretation to biblical poetry, especially the technique of close reading. Afterward came structuralism and poststructuralism. As biblical scholars learn of new literary and linguistic methodologies, they employ them in the study of the Bible.

Modern Descriptions of the Formal Features of Biblical Poetry

The recognition of poetry implies distinguishing poetry from other forms of literary discourse on the basis of formal criteria. Since the formal requirements of biblical poetry are not immediately apparent, the search for them has been the focus of most studies throughout history. Most often, the search has centered around meter.

It has been difficult, if not impossible, for many to conceive of poetry —or, more properly, verse—without meter; but what exactly was to be metered, or measured, and by what metrical system, has rarely met with scholarly consensus. Medieval authors looked for quantitative meter, for that was the kind they knew from their own poetry. Modern scholars have proposed various metrical systems, differing from each other and from the medieval conception. In general, these modern systems fall into one of three groups: accentual meter, syllabic meter, or word/thought meter.[6] All of these count phonological features, although the last moves toward semantic features. Most recently, as a result of the influence of linguistics, syntax has begun to replace phonology and semantics. In the system of word meter proposed by J. Kurylowicz, grammatical criteria are used to define a word complex, rather than semantic criteria;[7] and in M. O'Connor's metrical system, syntactic constraints, not phonological units, define a line of verse.[8] Then there have been those in all historical periods who rejected the notion of meter in biblical poetry altogether. The point of surveying these trends is not to decide which system is correct, but to appreciate the wide range of divergent views that have arisen over the years, and to understand the factors that led to their rise.

Since the time of Lowth, biblical poetry has been perceived as consisting of two formal features: meter and parallelism. Various descriptions give prominence to one or the other, but both are usually present to some degree (except where the existence of meter is rejected or where parallelism is considered a substitute for meter). Like meter, the study of parallelism has been affected by literary and linguistic trends. It began as a semantic phenomenon, in Lowth's three categories of synonymous, antithetic, and synthetic parallelism. This subdivision, based on the perception of semantic sameness or its lack in parallel lines, held sway for two hundred years and is still widely used, but it has recently been criticized by Robert Alter and James Kugel.[9] They reject Lowth's tripartite subdivision and speak instead of semantic continuity or consequentiality, putting the emphasis on the *difference* in the parts of the parallelism, rather than their similarity. Nevertheless, their criteria are still semantic ones. Other scholars have applied linguistic methods to the study of parallelism, describing the relationship between parallel lines in terms of syntax instead of semantics.[10] The influence of structural linguistics, especially of Roman Jakobson, is evident in these studies.

Although parallelism is an important feature of biblical poetry, it cannot, in and of itself, serve to identify a poem, since nonpoetic discourse also contains parallelism. The other mark of poetry, meter, has also proved to be elusive. For this reason, a few scholars have looked in another direction for clues to the identification of poetry. It has been known since at least 1910[11] that certain words and particles (the definite article, the relative pronoun *'ašer*, the particle *'et*) appear less frequently in poetry. Modern computer technology now makes the actual counting of these particles relatively easy, and their occurrence in the Bible has been tabulated.[12] The results seem to confirm the modern intuition about what is to be labeled poetry.

In addition to its formal requirements, much of the world's poetry —and, indeed, literary discourse in general—utilizes an array of tropes and figures. The Bible is no exception; it employs imagery, repetition, chiasm, assonance, and the like. These tropes and figures are in the domain of stylistics or rhetoric. They do not define poetry but are often present in poetry. They have been noted at least since medieval times, and have been discussed against the background of Arabic rhetoric (especially by Moshe ibn Ezra) and classical rhetoric (by Judah Messer Leon). Interest in biblical rhetoric is naturally high in societies in which rhetorical elegance is valued. Also, given that the Bible's rhetorical devices are more obvious than its formal poetic devices, and that they conform more to those in other literatures, it is not surprising to find that there is more agreement over the centuries concerning them. The question of metaphor, important in modern literary discussions, if not among biblical scholars, was a central issue in medieval times. The essence of poetry was thought to be the use of metaphorical, or figurative, language. This, in turn, has bearing on the crucial question of interpretation: what in the Bible is to be taken literally and what figuratively.

It is both the need to interpret the Bible in a satisfying way and the need to scrutinize it in light of contemporary literary standards that prompt studies of biblical poetry and poetics. In this regard, modern scholars are no different from their medieval and Renaissance counterparts. The frame of reference may change, but the goals are the same. The following chapters will present the medieval frame of reference, and some outstanding reflections on biblical poetry.

•3•

MEDIEVAL AND RENAISSANCE JEWISH ATTITUDES TOWARD POETRY AND THE BIBLE

The study of biblical poetry from the twelfth to the seventeenth centuries took place against a background of values and assumptions quite different from our own. The medieval world saw, first among the Arabs and then among the Jews, a rise of linguistic consciousness—a flourishing of the scientific study of language in the form of grammars and dictionaries[1]—and along with this a sense of linguistic pride. Elegance in spoken and written expression was a mark of distinction, both for the individual author and for the nation whose language lent itself to such elegance. Poetry, the most elegant form of language, was therefore highly valued. It was, especially in Muslim Spain, the vehicle for entertainment, encomium, eulogy, religious expression, and, on occasion, polemic; in short, poetry was widely employed and had a much higher status in medieval society than it does in our own.

At the same time, interest in the Bible was also high. The Masoretes had accomplished their monumental task of establishing the text of the Hebrew Bible, with its vocalization and accentuation, just prior to the period of the growth of Hebrew poetry in Islamic Spain. The work of the Hebrew grammarians and lexicographers drew on the work of the Masoretes (the principles of grammar were built on the masoretic vocalization), and so the grammar of Hebrew meant the grammar of biblical Hebrew. This, in turn, promoted even greater interest in the philology and grammar of the biblical text, which began to figure increasingly in exegetical writings. On its part, exegesis also flourished, and took an innovative turn toward the rational, both as a result of the general desire for more scientific pursuits and as a defense against Karaite, Christian, and Muslim polemics.[2]

Interest in language, poetry, and the Bible come together in the writings presented in this book. These writings also share the philosophical views of their day. Philosophy, no less than poetry, was a major intellectual pursuit (the two sometimes rivaled each other) and encompassed theories of language, poetics, and biblical interpretation. With all of this one must also keep in mind that many of the writings from Spain are written against the background of *'Arabiyya* and, consciously or unconsciously, manifest a reaction to it.

The Arab conquest brought into the orbit of Islam non-Arab peoples upon whom the Arabs sought to impose their cultural values along with their religious ones. Among the tenets of *'Arabiyya*, the doctrine of Arab supremacy, which pertain to our subject are (1) the best of all scriptures ever sent down from heaven is the Qur'an, (2) the best of all languages is Arabic, in which God spoke to his people, and (3) the best poetry is Arabic poetry, in which the angels render praise to God in heaven.[3] It is no accident, then, that Jewish interest in the Hebrew language, poetry, and Scripture increased in the Islamic world; the factors are internal as well as external. Jewish reaction to *'Arabiyya* is complex and not uniform.[4] It is not my intention to deal with it directly, but many of the medieval Jewish attitudes discussed here reflect the need to address the aforementioned tenets. They should not be understood as naively chauvinistic but as attempts at cultural self-definition and preservation by members of a minority culture.[5] As Raymond Scheindlin and Ross Brann have brilliantly set forth, the literature of this period should be viewed not only as a reaction to *'Arabiyya* but also as a reflection of cultural ambiguity, of the tensions felt by members of a subculture within a flourishing main culture.[6]

Drawing on representative excerpts and on other texts, this chapter offers an overview of medieval and Renaissance attitudes toward the Hebrew language, the Bible, and poetry.[7]

Attitudes toward the Hebrew Language

In the premodern world, antiquity conferred honor. There was no doubt in the medieval Jewish mind about the antiquity of Hebrew: it was accorded the place of honor in the lineage of the world's languages. Not only was it the most ancient of the languages known at that time (the extinct languages of the ancient Near East were centuries from rediscovery), but since it was the language in which the Bible was written, it was of necessity the original language, the language in which God first spoke—through which the world was created and its components named. The "proof," as Judah Halevi explains, is that proper names and the word plays on them make sense only in Hebrew.

If Hebrew was the language of God's revelation, the Bible, that most perfect of books, it must surely be the most perfect of languages. And *biblical* Hebrew was Hebrew at its finest. After all, does not the Bible express everything it wishes to express in exactly the right words? Would the prophets, masters of rhetoric, have used an inferior form of expression? Postbiblical Hebrew, especially medieval Hebrew, was then, by definition, of lesser merit; it had deteriorated and become constricted. The Hebrew language suffered the same fate as its speakers, Judah Halevi and others tell us. With the passage of time and the vicissitudes of exile, Hebrew lost its purity and amplitude. Profiat Duran, who voiced strong feelings about the preservation of Hebrew, noted that the progressive loss had already begun in preexilic times. Not only did "half their children speak Ashdodite and not know how to speak Judean" (Neh 13:24) after the Babylonian exile, but even in earlier days the Torah and its language fell into neglect, for when Josiah was presented with the scroll discovered in the Temple, it seemed unfamiliar to him, and instead of reading it for himself he had Shaphan read it to him. Along the same lines, Moshe ibn Ezra points to the fact that the government officials spoke Aramaic to Rabshakeh in the time of Hezekiah. This forgetting of Hebrew and the concomitant neglect of the Torah led, in Duran's opinion, to the destruction of Israel and to its dispersion and subjugation. Duran goes on to criticize scholars in his own day who preferred the study of the Talmud to the study of the Bible and the use of the vernacular to the use of Hebrew.

Perhaps the most moving expression of the attitude toward Hebrew is that of Judah al-Ḥarizi (ca. 1170–1235). In the opening section of the *Taḥkemoni* he explains how and why he came to compose this collection of *maqāmāt*, a Hebrew work in rhymed prose inspired by the work of the Arab poet al-Ḥariri. Al-Ḥarizi portrays himself, in a fictionalized fashion full of biblical images and allusions, as a prophet who has come to rescue the Hebrew language.

> I was asleep but my heart was awake and in a sea of fire desire raged and burned. My intellect aroused me from my sleep of folly. It instructed me saying:
> "O, you, son of man. . . . Gird up your loins and clothe yourself with zeal for the God of Hosts and for the holy tongue which was once the language of prophecy but which has now come down amazingly. . . ."
> And I said, "Alas my lord, the wandering [of exile] has confounded my speech and my thoughts. . . . Who am I that I should snatch a lost sheep out of the teeth of lions and that I should bring forth the holy tongue from its dire straits?" And he said to me: "Verily I will be with you. . . ."
> Then the intellect put forth his hand and touched my mouth and kindled the sparks of my flame, and said to me: "Behold, I have put my words in your mouth, and for the vision[8] of poetry I have assigned

you as a prophet unto the nations. See, I have appointed you to pull down and to destroy the houses of folly, and to build and to plant the houses of *meliṣa*."

God has stirred up my spirit to light from the splendor[9] of the holy tongue lamps to open blind eyes, and they will become sources of light so that all the people of the earth may know that the holy tongue is incomparable in the clarity of its diction and in the pleasantness of its metaphors [*mašal*]—that it is like a bride adorned with her jewels. *Meliṣa* is her robe and the spice of myrrh is on her skirts. . . .

And in days of yore the righteous of the world used to rejoice in the holy tongue. But today criminals and hooligans among our people have stabbed her with swords and with spears from the flint of their tongue. . . . All her sons have forsaken their tongue and become stammerers. . . .

The Hebrew language now speaks, reminding the reader that the Ten Commandments were written in Hebrew, and calling herself the queen who sat beside God in his sanctuary. To abandon her is like abandoning God; to use other languages is like worshipping idols.

They have enslaved the tongue of the Israelites to the tongue of Kedar [Arabic] and they said: "Come and let us sell it to the Ishmaelites." And they said to it: "Bow down, that we may pass over." And they took it and cast it into the pit until it perished among them. And the tongue of Kedar blackened[10] it, and like a lion, tore it. A wild beast devoured it. All of them spurned the Hebrew tongue and made love to the tongue of Hagar. . . . Their hearts were seduced when they saw how precious was the *meliṣa* that Hagar, Sarah's Egyptian handmaiden, had borne. And Sarah was barren.

Maiden Hebrew appears to the speaker in a scene in which the dominant image is Rebecca at the well. He betroths her, and from their union is born a son, the reborn Hebrew language, mighty and powerful.

Now the thing that stirred up my spirit to compose this book was that a wise man among the sages of the Arabs and one of the choicest of the enlightened whose tongue is fluent in Arabic rhetoric [*meliṣa*] and through whose mouth the vision of poetry is spread abroad—he is the famous al-Ḥariri. . . . He composed a book in the Arabic tongue that offers goodly words; albeit its themes are hewn from the Hebrew tongue and all its precious metaphors are taken and handed over from our books. If you were to ask every rhetorical figure, "Who brought you to the language of the Hagarites?" it would answer, "I was indeed stolen from the land of the Hebrews."

Now when I saw this book, the heavens of my delight were rolled

> together like a scroll and the streams of my sadness flowed, because every other people is careful of its rhetoric and takes care not to sin against its language. But our language, which was the delight of every eye, is now regarded as a brother of Cain. . . .[11] They said that our language is too narrow and its rhetoric is deficient. But they know not that the lack is in those who do not comprehend its speech and do not recognize its loveliness. . . .[12]

In al-Ḥarizi's words we find the ambivalence toward Arabic language and literature which characterized many of the Spanish Jewish writers. On the one hand, Arabic provided the model, the standard to imitate, and the task that Hebrew writers set for themselves was to show that Hebrew could meet the challenge of Arabic. But on the other hand, Hebrew was declared superior to Arabic, no less supple and ample, and the source of the metaphors and rhetorical devices found in Arabic literature. Although the speaking persona in the *Taḥkemoni* acknowledges the decline of Hebrew, he is battling against the inevitability of this decline. In fact, the agenda of the *Taḥkemoni* is to show that Hebrew lives, that it is fully capable, in skilled hands, of serving as the vehicle of literature that is every bit as good as that written in Arabic.

Actually, the *Taḥkemoni* reflects a double loss of Hebrew: that following the biblical period and that following the "Golden Age" of the tenth and eleventh centuries. The *Taḥkemoni* replays some of the views of poets such as Judah Halevi and Moshe ibn Ezra, who had brought the poetic use of the Hebrew language to new heights. Yet, as will be discussed below, this Arabic-inspired Hebrew poetry was not always considered an unmixed blessing, even by the poets themselves. At any rate, the rejuvenation of Hebrew caused a dichotomy between theory and practice: in theory, no later form of Hebrew could aspire to the heights of biblical Hebrew, while in practice, the literary Hebrew of medieval Spain did precisely that. Moreover, it found modes of expression that the biblical authors had never imagined. (Al-Ḥarizi mediates between this dichotomy with his figure of the prophet.) However, despite its accomplishments in the literary-poetic realm, Hebrew was not much used for expository prose by Arabic-speaking Jews. In al-Andalus, philosophical and exegetical works, grammars, medical and halakhic works continued to be written in Arabic or Judeo-Arabic; Hebrew was reserved for poetry or belles-lettres. Only as the influence of Arabic waned (in Christian Spain) did Hebrew come to replace Arabic for scientific and religious discourse.

In the Franco-German communities (Ashkenaz) the situation was different from the outset. As A. S. Halkin points out,[13] in these communities the written language, Latin, was quite different from the spoken vernaculars. While Jews spoke the languages of their areas, they did not write in Latin; they used Hebrew for their scholarly works. Neither did they have models of secular poetry as the Jews of the Islamic world had, or the phenomenon of *'Arabiyya*. As a result, secular Hebrew poetry did not develop there; and while Hebrew continued to be used in learned discourse, there was little concern for its rhetorical elegance, or for its revitalization. Furthermore, in Ashkenaz the Talmud reigned as the most important text;[14] and since it is in Aramaic, this lessened the prominence of Hebrew. It was the Franco-German talmudic scholars that Profiat Duran singled out for the harshest criticism for their neglect of Hebrew.

It is therefore understandable that we find little discussion of the Hebrew language and its poetry in medieval Ashkenaz. It is found mainly in al-Andalus (Muslim Spain), in Provence, and later in Italy. Provence, while not Islamic, was closer to the Spanish cultural orbit than the Franco-German one, and was populated by some Jews who knew Arabic. (It was here that many of the translators of Arabic works into Hebrew lived.) Renaissance Italy had inherited some of the traditions of Spain as a result of the migrations after the Reconquista and the Inquisition, and besides, it had developed its own models of language and literature deriving from the interest in classical authors and the flowering of Italian literature. In all of these places we find that Jewish attitudes toward the Hebrew language and literature combined traditions which were, through exegetical means, traced back to the Bible, but which, by the same token, were shaped and influenced by the attitudes of their non-Jewish neighbors toward their own languages and literatures.

We have touched on the general cultural attitudes toward Hebrew, and on one aspect of the relationship between Hebrew and Arabic. Now let us examine the broader "linguistic" conceptions of the relationship of Hebrew to other Semitic languages.

There was a common view that Arabic was "Hebrew somewhat corrupted." This needs to be understood both as a defense of Hebrew and as a recognition of the linguistic similarity between Hebrew and Arabic. The educated Jews of the Islamic world were well versed in Hebrew, Aramaic, and Arabic, and were well aware that these three languages had much in common. Indeed, one can apply the term *comparative Semitics* to a work such as the *Risāla* of Judah ibn Quraysh, which advocates the study of Hebrew, Aramaic, and Arabic in order to understand the Bible, and includes lexical and grammatical comparisons of biblical Hebrew, Mishnaic Hebrew, Aramaic, and Arabic.[15] Ibn Quraysh explains the relationship among the languages as arising both from the geographical proximity of their speakers and from the genealogical closeness of their origins. Both points are echoed elsewhere, but rarely do the two occur together. The first—the influence of proximate languages on each other—can be considered a synchronic explanation and is close to modern linguistic views. The second point, a diachronic explanation based on a "family tree" model, derives from linguistic isoglosses and ethnic lineages related to biblical figures. Ibn Quraysh tells us that "Teraḥ . . . was an Aramean and Laban, too, was an Aramean [i.e., speakers of Aramaic]. Ishmael and Kedar were speakers of Arabic since the generation of the Tower of Babel; while Abraham, Isaac, and Jacob . . . clung to the holy tongue [in an unbroken chain] since Adam."[16] *The Kuzari* (2.68) explains that originally everyone spoke Hebrew, each generation acquiring it from the previous one until Eber, for whom it is named, since he preserved it at the time of the Tower of Babel. Abraham preserved it after Eber. However, Abraham spoke Aramaic in Ur Kasdim, where it was the vernacular, reserving Hebrew as his holy tongue. Ishmael brought Aramaic to the Arab lands. Thus, concludes the Advocate in *The Kuzari*, did Aramaic, Arabic, and Hebrew become similar in their vocabulary, verbal systems, and usages.

Attitudes toward the Bible

The Bible is the central text in Judaism. This is so in theory, if not always in practice. (In practice, the Talmud—i.e., the oral law—often eclipses the Bible as the central text, but in theory the oral law is derived from and dependent on the written law of the Bible.) The Jews of Spain inherited a long tradition of Bible study and exegesis, going back at least to rabbinic times.[17] To this had been added several new foci during the Islamic period, the most notable of which, for our concern, was the linguistic-aesthetic focus. In large measure, this can be attributed to the work of Saadia ben Joseph al-Fayyumi (Saadia Gaon, 882–942), the brilliant exegete, translator, philosopher, and poet who headed the Jewish community of Babylonia. Saadia was a virulent opponent of the Karaites, and much of his work dealt with the Bible and the proper ways to interpret it. We also find in his works evidence of a reaction to *'Arabiyya*, especially the principle of *i'jāz al-qur'ān* (the wonderful inimitability of the Qur'an), Qur'anic exegesis (*tafsīr*), and Islamic attacks on biblical anthropomorphism. Among his influential writings are his Arabic translation (and commentary) of the Bible, his grammar, *Kutub al-Lugha*, and his poetic dictionary, *Kitāb 'uṣūl al-shi'r al-'ibrāni* [The Elements of Hebrew Poetics], known in Hebrew as *Seper Ha'egron*. The latter has been called "the first Hebrew dictionary, the first rhyming dictionary, and the first essay on Hebrew poetics."[18] He also wrote *Kitāb al-Sab'īn Lafẓa al-Mufrada* [The Book of the Seventy Isolated Words], in which some biblical *hapax legomena* are explained by recourse to the Mishna. (The purpose of this work was polemical: to show the Karaites that recourse to the oral law was necessary for a proper understanding of the Bible.)

In these and other works, Saadia promoted a program of rational exegesis of the Bible in which the establishment of the discipline of Hebrew grammar as an exegetical tool played a major role. Toward this end, he applied the terminology and modes of analysis of the eighth-century Arabic grammarians to the study of Hebrew grammar. Hand in hand with the study of grammar, and in the Arabic world not totally distinct from it, went the concern for style and rhetoric. The high esteem granted by the Arabs to aesthetic forms of linguistic expression and the principle of *iʿjāz al-qurʾān*, the wonderful inimitability of the Qur'an, motivated Jews to seek in their Scripture a similar eloquence of expression. The term for this eloquence was *ṣaḥot hallašon*,[19] "pure language," a term coined by Saadia, based on Isaiah 32:4. *Ṣaḥot* is a term applied to language which is clear and correct—based on biblical patterns and their accepted derivatives. It came to include various stylistic features and poetic ornamentations.

The intention of Saadia and his successors, and the effect of their work, was a double one: renewed interest in biblical grammar as a key to rational exegesis, and a revival of Hebrew language and poetry in which biblical language and style became the model. Indeed, Saadia may be seen as the earliest and perhaps most brilliant example of the beneficial effect that *'Arabiyya* had on Jewish intellectual development, and on the role that the Bible assumed in that development. The irony of the situation and its outcome is captured by Gerson Cohen:

> The fascinating feature of Arab influence on the Jews was not in the use of Arabic, in the cultivation of the sciences, or in the rise of religious skepticism. Paradoxically, the profoundest form of Arabization of the Jewish *intelligentsia* was betrayed in the flowering of Hebrew —grammar, poetry, and, above all, neo-classicism. The revival of classical Hebrew—*but only in poetry*—was accompanied by a revival of classical metaphor, classical panegyric, classical typology. The Quran gave new life to the Bible, and the children of Mecca rejuvenated the spirit of the seed of Jacob.[20]

A cursory perusal of medieval Hebrew poetry quickly shows to what extent biblical language permeated it. The various emulations of biblical style and constructions, and the types and uses of biblical allusion and metaphor, have been described by several scholars.[21] T. Carmi sums it up elegantly:

> Of the many ornamental techniques developed by the Andalusian school, one deserves special mention: the art of scriptural insertions. This consisted of an adroit and fluent weaving together of biblical quotations, from a short phrase to an entire verse. The quotation could be verbatim, slightly altered, or elliptical; it could create a broad spectrum of effects by assuming an altogether different, and even contradictory, meaning in its new setting. At times, an entire poem is chequered with quotations from a specific and relevant biblical passage. In such cases, the strands of quotations and allusions cease to be an ornamental device and become the very fabric of the poem, a sustained metaphorical texture.[22]

Of even greater interest for our concern is the articulation of the theory behind the practice—the principle of imitating biblical expression—and the effort to observe it in a radically different context. For after all, medieval Hebrew was not biblical Hebrew, and, most important, the rules of medieval Hebrew poetry were quite different from those of biblical poetry. There were times when biblical language was insufficient to express all that a poet wished to express, or when biblical style contradicted medieval canons or tastes. The struggle to remain true to biblical forms while still producing innovative poetry is best seen in the following excerpts from Moshe ibn Ezra's *Kitāb al-Muḥāḍara wa-'l-Mudhākara*. Note the delicate balance that ibn Ezra aims for, and the reluctant and respectful manner in which he departs from biblical usage. In reference to metaphor he tells us:

> Gather for yourselves from the verses of the Bible however much you like and find pleasing. . . . As for me, in every speech that I gave, and in every letter that I wrote, and in every poem that I composed, I followed this course when I found it in the Holy Scriptures. Therefore, I did not create my own metaphors, for it [the Bible] contains enough for the most part; except if its path was not apparent to me and its procedure was not clear to me. . . . [Halkin, 228–29]

In other words, it is preferable to limit oneself to biblical metaphors, but if the need arises one may create one's own.

Similarly, it is desirable that an adjective be used together with the noun that it describes, but, because of metrical requirements, medieval poets sometimes omitted the noun. The Bible, too, may use an adjective without its noun. Ibn Ezra remarks: "What you find there you may use, and if you do not find it, do not create analogous forms. Go where the language [of the Bible] leads you and stop where it stops" (Halkin, 202–203). A clearer case of when the Bible contravenes medieval rhetorical forms is the following:

> Beware of juxtaposing words [in which the first ends and the second begins] with similar letters—letters with the same point of articulation—for this is ugly in poetry and in the opinion of men of music . . . even though the Hebrew [i.e., biblical] language permits it, and does not refrain from it, as in *bin nun* [Exod 33:11]; *yaruṣ ṣaddiq* [Prov 18:10]; *we'ozel lo* [Prov 20:14]; *me'ereṣ zikram* [Ps 34:17]; *ki yeš šeber* [Gen 42:1]. . . . All that the Bible permits is permissible. However, since in poetry especially we follow Arabic practice, it is incumbent upon us to do as they do as far as we are able. [Halkin, 160–61]

From the last two citations we sense some discomfort on ibn Ezra's part when biblical usage went against medieval rhetorical norms; but he could not declare biblical usages unacceptable.

On a broader level, the Bible was not only the source of proper linguistic usage, it was the source of all knowledge. *The Kuzari* (2.66) tells us that Solomon discoursed on all knowledge, and that all the principles of science were transmitted from the Jews to the rest of the world. However, as a result of the long and complex chain of transmission, the Jewish origin was forgotten and was erroneously ascribed to the Greeks and Romans. The same thought is expressed several centuries later, by Judah Messer Leon in *Nopet Ṣupim* (book I, ch. 13): "In the days of prophecy [i.e., the biblical period] . . . we used to learn and know from the Holy Torah all the sciences and truths of reason. . . . What other peoples possessed of these sciences and truths was very little, compared to us." This line of reasoning sounds highly apologetic to us, but it fits nicely with the tenor of the times and the Jewish intellectual enterprise. It is not surprising, then, to find that among the branches of knowledge found in the Bible are poetry and rhetoric.

The case of rhetoric was the easier to substantiate. Two major works are of special interest in this regard: Moshe ibn Ezra's *Kitāb al-Muḥāḍara wa-'l-Mudhākara* (especially chapter 8) and Judah Messer Leon's *Nopet Ṣupim*. Both base their analyses on the accepted rhetorical models of their respective societies, and find that the Bible implicitly used these models long before they were current elsewhere. Ibn Ezra, who lived in medieval Spain, used Arabic models of rhetoric and, for each trope, found a biblical reference as well as medieval Hebrew and Arabic references.[23] Judah Messer Leon, who lived in Renaissance Italy, looked to the classical rhetoricians for his model, and showed how they had been anticipated by the biblical authors.

It was somewhat more difficult to view the Bible as the source for (medieval) poetry. There was, as we shall see in the following chapter, much disagreement on what constituted poetry in the Bible and whether the ancient Israelites had knowledge of rhyme and meter. This was due mainly to the fact that biblical prosody was quite different from medieval prosody, but perhaps also to the ambivalent attitude toward poetry.

Attitudes toward Poetry

Medieval Hebrew poetry, with its rhyme and meter, was an innovation. Before it (and continuing throughout the medieval period) there had been *piyyuṭ*, liturgical poetry with rhyme and word meter, but in the tenth century Hebrew poets began to adopt Arabic forms of monorhyme and quantitative meter. Like any innovation, this one did not meet with unanimous acceptance at the outset, especially since the use of quantitative meter demanded certain adjustments in Hebrew. The appropriateness of this metrical borrowing and its effect on the Hebrew language were the subject of fierce debate.[24] At first, opponents considered the adoption of Arabic style a threat to the integrity of the Hebrew language and its native poetry, as well as a sign of admission of the superiority of Arabic culture. But Arabic culture soon came to permeate Jewish intellectual society, and with it, Arabic poetic norms. By the twelfth century, the question was no longer whether Hebrew poetry should employ Arabic meters, but how to justify the fact that it did.

There were several ways to do this, and they will be explored further in the following chapter. In general, there are two approaches, each with its modifications: (1) to find Arabic-style meters in the Bible, or at least among Jews of biblical times if not actually in scriptural writings; (2) to acknowledge that quantitative meter was a later borrowing; this borrowing represented either decadence or natural development. Whichever approach was preferred, there was a distinct "anxiety of influence," a need to come to terms with medieval poetic practice vis-à-vis the poetic practices of the Bible. As in the case of the Hebrew language, so in the case of Hebrew poetry: How could medieval poetry depart from its biblical antecedents? How could the medieval poets surpass the psalms of David?

Another question which occupied medieval writers was how to evaluate poetry in comparison with other areas of knowledge. While, on the one hand, poetry was highly prized as a social and cultural skill, on the other hand, it was considered intellectually inferior to philosophy. This derives from the Aristotelian formulation, transmitted by al-Farabi and other Arab scholars, whereby poetry is placed at the bottom of the intellectual hierarchy. In addition, the very essence of poetry—its metaphorical nature as expressed by the oft-repeated phrase "The best of poetry is its falseness"—put it in diametric opposition to the philosophical search for truth.[25] Poetry misled the hearer by presenting things which were not there, by saying things which were not true. This thought is exemplified in one of the questions that Falaquera's Seeker puts to the Poet: "Why has it been said that poetry causes a man to err so that he mistakes an imaginary object for the real thing?" To this the Poet has no answer.[26] This notion about poetry versus reality was widespread among Jews and Arabs. To quote one example, al-Jurjani, an eleventh-century Arab grammarian, states:

> What I understand here by imaginative creation is that process in which the poet presents as existing an object which actually does not exist, and makes a statement for which there is no possibility of a scientific presentation, and uses an expression which he himself makes up, and shows himself as seeing what he does not see.[27]

This idea is put more metaphorically in Falaquera's *Seper Hammebaqqeš* [The Book of the Seeker]:

> I have now beheld that the words of the poets follow a crooked course which is alien to the wise of heart and foreign to men of truth. . . . He [the Poet] builds a house of thick darkness upon the foundation of falsehood and daubs its flimsy walls with whitewash, covering it over both inside and outside with dross.[28]

Thus from a philosophic perspective, poetry was felt to be frivolous. Maimonides, the foremost of the medieval Jewish philosophers, expressed his distaste for it on numerous occasions, considering it a trivial pursuit. Immanuel Frances, reflecting a similar thought with the irony of someone promoting poetry, has a character in his *Meteq Sepatayim* say: "The art of poetry is the dessert . . . ; but talmudic study is grain and bread and food for a hungry soul."

What the philosophers dismissed as frivolous, the jurists and theologians considered downright dangerous, among both the Jews and the Arabs.[29] The figurative nature of poetry presented problems in the interpretation of Scripture. If "the best of poetry is its falseness," what could be said about biblical poetry? It became difficult to speak of poetry in the Bible, in its generally accepted sense; it was better not to take a "literary approach" to the Bible.[30] At the same time, the use of biblical expressions and allusions in *secular* poems angered the theologians; for them this represented a desecration of the divine word—the sacred employed for the benefit of the profane. Indeed, it was the secular use of poetry, not only new poetic forms, that was novel and hence disturbing to some. Moreover, although they may not have expressed it, poetry might also interfere with the theologians' control of hermeneutics, for by using a biblical phrase a poet was interpreting it, or perhaps misinterpreting it. And each time a biblical phrase appeared in a new context, its interpretation was stretched a little further.

Even some of the poets themselves seem to have eschewed poetry, repenting for having wasted their youth composing it and vowing to forswear it. But this vow is not what it appears. It must, as Ross Brann has convincingly argued, be considered a literary topos—expressing a kind of self-conscious false modesty on the part of the poet vis-à-vis his profession.[31]

This is not to say that poetry was universally denigrated. On the contrary, a number of positive qualities were attributed to it. Poetry, like music, appealed to the listener's aesthetic side, or, as we would put it, his emotional side. Poetry could arouse the listener, stir his heart, motivate him to action more effectively than philosophical discourse. Moreover, words set to music or meter were easier to remember; poetry served as a mnemonic aid. Finally, in the Bible, poetry was the vehicle for praising God. These and other sentiments, showing the power of poetry and poets, are put apothegmatically in *Seper Happardes*, by Yeda'ya Hapenini (Bedersi) (ca. 1270–1340).[32]

> When a poet is skillful, he seems like[33] a prophet. . . . Beware of the enmity of a poet, for his lies will be believed more than your truth. . . . The advantage of a poet is that he can remain in his place and take revenge on his enemy across the sea. . . . If it were not for the sweet metaphors of poetry, religions could not be sustained, for it is the nature of every poem to strengthen one's religion, to increase one's faith through pleasing rhetoric and sweet metaphors. . . . If you wish to make a point,[34] put it in a poem; if you put it in a book, it will not be publicized.[35]

Poetry had many advocates besides Yeda'ya Hapenini, and, despite its detractors, the composing of poetry was not about to be abandoned, for it was too much a part of the cultural and social scene. The conflicting attitudes toward it reflect the need to come to terms with this new form of expression, and to justify it as a natural outgrowth of native Hebrew language and literature. The Bible played a central role in this process, for not only did biblical language provide the framework upon which medieval Hebrew poetry was constructed, but the authority and antiquity of the Bible were invoked to legitimize the medieval poetic endeavor. If there was poetry in the Bible, how could it be wrong to write it now, especially if it imitated biblical style? If ancient Israel had written poetry, it was not a recent foreign import but a true and venerable form of Jewish expression. The Jews of medieval Spain promoted the myth that they were the direct descendants of the tribe of Judah, part of which had settled in Iberia *before* the Babylonian exile.[36] They were, thus, the direct heirs of the biblical tradition, the revivers of the cultural heritage (and the Hebrew language) that had been lost during the exile. Their poets strode in the footsteps of Moses, David, and Solomon.

Thus we see that attitudes toward the Hebrew language, the Bible, and poetry were intimately intertwined, and were part of a complex cultural awareness. They could not help but influence the study of biblical poetry.

•4•

MEDIEVAL AND RENAISSANCE VIEWS OF BIBLICAL POETRY

Medieval and Renaissance discussions of biblical poetry arose in a variety of contexts. In some cases, the biblical text itself motivated study. Since the Bible was a "privileged text," a religiously and ethnically central text, engagement with it was encouraged, indeed demanded, for no one could fully participate in society without it. Discussions of its poetic sections are, in these cases, part of the larger framework of exegesis. In other cases, discussions of biblical poetry are a part of a separate agenda, be it literary, philosophical, or historical. Their purpose was not to explicate the Bible but to justify certain contemporary cultural phenomena or to advance a particular argument. One finds in these latter writings, sometimes even more than in the former, a sustained view about the nature of biblical poetry. Because many of the authors were themselves poets, and all were highly literate, their observations were acute. Their writings give us a picture of the literary theory of their time, and of how this theory was applied to the Bible.

The Bible contains no metaliterary discussion. It offers no definition of poetry and no list of poetic devices. Although it does employ terms, such as *šir* and *mašal,* that appear to designate literary genres, the Bible provides little clarification concerning these genres. It is left to the readers to discern what they represent. In order to do so, readers call upon their own experience and training in the literature of their time. In the case of medieval and Renaissance Jewish scholars, this meant calling upon Arabic literary theory, itself influenced to an extent by Greek literary theory twice removed,[1] and later upon the neoclassical theory of the Renaissance. In addition, of course, there was the Jewish exegetical tradition, which also preserved some ideas relating to language and literature.

The Spoken Word versus the Written Word

Judaism knew both the written law and the oral law. Ironically, the oral law was also written, that is, existed as a written text. Yet its "oralness" was preserved if not in its textual form then in the manner in which it was studied. For it was considered (and still is in certain circles) improper to study the oral law from a written text alone; one must learn it from a teacher. One must receive an oral explanation, for the written text alone is insufficient in the sense that it cannot fully convey the depth and complexity of its meaning.[2] This notion was captured in the expression "From the mouth of scribes, not from the mouth of books." Moreover, it was not confined to the oral law but was broadly applied to all communications. If, as was assumed, the purpose of language was to transmit the thought of the speaker to the mind of the listener, then a written text is less adequate to the task, for it cannot convey the intonation and gestures that are conveyed in oral delivery. In other words, a written text is a limited representation of the meaning to be transmitted.

Judah Halevi stated (*Kuzari* 2.72) that oral delivery is aided by pauses, linkages of phrases, raising and lowering of the voice, gestures, and other means of expressing surprise, questions, fear, pleading, and so forth. Samuel ibn Tibbon said that there are ways that a teacher may convey meaning through reading the words, without literally explaining or commenting on them. He compares this to the everyday occurrence in which a phrase such as "You did well" is understood in the opposite sense, if so indicated by the tone of the speaker, his facial expression, or the occasion on which the statement is made.

These statements were made in a specific context and, prescient as they were in their grasp of what modern linguists call pragmatics, they were not intended to suggest that written communication is inferior to oral communication in an absolute sense. After all, Judaism's central text, the Bible, was written, and the medieval authors themselves produced a superb written literature in which they took enormous pride. The context of Halevi's statement (Samuel ibn Tibbon's is preserved in Judah Moscato's commentary on Halevi's) is the defense of the masoretic accents, which he viewed as indicators of the proper oral delivery of biblical passages. This, he felt, was a system which was superior to formal metrical systems which distorted the proper syntactic and semantic phrasing and subverted proper recitation.

Samuel Archivolti has a slightly different model, a more philosophical one. He explains the distinctions between (philosophical) thought, speech, and written composition as follows: thought is the highest form in one sense, for in it there is no possibility for confusion of meaning or ambiguity. (A word may have more than one meaning, but a thought or idea has only one.) But thought is of lesser value in another sense, in that it is limited to the person who has it, whereas speech benefits not only the possessor of thought but others as well. Written composition surpasses speech, for speech is limited to contemporary listeners, while written composition benefits both contemporary readers and future generations. (Archivolti also adds the idea that the spoken word is accompanied by tone and gestures, and is for this reason better.) Thus in Archivolti's model there is a balance or trade-off between the accuracy of the communication and the extent of its transmission.

Discussions such as these are interesting because they reflect a high level of consciousness about language and the processes of communication and interpretation. They are an additional indication that this was a society in which words and books—ancient and contemporary—were taken seriously, a society in which contemporary works of literature and philosophy were produced and ancient works were studied and interpreted.

Types of Discourse

In connection with discussions of poetry, we sometimes find brief discussions of discourse in general, and classification of all or part of the Bible into types of discourse. The models are not original; they are classical or neoclassical models applied to the Bible.

Since the books of Proverbs (*Mišlê,* the plural construct of *mašal*) and Song of Songs (*Šir Hašširim*) open with two of the important terms in the discussion of poetry, and since both were ascribed to Solomon, they and the third book ascribed to Solomon, Ecclesiastes, are often compared. Both Moshe ibn Tibbon and Joseph ibn Kaspi cite the common view that these three books represent three different types of discourse: Ecclesiastes is literal, Proverbs is allegorical (*mašal,* in which the literal has a hidden meaning), and Song of Songs is metaphorical, or poetic.

Two of our Italian Renaissance writers reflect slightly different ways of organizing types of discourse. Samuel Archivolti speaks of four types: simple, rhetorical, enigmatic (discourse by means of riddle and *mašal*), and poetic. They are differentiated by their complexity of linguistic and stylistic features. Simple discourse must obey the rules of grammar but has no other requirement. Rhetorical discourse, in addition to being grammatical, chooses the best-sounding words, so as to be persuasive. This is the best type for praising kings and God. Enigmatic discourse observes the prior points and hides the meaning in a succinct allegory or riddle, thereby inducing the reader to solve the interpretation and derive further pleasure. Poetic discourse is mindful of grammar, rhetoric, and succinct wording and employs meter and rhyme. (Compare Profiat Duran's division of the science of language into grammar, rhetoric, and poetry. Rhetorical discourse has sweetness and beauty; poetic discourse has, in addition to sweetness and beauty, meter.)

Immanuel Frances's persona, Jachin, finds the origins of rhetoric and poetry in the Bible and presents the most comprehensive, and also the most modern-sounding, analysis of biblical discourse. There are three types: prose, rhetoric, and poetry. Prose is the common language used by all, and the books written in it are the Pentateuch, Joshua, Judges, Samuel, Kings, Jonah, Chronicles, Ruth, and Esther. Rhetoric constitutes the prophetic books—Isaiah, Jeremiah, Ezekiel, and most of the Twelve Minor Prophets (excluding Jonah). Poetry is exemplified by the Song of the Sea, Ha'azinu, the Song of Deborah, Psalms, and the like.

The Meaning of Šir and Mašal

The biblical terms *šir* (and *šira*) and *mašal* are a natural starting point for a discussion of poetry and figure prominently in a number of our texts. Actually, though, the terms present certain difficulties, for the Bible does not use them quite the way a medieval or Renaissance scholar would have liked. The terms needed to be defined in a manner that would do justice to their biblical contexts and at the same time fit medieval notions of discourse.

Šir, "song" or "poem," was often rendered in Arabic by *shi'r,* "poetry." The phonetic similarity between the Hebrew and Arabic terms (which are etymologically unrelated) helped to reinforce the notion that the two terms must refer to essentially the same phenomenon.[3] This had two consequences. The first was the search for Arabic-style poetry in the Bible. This would have happened even if the terms had not sounded alike, since Arabic poetic criteria set the standard for discussions of poetry, but the coincidental similarity of the terms must have made the effort more compelling. The second consequence was the broadening of the meaning of *šir,* and hence of the concept of poetry, for it soon became apparent that biblical *šir* did not always mean "poem" in the sense understood by medieval Arabs and Jews. Moshe ibn Ezra, citing biblical verses for support, notes that *šir* may mean "poem," "song," "lament," and that it may even be used of prose, as in "Song of Songs," the Song of the Well (Num 21:17–18), and "Let me sing to my beloved" (Isa 5:1), or to mean "thank," as in Exod 15:21. The fact that modern scholars may deem all or most of these passages poetic is immaterial;

for ibn Ezra, Song of Songs and passages such as Isa 5:1ff. did not meet the criteria of poetry.

Quite a number of others were troubled by the use of *šir* in connection with Song of Songs. They did not call it prose, as ibn Ezra did, but found it to be poetic by virtue of its metaphorical form of expression. That is, their definition of poetry included nonmetrical compositions which employed figurative language. (See, for example, Moshe ibn Tibbon and Judah Messer Leon. In the case of Song of Songs, this usually referred to the allegorical interpretation.) *Šir* could also refer to a nonmetrical composition set to music. (Judah Messer Leon explains Exod 15:21 in this way.) In fact, *šir* was generally assigned three basic meanings (see Moshe ibn Tibbon and Don Isaac Abravanel): (1) metrical poem, (2) nonmetrical poem set to music, (3) figurative or metaphorical discourse. These points then become the criteria for defining poetry.

The various meanings of *šir* are presented in a more complicated arrangement by Yoḥanan Allemanno in his *Ḥešeq Šelomoh*. Allemanno finds that the term *šir* has two basic meanings: (1) a melody or words set to music, and (2) a composition employing metaphor (not necessarily sung). He further subdivides the first category into three: (a) rhymed metrical poems, (b) poems lacking rhyme and meter but arranged in short and long lines—that is, written stichographically (he cites the Song of the Sea, Ha'azinu, Psalms, Job, and Proverbs), and (c) compositions which by virtue of their contents warrant the designation of poem.[4]

The term *mašal,* meaning "allegory, parable" and also "comparison, metaphor, simile," presented even greater problems. On one hand, to call a composition a *mašal,* in the sense of being metaphorical, was to equate it with poetry; on the other hand, *mašal* in the sense of allegory was not necessarily poetic (e.g., Ezek 17:1). Several of our authors touch upon this.[5] Joseph ibn Kaspi, for example, explains that the Book of Proverbs is called *Mišlê* because it employs many metaphors and similes; but, according to him, it is not to be taken as an allegory, as it was by some of his contemporaries. However, ibn Kaspi does, like everyone else of his time, take Song of Songs to be an allegory, that is, a *mašal,* and this helped to justify its label of *šir,* "poem." Moshe ibn Tibbon distinguishes types of discourse—literal, *mašal,* and poetic—from poetry in a formal sense—metered, sung, or metaphorical. One can have a metered or sung "poem," he says, that is written in literal or *mašal* discourse, as, for example, Proverbs.[6] This differs from true poetry, in the Aristotelian sense, which is expressed in figurative language. An example of the last is Song of Songs, a poem par excellence not for its meter or melody but for its metaphorical quality. Taking a more philosophical tack, Don Isaac Abravanel distinguishes a *mašal* composed through the Holy Spirit from a *mašal* composed through prophecy. The former is poetry, a human work with elements of inspiration, while the latter is not poetry but divine revelation. This allows him to consider Proverbs and Song of Songs poetry, as well as any other passages that he can prove were composed while the author was not in a state of prophecy (see his commentary on Isaiah 5).

The clearest expression of the problem, and the difficulty in solving it, is found in Immanuel Frances's *Meteq Sepatayim*. Jachin, the teacher, lists *mašal* (and also *šir)* as one of the names for poems. The student, Boaz, questions the use of *mašal* as a general term for poetry, since it can sometimes mean simply (nonpoetic) comparison. Jachin responds that poems are called *mašal* because in poetry and elegant prose one finds many comparisons (i.e., metaphors and similes). Boaz then cites Ps 49:5 "I will turn my ear to *mašal;* I will open my riddle with the lyre." He interprets this use of *mašal* as referring to "the doubling of meaning in different words"—that is, poetry; but he does not understand the relationship of the two meanings of *mašal:* "comparison"—a feature of prose and poetry—and "doubling of meaning in different words." Jachin is not able to provide a satisfactory explanation. He answers, impatiently, one imagines, that "the commentators have already explained that both are closed matters, understood only by men of intellect. Let us return to our subject."

Jachin's subject, and the real issue, is not the definition of *mašal* but the definition of poetry, specifically biblical poetry. The assumption shared by almost everyone—deriving from biblical terminology such as *šir,* the stichographic writing in masoretic Bibles, the special system of masoretic accents in the books of Psalms, Proverbs, and Job, and the exegetical tradition—was that the Bible contained poetic sections. However, exactly which sections were to be considered poetry, and what qualified them for this designation, was the subject of some difference of opinion. The problem was that biblical poetry, whatever it might be, did not have the same characteristics as medieval Arabic or Hebrew poetry; the differences of opinion in defining and identifying it arose mainly from the ways in which individuals brought into line the poetry they found in the Bible with their own conception of poetry.

Does Biblical Poetry Have Meter and Rhyme?

For some medieval writers, Arabic-style meter and rhyme were the sine qua non of poetry, for that is what defined poetry in their own day. Anything short of that was not true poetry. Others took a broader view and included syllabic meter and nonmetrical poetry in their definition. Whichever position was taken, it was heavily influenced by contemporary poetic norms, by previous statements on the topic, and by individual attitudes toward the Bible and toward poetry.

Hebrew secular poems in Spain from the tenth to the fifteenth centuries consisted of a number of lines (*bayit,* pl. *batim*), each containing two metrically equivalent half-lines (*delet* and *soger*). The meter was quantitative. It was composed of long and short syllables, "cords and pegs," arranged in set patterns. The cord contained one vowel; the peg contained a vowel plus a mobile *shwa* (or *ḥaṭep* or the conjunction *u*). This system disregarded the stress or accent of the word. There was also syllabic meter, used for some liturgical poetry, which required simply that the number of syllables in a line be the same. The *shwa* and *ḥaṭep* were not included in the syllable count.

Italian Hebrew poets at first adopted the quantitative meters of Spain, but later they developed their own quantitative-syllabic and then syllabic meters. In the syllabic meter of Italy, short vowels *did* count as syllables.[7]

Rhyme, which ran throughout the entire poem in Spain, or throughout a strophe in strophic poems, required that the final consonant plus vowel (plus consonant) be the same. This is a more limited condition than English poetry requires, in which only the final vowel (plus consonant) need rhyme. Whereas words such as *bad* and *lad* rhyme in English, they do not rhyme in medieval Hebrew poetry. Medieval Hebrew poets would, however, accept *lad* and *salad* as a rhyme (since accent is not taken into account in the metrical system). Actually, *bad* and *lad* was considered a low form of rhyme that might be used in rhymed prose but never in poetry. Instructions as to what constitutes proper rhyme are contained in a popular "poem" often ascribed to Abraham ibn Ezra.

לא תחרז בשור ובחמור יחדו
אך אמנם תשמר החמור
בהר המור
ואת השור תקשור
בערי המישור

lo' taḥaroz bešor ubaḥamor yaḥdayw
'ak 'omnam tišmor haḥamor
behar hammor
we'et hašor tiqšor
be'arê hammišor.

Do not rhyme ox [*šor*] with ass [*ḥamor*]
But keep [*tišmor*] the ass [*ḥamor*]

In the mountain of myrrh [*mor*]
And the ox [*šor*] tie [*tiqšor*]
In the cities of the plain [*mišor*].

Playing on Deut 22:10, which forbids plowing [*lo' taḥaroš*] with an ox and an ass yoked together, this ditty forbids the rhyming of *šor* and *ḥamor,* directing the reader to rhyme words which end with the same consonant plus vowel plus consonant.

No one could make a case for sustained meter or rhyme throughout a large section of biblical poetry, and quantitative meter, even within a verse, was impossible to find (except for the simplest of metrical patterns). But occasional verses were found to have syllabic meter or rhyme within two verse halves.[8] For some, this was enough to justify the label "poetry"; others denied that the Bible contained proper poetry, or sought their justifications elsewhere.

One of the earliest observations on the subject is contained in a fragment attributed to Saadia Gaon.[9] The author discusses a category called "prose poetry," or poetic prose, which he considers more praiseworthy than the previous category (presumably prose, but the text is missing this section). He divides poetic prose into seven subtypes: *khuṭba,* "rhetorical speech" (which has verses but no rhyme); *rajaz,* "rhymed verses" (the first half of a verse rhymes with the second half, but the rhyme does not continue throughout the composition); *saj',* "rhymed prose" (rhyming throughout with some meter); *shi'r al-musammā piyyuṭ,* "poetry called *piyyuṭ*" (rhymed and with definite meter);[10] *al-mansuj al-mushajjar,* "connected poetry" (a fabric of biblical and rabbinic phrases); *fawāsiq wa-qiṣaṣ,* "proverbs and fables"; and *ta'lif al-kalām fī tafsīr,* "composition with commentary."[11] The Bible is mentioned in connection with *rajaz:*

> The second type is called in Arabic *rajaz,* and it is found in the Bible. It rhymes but is not poetry [*shi'r*], as in: *lo' tesulleh beketem 'opir / bešoham yaqar wesappir* [Job 28:16]; *he'anoki le'adam siḥi / we'im madua' lo' tiqṣar ruḥi* [Job 21:4]; and *mime'ê 'imi / hizkir šemi* [Isa 49:1].

The three verses cited all contain rhyme, as defined in medieval poetry.[12] Yet these verses are distinguished from true poetry.

A statement quite similar, and obviously influenced by this one, is made by Moshe ibn Ezra in chapter 4 of his *Kitāb al-Muḥāḍara wa-'l-Mudhākara.*

> We find nothing [in the Bible] but prose, except for three books: Psalms, Job, and Proverbs. And even these, as you can see, do not employ fixed meter or rhyme, as Arabic poetry does. Rather, they

> resemble *rajaz* only. Indeed, occasionally some of them follow a feature of *rajaz,* as in Job 28:16; Job 33:17; Job 21:4, and others.

Ibn Ezra substitutes a verse in Job for Isa 49:1 cited in the fragment, because he does not consider Isaiah to be poetry. Poetry, such as it is, is limited in his view to Psalms, Proverbs, and Job, the books with a special system of masoretic accents. In chapter 8 of his *Kitāb al-Muḥāḍara,* he illustrates verses with *rajaz* meter (the simplest type of meter that the Arabs considered to be poetry), and again he limits himself to Psalms, Proverbs, and Job. In chapter 4, however, he acknowledges that "a few songs elsewhere in the Bible depart from prose, e.g., Exodus 15, Deuteronomy 32, 2 Samuel 22, Judges 5." These passages are cited apparently because they are written stichographically in masoretic Bibles; but ibn Ezra excludes other "songs" so labeled in rabbinic sources, claiming that most are prose.

Ibn Ezra's view constitutes a narrow view of biblical poetry—one that finds little or no true poetry (by Arabic and Judeo-Spanish standards) in the Bible. In fact, ibn Ezra is skeptical of the claims made by some based on 1 Kgs 5:12 that Solomon composed *qaṣīdas*—that is, that true poetry was composed in ancient Israel but not preserved; he pleads ignorance on the date of the origin of Hebrew poetry but clearly suggests that it was postexilic.

This view is echoed in Judah al-Ḥarizi's *Taḥkemoni* (ch. 18), which finds Heman the Ezrahite in Jerusalem sitting among the wise men and poets,

> discussing poetry and its secrets. To know how its foundations were originally constructed, and who brought forth its origins to the Jews and shone its light upon them. Some men among them replied: "Lo, we all know, and our fathers have told us, that poetry is the heritage of the Arabs, since they were first on their soil." But they did not know when the spirit of poetry alighted upon the Hebrews, or who first opened its gates to them. . . . For when our fathers were still residing in the Holy City, metrical poetry in the holy tongue was unknown to them. [They knew] only the books of Job, Proverbs, and Psalms. They have short and light verses [*pesuqim*]. They resemble poetic verses [*ḥaruzê šir*] but they have no rhyme or meter.

A similar view is expressed by Saadia ibn Danaan (fifteenth century):

> We do not know when our countrymen began to practice this art, but it seems to me that it is not an art [indigenous] to our fathers, but to it, as to other things, applies the verse "They mingled among the nations and learned their ways" [Ps 106:35]. I have inquired and searched extensively and have found that before the poems of the

> great rabbi R. El'azar Kallir[13] poetry [*ḥaruzim*] was unknown in our nation.[14]

One gets the impression that Moshe ibn Ezra and Judah al-Ḥarizi may have found biblical poetry to be inferior to medieval Hebrew poetry, although ibn Ezra makes a strong case that biblical stylistics and rhetoric are every bit as good as those of Arabic and medieval Hebrew literature, and al-Ḥarizi emphasizes that the poetic capabilities of Hebrew equal or surpass those of Arabic. Ibn Ezra's contemporary Judah Halevi took a more positive stand, making a virtue out of the deficiency. Halevi, too, found that the Bible lacked the requirements of medieval poetry (quantitative meter and rhyme), but he saw in this a sign of superiority. The Bible, he claimed, had forgone metrical poetry in favor of preserving the proper recitation (through the masoretic accents), which in turn conveyed the correct meaning of the verses. For metrical poetry goes against normal syntactic and semantic phrasing, forcing one to pause where one should continue or continue where one should pause. It also wreaks havoc, Halevi explained, with Hebrew grammar and accentuation.[15]

Halevi had numerous adherents (*The Kuzari* was a widely accepted book), and we find his arguments repeated elsewhere (in even stronger language by his student Solomon ibn Parḥon, and also by Samuel and Moshe ibn Tibbon). These authors make the point that the virtue of the Bible is that it does not sacrifice meaning for meter. This, in turn, relates to the division of songs or poems into two types: those in which the meaning, or words, was primary and those in which the melody, or meter, was primary. Samuel Archivolti considers the former to be more praiseworthy, for

> it is designed not only to give pleasure to the ear, but also to give spirit and animation to the words pronounced. This is the type that the Levites used, for without it they would not have been able to arrange musical accompaniments. And it is the appropriate one for the composing of songs in our holy tongue.

Indeed, as Archivolti reminds his readers, Halevi explained that lines of different length could be set to the same melody. That is, they could be "poetic" in the sense of being set to music and still not be metrical in the strict sense.[16]

Clearly, according to these authors, there was no readily identifiable quantitative meter in the Bible. But had there ever been? Had there been a meter other than quantitative? Despite Halevi's insistence that the absence of meter was a boon, many were reluctant to give up the search for remnants or traces of it, or for alternative metrical or quasi-metrical systems. For the urge to define biblical poetry in terms of a formal structure was very strong, and the failure to find such a structure in passages generally acknowledged as poetic must have been as frustrating to the medieval scholar as it is to the modern one.

One way out of the impasse was to say that the meter of biblical poems had once existed but, as the result of time and exile, had been lost. (This is similar to the argument made in reference to the deterioration of the Hebrew language—see chapter 3). As early as the tenth century the followers of Menaḥem ibn Saruq, who opposed the introduction of Arabic-style meters into Hebrew, argued that Hebrew had had its own native meter.

> If we had not been exiled from our land, and our language in its entirety were in our hands, as in months of old when we rested secure in peaceful dwellings, then we would know all the grammar [or: fine points] of our language and its various structures [or: effects], and we would know its measure [*miš qal*] and would abide by it. For every people's language has its own measure [*mišqolet*] and grammar, but ours was lost to us. . . .[17]

It is not clear what metrical system, if any, ibn Saruq had in mind. He was not out to recover one, but only to show that one borrowed from the Arabs was inappropriate, since it went against the native rhythmic structures of Hebrew. His argument, which has to do more with grammar than with meter, is similar to the one that Judah Halevi was to make.

Ibn Saruq's is an argument from silence. Moshe ibn Ḥabib, however, brought proof. First of all, he defines "meter" differently from his predecessors, for just shortly before he wrote *Darkê No'am,* syllabic meter, in which a mobile *shwa* counted as a full vowel, came onto the Italian Hebrew scene. Ibn Ḥabib spoke of three types of meter: (1) syllabic meter in which the first half-line has the same number of syllables as the second half-line; there is no pattern of feet or rhyme; (2) syllabic meter in which there may not be an exact match between the number of syllables in the two half-lines; the lack is filled in by the melody (borrowing the point made by Judah Halevi); (3) quantitative meter. Biblical poetry (Psalms, Proverbs, Job, Song of the Sea, Ha'azinu, Song of David, and Song of Deborah) belongs to the second category. That is, in ibn Ḥabib's view, biblical poetry is metrical, although others would not call this kind of meter true meter. But he does not stop there. Feeling that quantitative meter is the superior form, he declares that this form is very ancient and cites a tombstone inscription to prove that, despite its absence in the Bible, this type of poetry was composed in ancient Israel.

Ibn Ḥabib's view that *quantitative* meter dates from biblical times is a minority opinion, but it had a strong advocate in the author of *Šeqel Haqqodeš*, who wrote: "I have no doubt that all that the Arabs knew of it [the art of poetry] they took from the sages of our nation, just as they took their inferior language from our holy tongue."[18] While several of our authors make this claim about metaphor, which abounds in the Bible, or about knowledge in general (see chapter 3), it was much more common to give the Arabs credit for the invention of poetry with quantitative meter.

The answer to the question whether biblical poetry was metrical depended on one's definition of meter and on one's need to find meter in the Bible. Those for whom quantitative meter was the norm, and who could readily admit that quantitative meter was borrowed from the Arabs, generally did not find meter in the Bible. This is true of both those who applauded Arabic-style poetry in Hebrew, such as Moshe ibn Ezra, and those who were more ambivalent, such as Judah Halevi. On the other hand, those who sought the origin of meter in the Bible were likely to find at least a few examples of it, but the type of meter was usually syllabic. This would have been only partially reassuring to those who considered quantitative meter to be the only true meter, but as syllabic meter became popular in secular poetry, e.g., Renaissance Italy, the advantages of finding it in the Bible became greater.

The Renaissance saw the growth of vernacular literature, especially poetry, and with it the legitimation of poetry. Among the defenses of poetry are, as James Kugel mentions, the divine origin of poetry and the metrical constructions in the Psalter and other poetic passages of the Bible.[19] This suggests a renewed effort to discover the source of metrical poetry in the Bible, this time among Christians. While at first the metrical models were classical ones, the quantitative meters of Greek and Latin poetry, they were later replaced, especially in Italy, by the models of vernacular poetry, which employed syllabic rather than quantitative meters. Biblical poetry, then, came to be seen as based on *numerus* rather than *metrum.* That is, the meter was in the number of the syllables, not in the quality of the syllables. As we have seen, and as Christian Hebraists also learned, there were precedents among the Jews for this idea. It is difficult to establish the extent of the Jewish influence, but quite a few of the Jewish advocates of syllabic meter in the Bible, or something like it, had lived at least part of their lives in Italy (Abravanel, ibn Ḥabib, Portaleone, Archivolti; and Moshe ibn Tibbon's introduction to Song of Songs was reproduced almost word for word by Immanuel of Rome). Kugel suggests that "it is reasonable to suppose that this notion, soon widespread, of Hebrew's 'system' as *numerus* but not *metrum* was essentially an Italian synthesis based on earlier and contemporary Jewish writings plus the distinction . . . between mere 'numbers' and true 'meter.'"[20] At the same time, it is equally plausible to assume that the later Jewish writers, such as Archivolti and Portaleone, were influenced by their surroundings, that they were spurred on to find syllabic meter not only because there were Jewish precedents but because their Christian neighbors were doing likewise. Portaleone, who denies that the Bible contains quantitative meter, and who therefore remains puzzled about the stichographic writing of certain sections, goes on to observe some examples of rhyme and syllabic meter in Numbers 21. Archivolti, too, finds rhyme in the Bible, whence it originated, and hints that there may be a simple form of meter in it, too.

The man who made the most brilliant synthesis of his time, who took the concept of *numerus* beyond his contemporaries and his successors, was an Italian Jew with humanistic leanings who had access to the long traditions of both Jewish and Christian thought. He was Azariah de' Rossi, and his work marks a turning point in the history of the study of biblical poetry.

In the sixtieth chapter of his *Me'or 'Ênayim,* de' Rossi discusses biblical poetry. He begins by citing Jewish sources who deny the existence of Arabic-style quantitative meter in the Bible, Judah Halevi and Don Isaac Abravanel (see below on Abravanel). He then quotes classical sources, many of which were being quoted by his Christian contemporaries, to the effect that biblical poetry does have meter similar to the quantitative meter of classical poetry. Finally, he mentions the "proof" of ibn Ḥabib regarding the existence of quantitative meter in ancient Israel. Seeking to mediate between these contradictory opinions, and to solve the metrical question, de' Rossi observes that the Hebrew language does not preclude metrical poetry. The meter may be a product of the melody or even inherent in the words themselves.[21]

This suggests a strong predilection on de' Rossi's part to find some type of meter in the Bible, probably because this was something of a Renaissance preoccupation. But, siding against the classical authors and with the Jewish ones, he senses that the meter of biblical poems is not quantitative. (This is in line with the Renaissance conclusions that the meter of the Bible was not like classical meter.) Rather, he says, "their structures and measures are in the *number of ideas* [*'inyanim*]." Here we have the synthesis. De' Rossi has accepted the concept of "number," *numerus,* but does not apply it to syllables, as others had done and continued to do. He applies it to *'inyanim,* "ideas" or "semantic units," a term that he seems to have gotten from Judah Halevi (*Kuzari* 2.72), who used it to refer to the fact that in biblical poetry meaning took precedence over meter, and that the masoretic accents, which indicated the meaning, were a kind of substitute for meter. De' Rossi does not accept Halevi in toto; he does not mention the masoretic accents in this context, and, more important, he speaks of the *number* of ideas. In other words, he counts ideas as others would count syllables (something quite far from Halevi's thought).[22]

The advantage of de' Rossi's system is that it works for many more examples than syllabic meter does. Yet we should not lose sight of the fact that de' Rossi wanted to discover in biblical poetry a metrical system, one no less metrical than that of classical poetry or Italian poetry. Indeed, de' Rossi declares the Bible's system to be superior, for it is possible to translate the Bible without losing its meter—something not possible in quantitative or syllabic systems (this is a variation on Judah Halevi's theme of meaning over meter, and the translatability factor was also noted by Moshe ibn Tibbon [see note 31 of this chapter]). Furthermore, de' Rossi gains prestige for the Bible by showing that it had a most ancient metrical system. The beauty of Azariah de' Rossi's synthesis, irrespective of its correctness, is that it incorporates Jewish traditional views along with the most advanced views of the Italian Renaissance. Unfortunately, it was largely ignored for two centuries until Robert Lowth utilized it in his *Lectures on the Sacred Poetry of the Hebrews.*

Although de' Rossi's main concern was meter, a by-product of his system was to demonstrate the binary structure of biblical verses, for the number of ideas was always the same in the two verse halves. This is not a new idea. In fact, all of the previous counting, be it quantitative or syllabic, was done by comparing the first verse half with the second. There were two reasons for this: (1) the masoretic accents generally subdivide a verse into two halves (not always equal in length), and (2) Hebrew secular poetry was composed of lines with two metrically equal halves (*delet* and *soger*). It was therefore quite natural to look for a metrical system in the relationship between the halves of a biblical verse. Yet rarely was this apprehended as a poetic structure in and of itself; it was usually taken as an assumption upon which to build the search for meter.

There are, however, three authors who point to the binariness of biblical verses as being significant as a mark of poetry. Moshe ibn Tibbon (thirteenth century) states that perhaps Proverbs, Job, and most of Psalms are poetry because "they have divided verses [*pesuqim*], like verses [in medieval poetry; *batim*], although the parts are not equal." Joseph ibn Kaspi, in explaining the style of the Book of Proverbs, starts from the assumption that the verses have a binary structure and analyzes the relationships between the two halves. He finds, in a manner that anticipates Lowth, that there are four types of verses: those in which the entire verse continues the same idea; those in which the second half contains antonyms of the first; those similar to the preceding but containing ellipsis; and those in which the first part is the *mašal* and the second part the *nimšal.* Ibn Kaspi's modern-sounding analysis was not picked up by his successors, but several centuries later Immanuel Frances observed that "although we do not find in their [the Bible's] poems meter or rhyme, nevertheless, there is a caesura in every line." He also identified biblical poetry at least in part by "the doubling of language in different words."[23] This phrase is not new, but it generally referred to a stylistic or rhetorical device, not an indicator of poetry.

Thus from a concern with the formal structure of biblical poetry emerged the beginnings of an awareness of the feature that later came to be known as parallelism. Azariah de' Rossi, too, seemed on the brink of discovering it, but he stopped short of it, as his concern was meter. It remained for later generations to develop parallelism into the important concept that it is today. But the basic assumption underlying discussions of parallelism—namely, that most biblical verses manifest a binariness—was a long-standing one in the history of the study of biblical poetry.[24]

Music and Poetry

Regardless of whether biblical poetry was thought to have had meter, there was a pervasive sense that in some, perhaps unquantifiable, way, biblical poetry was different from biblical prose. It was different in its rhythm or melody—in the way it sounded when recited. Azariah de' Rossi tells us that he

> inquired of many contemporary sages whether they knew how to find and identify in them [biblical poems] any measure or meter, but no one could. But while everyone acknowledges that the euphony of the poetry resounds in the recitation, no one could account for the difference between them and the rest of the words of the Torah, Prophets, and Writings in respect to melody.

Abraham Portaleone admits that he cannot explain the stichographic writing of certain biblical poems and the block writing of others, since he cannot find true meter in any of these biblical poems.[25] At best, he suggests that "the ancient songs are recognizable to the ear simply by virtue of the pleasantness of reciting them, even when there is no difference in the way they are written."

Behind these words lies the idea that poetry is words that can be set to music.[26] We have met it before: in the definitions of the term *šir,* in Judah Halevi's observation that lines of differing lengths could be sung to the same tune, and in variations on Halevi's theme. Often the "solution" that a poem is something set to music is enough to halt the quest for meter, but occasionally this leads to a reinvigorated quest, as in the case of Don Isaac Abravanel.

Abravanel distinguishes three types of poetry: (1) metrical poetry of the kind known in medieval Hebrew (and not found in the Bible), (2) nonmetrical poetry which once was sung, (3) poems which employ figurative language. This typology is similar to other definitions of *šir.* What is interesting is what Abravanel does with his second category, into which he places the stichographic sections of the Bible (including, as he notes, Psalms, Proverbs, and the dialogues of Job, which in carefully written Bibles are arranged stichographically). The purpose of the stichographic writing, according to Abravanel, was to indicate the melody, now lost, to which the words were originally sung. In other words, Abravanel sees in the stichography "proof" that the words were set to music, hence poetry. Furthermore, he attempts to reconstruct the general features of the melody of Exodus 15, assigning lengths called "short," "medium," or "long" to the lines. His method is far from clear, but it may be based on the medieval system of eight melodic modes. Thus far Abravanel seems in agreement with others, including Halevi and Archivolti, who suggested that biblical poems had been set to music. But in a radical departure from them, he opines that the melody controlled the words, and not the reverse. For the sake of the measurement (of the melody), Abravanel tells us, some words had to be contracted and others lengthened. What Judah Halevi suggested happened in the recitation, Abravanel says happened in the actual writing. By so saying, he undoes the gain that Halevi obtained for biblical poetry, namely, that it was not hampered by metrical constraints. Abravanel hampered it not by metrical constraints but by musical constraints. At least one author recognized that Abravanel was imposing the equivalent of a metrical system upon certain poems. Immanuel Frances, who acknowledged the possibility of forgotten melodies, chided Abravanel for trying to discover meter in the Bible.

> I am amazed that from his [Abravanel's] holy mouth such a thing could come—that the greatest of prophets [Moses] would have to constrict his discourse and pervert the meaning for the sake of the melody. For it is known that it is considered a disparagement to say of a poet that he constricts his words for the sake of the meter.

More than five centuries later, Judah Halevi's point about meaning versus meter still had an adherent in Immanuel Frances. This is not to say that the musical aspect of poetry was abandoned. On the contrary, music and poetry were considered related arts, often discussed together (e.g., *The Kuzari* and *Šilṭê Haggibborim*), and one of the definitions of *šir* was words set to a melody. But most scholars differentiated between a poem's musicality and actual poetic meter.

The Best of Poetry Is Its Falseness

While much emphasis was put on the formal structure and tropes of Hebrew poetry—its meter and rhyme, and its rhetorical figures—the essence of poetry was thought to be its figurative language. "*Mêṭab haššir kezabo*," "The best of poetry is its falseness," was the way it was expressed, meaning that the essential quality of poetry was its fictitiousness, its feigning, its use of metaphor and hyperbole. The idea was not original; it appears in Arabic sources and has its origin among the Greeks.[27] In fact, it is often quoted in the name of Aristotle.

The phrase was a two-edged sword, for, as was mentioned in chapter 3, it was used to cast suspicion on the veracity of a poem's contents, and to denigrate the writing of poetry. In order to avoid this problem, one had to distinguish, as Moshe ibn Ezra did, between the mode of discourse, which was "false," and the contents, which were true.[28]

The problem is dealt with in a slightly different manner by Avshalom Mizraḥi in his *'Imrê Šeper.* There the distinction is between the truth of biblical poetry and the falseness of medieval poetry.

> Now I will explain to you about exaggeration and hyperbole in the art of poetry. Know, my brother, that in the art of poetry there are exaggerations and nonsense and untrue things. For the poets were not constrained except to make their words equal in long and short vowels in order to make the discourse more beautiful, and they were careful in respect to mobile and quiescent *shwas,* and they used ungrammatical words and added things and subtracted words even though they were not necessary for the meaning, and they falsified the matter. . . . You know what the Logicians have said—that things are divided according to their nature into three parts: totally true; totally false; or a combination of false and true. The last is divided into three parts: mostly true; mostly false; or equal in truth and falseness. Totally true is demonstration; totally false is poetry; mostly true is dialectic; mostly false is sophistic speech—as the chief of the philosophers, Aristotle, explained. You know what the sage said: the best of poetry is its falseness. The sages said about the poets: What do

> you think of men for whom truth is deemed meritorious for all except them and falseness is deemed reproachable except for them?[29]
>
> Therefore, the poems of David, Solomon, Asaph, Heman, and Yeduthun are all truthful utterances, but our poems are totally or mostly lies and falsehoods. The poems of former generations distinguished truth from falsehood, but we distinguish good from bad.[30] And from this you will rightly understand that the gap that exists between our poetry and theirs is like the gap of Adam, the hiatus before he sinned. . . . [31]

Despite the danger of attributing falseness to the Bible (which Mizraḥi is at such pains to avoid), the idea that poetry is false, in the sense of metaphorical, had the advantage of defining poetry by other than the formal criteria of meter and rhyme. Metrical discourse lacking metaphorical language was not poetry; conversely, a poem lacking meter and rhyme might still be a poem. The latter was important in reference to the Bible, for it could be invoked to justify the designation "poem" [*šir*] for passages which lacked formal poetic characteristics. "The best of poetry is its falseness" was often applied to Song of Songs, which began with the word *šir*, but which lacked the formal markers used by medievals to identify biblical poetry: it was not written stichographically and did not have a special system of masoretic accents. Song of Songs was deemed poetic by virtue of its metaphorical language, which meant to the medieval interpreter something slightly different from what it means to us. The metaphorical aspect of Song of Songs was usually taken to refer to its allegorical interpretation: it was not about a human lover but about God (or, in philosophical interpretations, about the Intellect). Moshe ibn Tibbon goes one step further, piling metaphor upon allegory. He says: "He [Solomon] began with 'song of songs' to escape from [taking literally the] concrete descriptions by which the lover is described, when it says . . . 'his locks are curled' . . . 'his eyes' . . . 'his cheeks' . . . just as it says 'To whom can you liken me; to whom can I be compared' [Isa 40:25]." Apparently ibn Tibbon is concerned that, since the lover represents God, taking the descriptions of him literally will produce anthropomorphisms. He can avoid this by taking the descriptions figuratively, as one would expect in poetic discourse, which is by nature metaphorical.

The equation of metaphor with poetry was not, however, applied consistently, for there remained formal or traditional constraints on what could be considered poetry. So, while metaphors were found in books of the Torah and the Prophets, this was not sufficient to warrant calling them poetry (especially if they were not called *šir*). One must distinguish between metaphor as a rhetorical trope and metaphorical language as the essential component of poetry. Moshe ibn Ezra, for example, has a long list of biblical metaphors from various books, but he does not consider these signs of poetry. The one pericope that some authors (but not ibn Ezra) do consider a poem by virtue of its metaphorical expression is Isaiah 5; but this pericope is called *šir* in the Bible, and it is a parable, a *mašal* followed by the *nimšal*.[32] In summary, the metaphorical aspect of poetry was used to bolster the poeticity of pericopes which had, for other reasons, claims to the designation of poem, especially if they did not have meter or were not set to music; it was not, however, a sufficient criterion in and of itself to identify poetry in the Bible.

Poetry and Prophecy

Many modern biblical scholars, following in the footsteps of Robert Lowth, see a strong connection between prophecy and poetry. Prophetic speech is considered a form of poetic discourse, and the prophetic experience is explained by analogy with poetic inspiration.[33] But ancient and medieval thought distinguished sharply between prophecy and poetry.[34] Prophecy was the conduit for divine revelation; indeed, prophecy was the word of God. Poetry was a product of human creativity. Given that the Bible contained poetry, it was confined for the most part to the Writings (Psalms, Proverbs, and Job), which made no claims to prophetic origin but which was composed through the Holy Spirit—that is, by nonprophets, for the most part, such as David and Solomon, who, though divinely guided in some way, composed freely in their own words, not in God's. Moshe ibn Tibbon applies this generally accepted view to the Song of Songs. "It is known that King Solomon, peace be upon him, composed the scroll through the Holy Spirit, like the rest of the books termed 'Writings,' for he was not a prophet."

More problematic were poems in the Torah and the Prophets, for these parts of the Bible were ascribed to prophets and were, presumably, the word of God. (And God did not compose poetry.) There is some disagreement about the status of the poems in the first two sections of the Bible. Falaquera's poet explains that

> poems fall into three levels. Some poems are conveyed through prophecy, like Ha'azinu and the Song of Moses; these are of the highest level. Some poems are composed through the Holy Spirit, like the songs of David and others in Psalms, Proverbs, and the Song of Songs; these are of the second level. Some poems extolling God and his wondrous deeds have been composed by skilled [postbiblical] poets. These are of the lowest level.

Abravanel, however, had a different way of seeing things. He maintained the distinction between prophecy and poetry in all parts of the Bible, and was then compelled to explain how prophets could write poetry, and to present criteria for discerning when a prophet was composing poetry (that is, through the Holy Spirit—in his own voice) and when he was speaking words of prophecy (in God's words).[35] And if, indeed, a prophet such as Moses did compose poetry, how did it come to be included in the Torah, which purports to be the word of God?

Abravanel's discussion grows out of his need to ascertain whether all figurative language, especially the allegories and parables found in the Prophets, is ipso facto poetry. (This derives from his third category of poetry, which defines poetry as metaphorical discourse.) His answer is that they are not. Prophets, according to Abravanel, would sometimes compose in a state of prophecy, at which time they lost control over their words and spoke the words of God, and at other times through the Holy Spirit, at which time they maintained control of their words. His proof is that certain prophets, including Samuel and Jeremiah, composed prophetic books and also books that were included in the Writings (Ruth, ascribed to Samuel, and Lamentations, ascribed to Jeremiah).[36] The fact that these books are in the Writings shows that they were composed through the Holy Spirit. As for other parts of the Bible, the clue to differentiating the prophet's own words from God's words is in the textual attribution of the passage. When the text says "Then Israel sang" or "And Deborah sang," this is a sign of composition through the Holy Spirit. The poems which are found in Scripture are attributed to their human authors, and hence we know that they were composed through the Holy Spirit. Some were included in the Torah and the Prophets because "God accepted them and delighted in them. . . . The arranging of [Exodus 15] was done by Moses, and its writing in the Torah was at the command of God." In this way Abravanel was able to account for the existence of poetry in the Torah and the Prophets.

The foregoing chapter has provided a summary of the main concepts and lines of argument in medieval and Renaissance discussions of biblical poetry, and a few of the idiosyncratic divergences. In general, the main issues are the forms of verse, the rhythm of poetry, and metaphorical language—issues not unlike those brought to bear on poetry by modern literary critics. The texts themselves, however, are richer and keener than a summary can convey; they speak in their own voice in part II.

NOTES

1. Introduction

1. A perusal of the collection of material in Preminger and Greenstein, *The Hebrew Bible in Literary Criticism*, will quickly bear this out.

2. Among the most influential non-Jewish authors are Aristotle, Averroes, and al-Farabi.

3. The excerpts are Don Isaac Abravanel's commentary on Exodus 15; Azariah de' Rossi's *Me'or 'Ênayim*, chapter 60; Samuel Archivolti's *'Arugat Habbosem*, chapter 31; a section from Samuel ibn Tibbon's commentary on Ecclesiastes, quoted in Judah Moscato's commentary on *The Kuzari;* and a section from Abraham Portaleone's *Šiltê Haggibborim*.

4. *The Kuzari* was one of the most influential works of its time, not because of its views on poetry but because of its philosophical and nationalistic views. It and Maimonides's *Guide of the Perplexed* can be considered the two most important medieval Jewish texts. Both are quoted repeatedly in other medieval works.

5. For the full text, see part II, "Joseph ibn Kaspi."

6. His categories of types of discourse are not original. See below, chapter 4, "Types of Discourse."

2. Trends in the History of the Study of Biblical Poetry

1. For the history of the premodern period see Kugel, *The Idea of Biblical Poetry*, and for the modern period see O'Connor, *Hebrew Verse Structure*, 24–54. I have written an article on this subject to appear in *Dictionary of Biblical Interpretation.*

2. These books are often referred to as *siprê 'emet*, "the books of ', *m*, *t*," after the initial letters of *'Iyyob* [Job], *Mišlê* [Proverbs], and *Tehillim* [Psalms].

3. Lowth thought that biblical poetry had meter, but that it was irretrievable. He therefore concentrated on what was easier to analyze—parallelism.

4. Quoted in Cheyne, *Founders of Old Testament Criticism*, 73.

5. In one sense, the idea of discovering the occasion on which a poem originated is not entirely novel. Some of the psalms bear superscriptions assigning them to a historical context (e.g., Psalm 63: "A psalm of David, when he was in the wilderness of Judah"). But modern scholars, unlike the medievals, do not take these literally.

6. For a description of these systems, see my article in *Dictionary of Biblical Interpretation.*

7. See Kurylowicz, *Metrik und Sprachgeschichte* and *Studies in Semitic Grammar and Metrics.*

8. See O'Connor, *Hebrew Verse Structure*.
9. See Alter, *The Art of Biblical Poetry*, 3–61, and Kugel, *The Idea of Biblical Poetry*, 1–58.
10. For a summary of these studies see Berlin, *The Dynamics of Biblical Parallelism*, 18–30.
11. See Smith, *The Early Poetry of the Hebrews in Its Physical and Social Origins*, 11.
12. Cf. Andersen and Forbes, " 'Prose Particle' Counts of the Hebrew Bible," *The Word of the Lord Shall Go Forth*, 165–83.

3. Medieval and Renaissance Jewish Attitudes toward Poetry and the Bible

1. For a summary of medieval linguistic studies see Tene, "Linguistic Literature, Hebrew," and, for a simplified account, Waltke and O'Connor, *An Introduction to Biblical Hebrew Syntax*, 31–43.
2. See Baron, *A Social and Religious History of the Jews*, VI 235–313.
3. The entire program of *'Arabiyya* is outlined in Katzew, "Moses ibn Ezra and Judah Halevi," 181. See also Allony, "The Reaction of Moses ibn Ezra to 'Arabiyya (Arabism)."
4. See Allony, "The Reaction of Moses ibn Ezra to 'Arabiyya (Arabism)"; Brann, "Andalusian Hebrew Poetry and the Hebrew Bible"; Katzew, "Moses ibn Ezra and Judah Halevi"; Roth, "Jewish Reactions to the *'Arabiyya* and the Renaissance of Hebrew in Spain."
5. Compare the *Shu'ubiyya*, the movement by non-Arab Muslims which aimed to undercut the doctrine of Arab supremacy by claiming that all peoples were equal or even that certain non-Arab peoples, e.g., the Persians, were superior.
6. See Scheindlin, "Rabbi Moshe ibn Ezra on the Legitimacy of Poetry" and *Wine, Women, and Death*. The idea is further developed by Brann in *The Compunctious Poet* and "Andalusian Hebrew Poetry and the Hebrew Bible."
7. I make no claim to completeness here, nor do I attempt to cite all references for each point. I have lumped together views spanning several countries and centuries, since they are more similar than disparate, and, in any case, it is the general mindset that is of interest here. Much of this chapter draws on the work, published and unpublished, of Ross Brann.
8. Toporowsky: "vision" [*ḥazon*], and so the translation of Reichert. However, the 1578 Constantinople edition reproduced in Reichert reads *herayon*, "conception," or, perhaps better, "rebirth."
9. Toporowsky: "splendor of the Divine Presence to the holy tongue."
10. The word for "blackened" is *q.d.r.*, thus forming a word play with "Kedar" [Hebrew: *qedar*].
11. That is, *hebel*, "vanity."
12. The translation is based on the Constantinople, 1578, edition reproduced in Reichert, *The* Taḥkemoni *of Judah al-Ḥarizi*. Cf. Reichert's translation on pp. 30–35 of that volume. The *editio princeps* is Y. Toporowsky, *Taḥkemoni* (Tel Aviv, 1952).
13. "The Medieval Jewish Attitude toward Hebrew," 233.
14. As Brann notes (*The Compunctious Poet*), Immanuel Frances alludes to this ironically by referring to the study of Gemara as the main course and Hebrew poetry as the dessert.

15. Ibn Quraysh was not alone in employing the methodology of comparative philology to the Bible; it was widespread. But, as Halkin reminds us ("The Medieval Jewish Attitude toward Hebrew," 242–43), not everyone was comfortable with this approach, for to consider Hebrew to be just one of a number of languages in a family was to negate its status as a special and holy tongue. The same problem exists nowadays in relation to the question of the Bible as literature.

16. There are variations on this line of development. According to *b. Sanhedrin* 38b, Adam spoke Aramaic.

17. Fishbane, *Biblical Interpretation in Ancient Israel*, has indicated that some of the principles of rabbinic exegesis are present within the biblical text itself, having originated in the prerabbinic period.

18. Carmi, *The Penguin Book of Hebrew Verse*, 22. For a summary of the poetics that Saadia applies to the Book of Job, see Goodman, *The Book of Theodicy*, 415–26.

19. According to Allony, *Ha'egron*, 27, the proper vocalization is *ṣaḥot*, as in Isa 32:4. However, in conformity with the nominal pattern for abstracts ending in *-ut*, it came to be pronounced *ṣaḥut*.

20. *The Book of Tradition (Sefer Ha-Qabbalah) by Ibn Daud*, 285.

21. See Brann, "Andalusian Hebrew Poetry and the Hebrew Bible," and Pagis, *Ḥiddush Umasoret*, 51–64.

22. *The Penguin Book of Hebrew Verse*, 27.

23. As Raymond Scheindlin points out ("Rabbi Moshe ibn Ezra on the Legitimacy of Poetry," 110), the extensive use of illustrative material from the Bible not only proves that Jewish scripture has as much literary merit as Arabic scripture, if not more—and also has the merit of being older—but it also puts to rest the doubts about the propriety of importing Arabic rhetorical style into Hebrew poetry. It is, after all, not a foreign import if it is already present in the Bible.

24. This is recorded in the dispute between Menahem ibn Saruq and Dunash ibn Labrat. See *Tešubot Talmidê Menahem ben Ya'aqob 'ibn Saruq*.

25. For a fuller discussion of "The best of poetry is its falseness," see below, chapter 4, with references cited there.

26. *Sefer Hammebaqqesh*. See below, part II.

27. Cantarino, *Arabic Poetics in the Golden Age*, 167–68.

28. Levine, *Falaquera's Book of the Seeker*, 81.

29. See Bonebakker, "Religious Prejudice against Poetry in Early Islam."

30. Indeed, some moderns of various religious persuasions have the same difficulty with a literary approach to the Bible.

31. Brann, *The Compunctious Poet*. See also his earlier articles "The 'Dissembling Poet' in Medieval Hebrew Literature" and "Judah Halevi: The Compunctious Poet."

32. Originally published in Constantinople, 1516. A modern edition by J. Luzzatto was published in *'Oṣar Hasifrut* 3 (1889–90) 1–18. The excerpts here are from chapter 8 (pp. 12–13).

33. So the reading in an edition lacking bibliographic information located in the Jewish National and University Library, Jerusalem. Luzzatto: "they call him."

34. So the edition in the Jewish National and University Library. Luzzatto: "to publicize a point."

35. For other positive comments about poetry see Kugel, *The Idea of Biblical Poetry*, 181–82.

36. The "prooftext" for this was Obad 1:20: "And the exiled force of Israelites [shall possess] what belongs to the Canaanites as far as Zarephath, and the exiled community of Jerusalem which is in Sepharad shall possess the towns of the Negev." "Sepharad" here probably refers to a place in Asia Minor, but it was taken in its later sense (based on Targum Jonathan to the verse in Obadiah) of "Spain." The tombstone inscription cited by ibn Ḥabib should be understood in the context of this tradition.

4. Medieval and Renaissance Views of Biblical Poetry

1. Many Greek texts were transmitted into Arabic via Syriac. The extent of Greek influence on Arabic literary theory is not clear. There was also native Arabic theory developed independently.

2. Modern theorists would say that all texts have multiple meanings, and no text can fully convey its meanings. Our medieval authors did not have quite the same view. More likely they were interested in preserving the tradition of oral study simply because it was traditional and because it tended to channel the interpretation in acceptable ways.

3. See Kugel, *The Idea of Biblical Poetry*, 185.

4. The idea here is that certain genres deal with specific subjects. He goes on to cite the view that each national poetry has its own characteristic subject matter: Arabic poems are about love, Latin poems are about war, and so forth. Cf. the poem by Abraham ibn Ezra in Schirmann, *Haššira Ha'ibrit* I, 578.

5. The question of parables is dealt with extensively in Maimonides, *The Guide of the Perplexed*. Maimonides was primarily interested in prophetic parables from a philosophic point of view, and subdivides them into types. *The Guide* had great influence on other discussions; ibn Kaspi, for one, acknowledges his debt to it.

6. Ibn Tibbon does not find meter in Proverbs, but a binary structure which he equates with meter.

7. For more on these metrical systems see Schirmann, *Haššira Ha'ibrit* II 719–34; Pagis, *Ḥiddus Umasoret*, 108–24, 290–314; and Hrushovski in Carmi, ed., *The Penguin Book of Hebrew Verse*, 63–65.

8. For examples of meter see *Quntres Bediqduq Sepat 'Eber* and Portaleone; for rhyme see Archivolti and Portaleone.

9. Allony, *Ha'egron*, 386–87. See also pp. 79–82, 111–18. On disagreements about the author of this fragment see Kugel, *The Idea of Biblical Poetry*, 131, note 85.'

10. This would seem to refer to early liturgical poetry in which the characteristics of later medieval Hebrew poetry were found. See Allony, *Ha'egron*, 81. The entire passage is difficult.

11. This category is obscure. See Allony, *Ha'egron*, 82.

12. There are other biblical verses which meet this criteria, but not many. Allony (*Ha'egron*, 80, note 320) notes several others.

13. A prominent composer of *piyyuṭim* in the sixth (?) century.

14. Neubauer, *Mele'ket Haššir*, 6.

15. Judah Halevi's attitude toward medieval Hebrew poetry is complex. See

Brann, *The Compunctious Poet,* chapter 4. On Moshe ibn Ezra see ibid., chapter 3.

16. It is not altogether clear which parts of the Bible Halevi considered poetic. Archivolti, despite his general sense that biblical poetry put meaning before meter, did suggest that meter had its origin in the Bible.

17. *Tešubot Talmidê Menaḥem ben Ya'aqob 'ibn Saruq,* 27–28. The passage is cited by Profiat Duran, who uses it to prove that the Hebrew language has declined.

18. Yalon, *Šeqel Haqqodeš,* 52. The author of this work is, according to Yalon, Solomon Almoli (late fifteenth–early sixteenth century). It was previously ascribed to David ibn Yahya.

19. *The Idea of Biblical Poetry,* 216.

20. Ibid., 240.

21. This reflects the notion that meter may be primary, with the words chosen to fit it, or it may be secondary, with the words chosen first and the melody arranged to fit the words. See below, "Music and Poetry."

22. See below, part II, "Azariah de' Rossi," for a fuller discussion.

23. Frances also identified poetry by the tendency of the poet to speak of himself in the third person.

24. For more on this see Kugel, *The Idea of Biblical Poetry.*

25. He does offer examples of rhyme and syllabic meter.

26. Actually, it is more than that. As Werner and Sonne observe: "We may conclude that, though it has at times been overlooked, musical and metrical theories in Hebrew literature are closely interwoven and can hardly be separated from each other" (p. 303).

Some modern literary critics and musicologists also relate prosody to music; cf. *The New Harvard Dictionary of Music* (Cambridge, Mass.: Belknap, 1986), 529: "The rhythm of non-metric music is closely related to the prosody of Middle Eastern poetry." J. C. de Moor says that "we have to bear in mind that people used to sing or chant poetry to the accompaniment of music. . . . The solution [to the question of meter] that lies readiest at hand, then, is to assume a connection between the *rhythm* of the poetry and the music" (*Studies . . . Presented to Samuel E. Loewenstamm,* 129; see also Korpel and de Moor, "Fundamentals of Ugaritic and Hebrew Poetry," 174). M. O'Connor takes exception with the methodology that uses music to explain prosody, remarking that "music, when used in describing poetic systems, is a way of covering over variations in verse. [Shades of Judah Halevi!] . . . Reference to music has general explanatory power, but no descriptive usefulness. To claim that variation in a language subsystem is due to music is to claim that it is unanalyzable. . . ." (*Hebrew Verse Structure,* 40).

27. See Pagis, *Širat Haḥol,* 46–50, with previous references; Kugel, *The Idea of Biblical Poetry,* 187–89; and Brann, "The 'Dissembling Poet' in Medieval Hebrew Literature," esp. 40 with note 3. The source has been identified as Plato's *Republic,* Book 10, Aristotle's *Poetics,* chapter 9, and *Metaphysics.*

28. Halkin, *Kitāb al-Muḥāḍara,* 116–18. See Scheindlin, "Rabbi Moshe ibn Ezra on the Legitimacy of Poetry," 106–107.

29. Cf. the statement from Ibn Rashiq al-'Umda, quoted in Cantarino, *Arabic Poetics in the Golden Age,* 147: "One of the ancients was asked about the poets, and he said, 'One thinks people of moderation to be praiseworthy except when they are poets, and that the lie is blameworthy except for them.' "

30. That is, we evaluate poetry as being either good or bad, from a formal

or aesthetic point of view, and are not concerned with whether it is true or false.

31. Carmoli, *'Imrê Šeper*, 13. Moshe ibn Tibbon also makes a distinction between the truth of biblical and the falseness of medieval poetry; he puts it in terms of meaning versus meter, which echoes Judah Halevi.

> The poems of the early [poets] were true utterances and their value was in their contents, not in their rhetoric. And if they were paraphrased in different rhetoric, or a different language, nothing of their meaning would be changed or lost, for the essence is permanent. It is [only] the discourse and rhetoric that are changed and lost. Thus, if the utterance is good and true, the meaning will not be changed with the change or loss of the rhetoric. But [as for] the poems of the later [poets], their value is in their rhetoric; they are for the most part exaggerations and unreal things, so if they are paraphrased in other rhetoric, even in the same language—and how much the more in a different language—their meaning will be totally lost, or at the least the poem's value and beauty will be destroyed. It is even possible that the early [poets] minimized the melody [i.e., the second type of poetry: words recited to a melody] also, so that their hearts and minds would concentrate on the meaning of the utterance, not on its words and rhetoric.

32. Allemanno also considers the Song of Deborah poetic because it is metaphorical. Most authors consider it poetic because it is written stichographically and is termed *šir*.

33. For some references and an extensive discussion see Heschel, *The Prophets*, 367–89.

34. See Kugel, *The Idea of Biblical Poetry*, 280–81. An apparent exception is Moshe ibn Ezra, who explains that the Arabic term *shā'ir* is in Hebrew *nabi'*, "prophet," and that the band of prophets mentioned in 1 Samuel 10:5 is a group of poets and the phrase "you shall prophesy with them" spoken to Saul means "you shall compose poetry with them" (Halkin, *Kitāb al-Muḥāḍara*, 24–25). This is not, however, an equation of prophecy and poetry. The Arabic term *shā'ir*, "poet," comes from the root meaning "to know, sense," and also has the meaning "sorcerer, soothsayer." It is the latter meaning, I think, which provoked the connection with *nabi'*; then the other, more common, meaning of *shā'ir* was applied to *nabi'* as well.

For another hint of the connection between prophecy and poetry in ibn Ezra's writings, see Scheindlin, *Wine, Women, and Death*, 66. Here, too, poetic inspiration, prophecy, and music are related. But, to quote Scheindlin, "Ibn Ezra ultimately rejects the view that the spiritual power of prophecy is the same as that of poetry."

35. This may be considered part of the larger question of the human element in prophetic discourse. On this see Greenberg, "Jewish Conceptions of the Human Factor in Biblical Prophecy."

36. This is not to suggest that Ruth and Lamentations were poetry, only that they were composed through the Holy Spirit, that is, human products, not divine discourse.

II

AUTHORS AND TEXTS

JUDAH IBN QURAYSH

Judah ibn Quraysh (ninth century) was a grammarian, lexicographer, and physician in Tahert, Algeria. He was one of the early advocates of comparative Semitic linguistics. His Risāla *[Epistle] is addressed to the Jewish community of Fez and urges them not to abandon the reading of the Targum in the synagogue, for the Aramaic language, as well as Arabic, is helpful in understanding biblical Hebrew. While the main purpose is purported to be the preservation of the custom of reciting the Targum, the real purpose of the* Risāla *is to encourage the comparative study of Hebrew, Aramaic, and Arabic, in order to better understand the Bible. The main body of the work includes comparisons of the vocabulary and structures of biblical Hebrew with those of Aramaic, Mishnaic Hebrew, and Arabic. Ibn Quraysh offers two explanations for the similarities among these languages: the geographic proximity of their speakers and the genealogical closeness of their origins. Others who came after him, for example Judah Halevi and Moshe ibn Ezra, give only one or the other of these reasons.*

Edition: Dan Becker, The *Risāla* of Judah ben Quraysh *(Tel Aviv, 1984).*

Introduction to the *Risāla*

I saw that you have abolished the custom of reciting from the Aramaic Targum of the Torah in your synagogues, and in the matter of its neglect you follow the most boorish among you who claim they do not need it, and that they know all of the Hebrew language without it. Some among you even told me that they have never read the Targum of the Torah or the Prophets. The Targum is something that your predecessors did not leave, your ancients did not discard, your sages did not cease to study it, your forebears did not forgo it, its value was not hidden from your fathers, your predecessors in Iraq, Egypt, Africa, and Spain did not belittle its study. When I told one of you, who rejected the Targum, about the exceptional words from it found in the Bible [biblical Aramaic], and about Aramaic, which mixed in with Hebrew and branched out in it like branches on a tree or veins in a body, he was greatly startled by this, and gave it his full attention, and understood well the value of the Targum and its many benefits—the useful interpretations and the convincing explanations that it is possible to achieve by means of it. Then he was remorseful that he had missed studying it, and regretted his lack of the sweetness of its language.

For this reason I decided to write this book for men of understanding and knowledge, so that they would know that throughout all of the holy tongue found in the Bible, Aramaic words are strewn, Arabic words are interspersed, and foreign and Berber words, especially Arabic, are scattered. Indeed, there are in it many exceptional words, which we have found to be pure Arabic, so much so that there is no difference between Hebrew and Arabic except the substitution of *ṣade* for *ḍad*, *gimel* for *jīm*, *ṣade* for *ṭā'*, *'ayin* for *ghayn*, *ḥet* for *ḥā'*, and *zayin* for *dhāl*. The cause of this similarity and the reason for this intermingling are the neighboring proximity of the lands [in which these languages were spoken] and the genealogical closeness [of the original speakers]. Indeed, Terah, the father of Abraham, was an Aramean, and Laban, too, was an Aramean. Ishmael and Kedar were speakers of Arabic since the generation of the Tower of Babel; while Abraham, Isaac, and Jacob, peace be upon them, clung to the holy tongue [in an unbroken chain] since [the time of] Adam. The [Hebrew] language came to resemble [the others] by means of the intermingling, as we see in every land adjacent to a land having a language different from it the exchanging between them of some words, and linguistic borrowing one from the other. This, then, is the reason for the similarity between Hebrew, Arabic, and Aramaic, which we found, except for the nature of the letters. . . .

JUDAH HALEVI

Judah Halevi (ca. 1075–1141) was among the most notable Hebrew poets of the "Golden Age" of Spanish Jewish culture. He was also the author of the philosophical work that came to be known as The Kuzari. A contemporary of both Moshe ibn Ezra and Abraham ibn Ezra, Halevi was born in Tudela, in Christian Spain, but while still young was drawn by the cultural magnet of al-Andalus. He lived in Granada and in several other Jewish communities in Muslim Spain, where he was quickly accepted into their literary circles. Toward the end of his life he began to voice doubts about the cultural values that had once seemed so attractive, and he became determined to leave the society in which he had found so much success and emigrate to Israel (which was then under Crusader rule). His route took him to Egypt, where he sojourned for a while before finally setting sail for Israel.[1]

The Kuzari, or, as it is properly titled, Kitāb al-Ḥujja wa-'l-Dalīl fī Naṣr al-Dīn al-Dhalīl [The Book of Argument and Proof in Defense of the Despised Faith], was written in Judeo-Arabic over a period of twenty years and completed in 1140, shortly before Halevi's departure from Spain. It was translated into Hebrew about thirty years later by Judah ibn Tibbon and was thence commonly known among Hebrew readers as The Kuzari.[2] It is a polemical work, a defense of Judaism against Aristotelianism, Christianity, and Islam; it became immensely popular among Jews because it provided a unified and appealing conception of Judaism. Its influence is evident from the many references made to it in later literature, not only in philosophical contexts but, as we shall see, in literary discussions as well.

The Kuzari takes its name from the king of the Khazars, who seeks to discover the path in life that he should follow. He invites an Aristotelian philosopher and spokesmen for Islam, Christianity, and Judaism to discuss their respective beliefs. He hears from the first three men in the first part of the book, and in the remaining four parts the Jewish representative (whom I have called the Advocate; the Hebrew is ḥaber) presents the case for Judaism in the form of a dialogue with the Kuzari. Of interest to us here is the end of the second part where the Advocate discusses the Hebrew language. He proclaims the superiority of Hebrew over other languages, especially in its pristine, biblical form, and rather than attempting to find meter in biblical poetry, as later scholars were to do, he finds that the nonmetrical poetry of the Bible has virtues that metrical poetry lacks.

Editions and Translations: The Kuzari was first printed in Fano in 1506.

J. Buxtorf's Liber Cosri *(1660) contains a Latin translation along with the Hebrew text. Popular editions of ibn Tibbon's translation, along with Judah Moscato's commentary,* Qol Yehuda, *and Israel Zomosc's* 'Oṣar Neḥmad, *were published in Warsaw (1880) and Vilna (1904). H. Hirschfeld prepared a critical edition of the Arabic text and ibn Tibbon's translation (Leipzig, 1887). A modern Hebrew translation was prepared by Y. Even Shmuel,* The Kosari of R. Yehuda Halevi *(Tel Aviv, 1972); cf. p. 50, note 4 and p. 55, note 6 of this work for a list of other editions and translations. A new edition of the Arabic is found in D. Baneth,* Kitāb al-Radd wa-'l-Dalīl fī 'l-Dīn al-Dhalīl *(Jerusalem, 1977). English translations have been made by H. Hirschfeld (London, 1905; reprint, 1930; New York, 1946) and I. Heinemann (Oxford, 1947). Before his death, Lawrence V. Berman was preparing a new English translation. A most enlightening discussion of parts of the excerpt presented here is found in R. Brann,* The Compunctious Poet, *chapter 4.*

The Kuzari

2.63 The Kuzari:

I see that your teaching includes every refinement and marvel of knowledge, such as no other teaching has.

2.64 The Advocate:

He begins with a discussion of various branches of knowledge, concluding with music.

As for the knowledge of music—imagine a people who value music and assign their songs to their most important men, the Levites, who engage in music as in holy service in the holy Temple on holy festivals. These men are free from the concerns of earning a livelihood since they partake of the tithes, and they have no other business except music. This art, important in its own right in all societies, is especially revered in the eyes of this aristocratic and purebred people; and at the head of those who engage in it were David and Samuel. What do you think, then—did they have knowledge of music, or not?

2.65 The Kuzari:

Without doubt there [i.e., in biblical Israel] it [the art of music] reached perfection, and there it aroused the soul—as is said of it—for it transports the soul from one mood to its opposite. However, the degree of its importance today cannot be compared to its level then, for its value has diminished, and only servants and the simple-minded engage in it now. Indeed, it has surely declined, Advocate, despite its aristocratic nature, just as you have declined despite your aristocratic nature.

2.66 The Advocate:

What do you think of Solomon's wisdom? For he discoursed, through divine, and intellectual, and natural power, on all knowledge. Men the world over would come to him in order to convey his knowledge to the nations, even as far as India. Now all the roots and principles of knowledge [or science] were transmitted from us, first to the Chaldeans, then to Persia and Media, then to Greece, and then to Rome. But because of the length of time and the multiplicity of transmissions, it was not mentioned in the [books of] knowledge that they were transmitted from the Hebrews—only that they were transmitted from the Greeks and the Romans. To Hebrew, however, belongs the pride of place both in the form of the language and in its contents.

2.67 The Kuzari:

And is Hebrew, then, superior to other languages? Are there not languages that are fuller and richer than it is, as we can see with our own eyes?

2.68 The Advocate:

It had the same fate as its bearers; it became impoverished when they became impoverished, and it became constricted when they became fewer. But in respect to its form, it is the noblest of languages, as we know from tradition and from logic [i.e., from the interpretation of scriptural verses and from logical inference].

The [proof from] tradition is that it is the language in which God spoke to Adam and Eve, and in which the latter two conversed. This is demonstrated by the name Adam, which is derived from *'adama* ["ground, earth"], and *'išša* from *'iš* ["woman" from "man"], and *ḥawwa* from *ḥay* ["Eve" from "living"], and *qayin* from *qaniti* ["Cain" from "I acquired"], and *šet* from *šat* ["Seth" from "put"], and *noaḥ* from *yenaḥamenu* ["Noah" from "he will comfort us"].[4] Besides this, there is evidence from the Torah. Each generation received it [the language] from the preceding one: Eber—Noah—Adam. For Hebrew was Eber's language; it was called Hebrew after his name, for he retained it during the time of the Tower of Babel and the confusion of the tongues. Abraham already spoke Aramaic in Ur of the Chaldees, for Aramaic was the language of the Chaldeans, but he used Hebrew as a special language, a holy language, while Aramaic was his language for secular purposes. And thus Ishmael brought it to the Arabs, and as a result these three languages—Aramaic, Arabic, and Hebrew—are similar in their vocabulary, grammar, and usages.

As for the [proof from] logical inference, the superiority of Hebrew is manifest in the fact that it was used by the nation that had a need for elevated speech, especially when prophecy was prevalent among that nation. They also required exhortations, songs, and hymns; their leaders were Moses, Joshua, David, and Solomon [i.e., those credited with composing in these genres]. Is it possible that they lacked the right word to express what they wished, as we lack it today since the language is lost to us? Look how the Torah, in describing the Tabernacle, the ephod, and the breastplate, and the like, when it requires an uncommon term, it finds the one exactly appropriate. And how well composed the narrative is. The same is true for the names of the nations, the species of birds, and the types of stones. Consider also the hymns of David, the complaints of Job when he argues with his friends, Isaiah's prophecies of doom and comfort, and similar passages.

2.69 The Kuzari:

So far you have shown only that Hebrew is as good as other languages, but wherein is its superiority? On the contrary, other languages surpass it in metrical poems set to melodies.

2.70 The Advocate:

It is obvious that melodies do not require a specific meter. One can sing a short verse, "Praise the Lord, for he is good" [Ps 136:1], to the same melody as a long verse, "Who alone works great marvels" [Ps 136:4]. Such is the case for melodies which are intended to be affective. But as for poems which are recited aloud, in which meter is desirable, they [the Hebrews] forwent this [form of poetry] in favor of a more excellent and useful feature.

2.71 The Kuzari:

And what is that?

2.72 The Advocate:

The purpose of language is to transmit that which is in the mind of the speaker to the mind of the listener. This purpose can be fully realized only when speaking face to face, for spoken words are better than written words. The saying is "From the mouth of scribes [or scholars], not from the mouth of books," because oral delivery is aided by pauses, linkages of phrases, raising and lowering of the voice, gestures, and other means of expressing surprise, questions, narrative, expectation, fear, pleading, and other means which discourse itself is unable to convey. The speaker may even be aided by the movement of his eyes, his eyebrows, his whole head, and his hands to express anger, pleasure, supplication, or pride, to the extent that he wishes. In the remnant that remains of our language [i.e., the Bible], a divine creation and product, subtle but profound signs are imbedded to promote the understanding of the meaning; they serve in place of the aids in oral delivery. These are the [masoretic] accents according to which the Bible is recited. They indicate where to pause and where to continue, they distinguish question from answer, subject from predicate, things said in haste from those said with deliberation, command from request—on these matters books could be written. Whoever aspires to this must, of course, forgo metrical poetry, for metrical poetry can be recited in only one way, thereby forcing one to connect what should be separated and to pause where one should continue; and this cannot be avoided except with great effort.

2.73 The Kuzari:

They rightly gave up the advantage of sound in favor of the advantage of meaning; for prosody pleases the ear, but the [masoretic] accents serve the meaning. But I see that you, the Jewish community, aspire to the advantage of prosody, and imitate the other nations by imposing their meters upon Hebrew.

2.74 The Advocate:

This is due to our erring and obstinacy. Indeed, we were not satisfied with abandoning that advantage [of the accents], but we even caused loss to the structure of our language, which was meant to unify, but we made it divisive.

2.75 The Kuzari:

How?

2.76 The Advocate:

Have you not seen a hundred men reciting the Bible as one man, stopping at the same instant and continuing as one?

2.77 The Kuzari:

I have observed this, and I have never seen anything like it, either among the Persians or among the Arabs. This is not possible in the recitation of poems. Tell me how this language achieved this advantage, and how does meter cause it to be lost?

2.78 The Advocate:

Because in Hebrew two vowelless consonants can be grouped together, but not three voweled consonants, except in rare instances. The discourse thereby tends toward rests, and in this way it acquires that advantage, namely, uniformity and carefulness of recitation. This makes it easier to remember and to grasp the meaning. The first damage that metrical poetry causes is in the matter of the two vowelless consonants, and [then] the correct accentuation is lost, so that *'okla* ["eating"; 1 Sam 1:9] and *we'akela* ["eat" (imperative, paragogic); Gen 27:19] sound the same; *'omro* and *'omero* are metrically equivalent; *'omér* ["he says"; Isa 52:7] and 'omer ["a word"; Ps 68:12]; *sámti* ["I placed"; Gen 28:22] and *wesamtí* ["I will place"; Gen 13:16], and the distinction in tense will be lost.[5] There was some leeway in the ways of *piyyut*, which does not contravene the [rules of the] language even though it employs rhyme;[6] but when it comes to metrical poetry, the same befell us as befell our fathers, about whom it is said, "They mingled among the nations and learned their ways" [Ps 106:35].[7]

NOTES

1. There has been some doubt as to whether Halevi ever reached Israel. See Goitein, "Did Judah Halevi Reach the Shores of the Land of Israel?"

2. There are several different versions of the Arabic title. Baneth has *Kitāb al-Radd wa-'l-Dalīl fī 'l-Dīn al-Dhalīl.* Cf. ibid., p. 11 of the Hebrew introduction for the variants.

3. Even Shmuel departs from the usual pronunciation, preferring כּוֹזָרִי (which is romanized as *Kosari*). He cites Buxtorf's *Cosri* for support. For the various Hebrew renderings of the official Arabic title, see Even Shmuel, *Kosari,* 47, note 1, and 243.

4. These are all biblical word plays. Cf. Gen 2:7; 2:23; 3:20; 4:1; 4:25; 5:29. The notion that the world was created in Hebrew is made explicit in *Genesis Rabbah* 18:4.

5. The precise reading of Halevi's examples of the corruption of Hebrew when it is subjected to the Arabic metrical system is not altogether clear. I follow the reading of Even Shmuel. Baneth and Hirschfeld differ, as the chart below shows.

	Baneth	*Even Shmuel*	*Hirschfeld*
1.	אָכְלָה	אָכְלָה	*ŏkhlāh,* "food"
	אוֹכְלָה	וְאָכְלָה	*ōkhelāh,* "eats"
2.	אִמְרוּ	אָמְרוֹ	*ŏmro,* "his word"
	אָמְרוּ	אֹמְרוֹ	*āmerū,* "they spoke"
3.	אוֹמַר	אֹמֵר	*ōmēr,* "speaking"
	אוֹמֵר	אֹמֶר	*ōmer,* "word"
4.	שַׁבְתִּי	שַׂמְתִּי	*shábti* (past tense)
	וְשַׁבְתִּי	וְשַׂמְתִּי	*we-shabtí* (future tense)

Brann, *The Compunctious Poet,* 102, translates: "(With Arabicizing Hebrew prosody) penultimate and ultimate accents distinguishing nouns from verbs are lost. For example: *omer* (word) and *omer* (says); and what distinguishes past tense from future tense (is lost). For instance: *samti* (I put) and *we-samti* (I will put); and what distinguishes the indicative from the imperative mood (is lost). For example: *okhlah* (I will eat) and *okhlah* (eat!). Similarly, *omero* (his saying) and *omro* (his word) are reduced to a single metrical form."

6. Even Shmuel has a different reading here.

7. As Scheindlin has noted (*Wine, Women, and Death,* 182, note 27), this verse lends itself to use as a prooftext on the dangers of cultural assimilation in Muslim Spain because of the double entendre on *wa-yit'arebu,* which can be understood as "they mingled" and "they became Arabized."

MOSHE IBN EZRA

Moshe ben Jacob ibn Ezra (ca. 1055–1140), like his younger contemporary and friend Judah Halevi, lived in Spain during the period of the flowering of Hebrew poetry and was one of the outstanding contributors to it. He was born in Granada into a respected family and received a classical Jewish education, including traditional sources, Jewish and Arabic philosophy, and their Greek antecedents. The first half of his life was peaceful and prosperous, but in 1090 the Almoravides invaded and the Jewish community of Granada was destroyed. Many of his family and friends fled. Ibn Ezra remained in Granada for a time, then fled to Christian Spain, wandering from place to place—Castile, Aragon, and Navarre. The last half of his life was full of bitterness and disillusion, both over his own personal fate and over the apparent decline of the glorious Spanish Jewish culture that had flourished in Muslim Spain.

Despite his dislocations and discomforts, ibn Ezra was a prolific poet, producing both secular and religious poetry. He, Judah Halevi, Solomon ibn Gabirol, and Samuel ibn Naghrela (Hanagid) are considered the four major poets of the Golden Age of Jewish culture in Spain. In addition to his poetry, ibn Ezra wrote, near the end of his life, one of the few surviving medieval works on Hebrew poetics, Kitāb al-Muḥāḍara wa-'l-Mudhākara [The Book of Discussion and Conversation]. *The book was written in Judeo-Arabic and, unlike many philosophical and exegetical works in this language, was not translated into Hebrew until modern times. Another work, apparently written about the same time,* Maqālat al-Ḥadīqa fī Ma'nī 'l-Majāz wa-'l-Ḥaqīqa [Dissertation of the Garden on Figurative and Literal Language], *was partially translated into Hebrew in medieval times under the title* 'Arugat Habbosem. *This book contains, among other things, an extensive discussion of biblical metaphor in a philosophical-theological context.*[1]

Kitāb al-Muḥāḍara wa-'l-Mudhākara *discusses secular Hebrew poetry from the perspective of Arabic poetics. Its eight chapters are answers to eight inquiries concerning poetry and rhetoric, the excellence of Arabic poetry, the history and current practice of Hebrew poetry, and Hebrew and Arabic poetic technique. The last chapter, the longest by far, contains a list of poetic tropes and figures with illustrations from the Bible, Hebrew poetry, and Arabic poetry. In addition to its contribution to the history of Hebrew poetic theory, the book is a gold mine of contemporary references and traditional biblical exegesis. It is a window onto the literary culture of the Spanish Jewish community and reflects the tension that was felt by its poets: the drive to imitate and assimilate the values of the vernacular Arabic poetry and, at the same time, the struggle to develop a Hebrew poetic style which could be perceived as distinctive yet continuous with Hebrew poetry of the past, reaching back to the Bible.*

Since my interest is ibn Ezra's view of biblical *poetics, I have selected those passages which discuss the biblical text. In so doing I risk skewing the reader's perception of the work, of which there is no complete English translation, for its main concern is not the Bible but the Hebrew poetry of its author's day. Nevertheless, it becomes evident that while the rhetoric of the Bible is quite different from that of medieval Hebrew poetry, ibn Ezra was at pains to demonstrate the continuity between the two, and to confirm the Bible as a model of rhetorical excellence.*

Editions and Translations: The critical edition is A. S. Halkin, Kitāb al-Muḥāḍara wal-Mudhākara (Liber Discussionis et Commemorationis; Seper ha'iyyunim wehaddiyyunim) *(Jerusalem, 1975). An earlier, inferior Hebrew translation is B. Halper,* Seper Širat Yisra'el *(Leipzig, 1924). English excerpts appear in A. Preminger and E. L. Greenstein,* The Hebrew Bible in Literary Criticism, *72, 105, 185, 222, 251. An extensive analysis, in Hebrew, is contained in J. Dana,* Happo'etiqa šel Haššira Ha'ibrit. *See also D. Pagis,* Širat Haḥol Wetorat Haššir Lemoše 'ibn 'Ezra' Ubene Doro; *R. Scheindlin, "Rabbi Moshe ibn Ezra on the Legitimacy of Poetry"; R. Brann,* The Compunctious Poet, *chapter 3.*

Kitāb al-Muḥāḍara wa-'l-Mudhākara

Chapter 1

Toward the end of chapter 1 ibn Ezra discusses various genres and their terminology. Of interest to us are his comments on the word šir.

Šir is the term for poem,[2] as it is written in 1 Kings 5:12: "his poems [*širo*] were one thousand and five." It also refers to song, as in Isa 24:9: "they drink their wine without song [*šir*]." In addition, dirges and laments are called *šir*: "all the male and female singers [*šarim wešarot*] recited in their laments" [2 Chr 35:25]. The term *šir* is also applied to prose, as in Song 1:1: "song of songs [*šir hašširim*]," Isa 5:1: "Let me sing ['*ašira*] to my beloved," and elsewhere. And recited poetry occurs in the sense of "thank"—Exod 15:21: "Sing [*širu*] to the Lord."

Chapter 4

Was poetry known to our nation in the time of its glory, during the First Commonwealth? This is the answer to the fourth inquiry.

I say: We find nothing [in the Bible] that departs from the category of prose, except for three books: Psalms, Job, and Proverbs. And even these, as you can see, do not employ [fixed] meter or rhyme, as Arabic poetry does. Rather, they resemble *rajaz* only.[3] Indeed, occasionally some of them follow a feature of *rajaz*, as in

Job 28:16 *lo' tesulleh beketem 'opir / bešoham yaqar wesappir.*
[The verse halves end in *-pir* and *-pir*]
Job 33:17 *lehasir 'adam ma'aseh / wegewa miggever yekasseh.*
[The verse halves end in *-seh* and *-seh*]
Job 21:4 *he'anoki le'adam siḥi / we'im maddua' lo' tiqṣar ruḥi.*
[The verse halves end in *-ḥi* and *-ḥi*]

and others. A few of the "songs" elsewhere in the Bible depart from prose, e.g., Exodus 15, Deuteronomy 32, 2 Samuel 22, Judges 5.[4] I said "*a few* of the songs" because there are also prose passages labeled "song," such as Song of Songs, the Song of the Well [Num 21:17–18], and others, as I mentioned previously. The rabbis enumerated nine such passages,[5] and most of them are prose. The Bible attests [1 Kgs 5:12] that Solomon, the Sage, peace be upon him, wrote poetry and prose, the latter being proverbs: "He spoke three thousand proverbs" refers to prose; "His song was one thousand and five" refers to poetry. There are some learned men[6] who believe that these poems were *qaṣīdas*. But about the true nature of these poetic compositions or even their existence, I do not know, for we have nothing of them, not even a trace.

As for the question of when the Jews of the diaspora began to compose poetry and *rajaz*, with meter and rhyme and the measurement of cords and pegs—called by the Greeks metrical feet—and rhyme of the final letters, according to the rules of Arabic prosody, and two verse halves, to the extent that is possible with the part of the Hebrew language that has come down to us—this date I do not know, for our people were dispersed in various countries among different nations at wide intervals, and I do not know which province preceded which in this matter, or which community preceded another. I would point out only that since our sovereignty was brought to an end, and our people dispersed, and [nations of] other faiths took us into captivity and [nations of] other creeds subjugated us, we imitated their ways and life-style, and adopted their characteristics, and spoke their languages, and followed their ways in most matters, as it is written: "They mingled among the nations and learned their ways" [Ps 106:35]. Elsewhere it is written: "The holy seed mingled among the peoples of the lands" [Ezra 9:2], except for the commandments of the Torah and religious laws. As a result of the length of the exile and the change of conditions, circumstances forced us to become similar to them. Look, Daniel, Hananiah, Ezra, and Nehemiah, peace be upon them, wrote some of their words in Aramaic. During the First Commonwealth government officials and nobles spoke that language, for they said to Rabshakeh, "Please speak to your servants in Aramaic" [2 Kgs 18:26]. Likewise, there is no doubt that Rabshakeh could speak Hebrew, as it is written: "Do not speak to us in Judean." But he did not heed them; on the contrary, he wanted to incite the mob, as it is written: "He called out in a loud voice." There are some Aggadists who thought that Rabshakeh was a convert [*mešummad*], but this cannot be, for the form of this word, as R. Hai Gaon explained, is missing an *'ayin*—its correct form is *mešu'amad*, that is, "one who adheres to the practice of baptism." Baptism, among those who hold to this practice, is the submerging in water, as John the Baptist did to their lord in the Jordan, as they tell it. This is an essential part of their religious practice. But in the time of Rabshakeh this practice had not yet come into existence.

It suffices to point out that the exiles who returned from Babylonia spoke Aramaic dialects until Nehemiah chided them for it, as it is written: "Half of their children speak Ashdodite and the language of various other peoples, but do not know how to speak Judean" [Neh 13:24]. This occurred despite the relatively short span of time there [in Babylonia] compared with the longer duration of our present exile. This had already befallen the exiles from the Northern tribes of Samaria who were exiled to Khorasan, as it is written: "He brought them to Halah and Habur, the river Gozan and the cities of Media" [cf. 2 Kgs 17:6; 18:11; 1 Chr 5:26]. There is no doubt that these are the districts of Khorasan, and it is possible that Gozan is the city Guzana, written with a *jim* without a dot,[7] which is the capital of Khorasan. And Habur is apparently the Khabur River, with a dotted *kap*, and it is well known there. All this is on the authority of R. Saadia, from his book *The Attainment of the Traditional Commandments*.[8] Moreover, the languages of the people have become a jumble, as is evidenced concerning them. And I have been told by them and others, although I cannot verify it, that in the aforementioned capital Guzana there are about forty thousand of our Jewish brethren on the obligatory head-tax rolls, and a like number in the other cities of Khorasan.

And when God decreed the second exile, the one in which we find ourselves, the very same thing happened to us in Christendom and Islam in which most of us live. Our predecessors and forefathers, of blessed memory, are to be faulted, even condemned, for failing to hold onto their language and to attend carefully to their Hebrew; they did not have the foresight to refine their language and to set down the events that befell them and to record their history and their traditions. They should not have let these things fall into such neglect. Did they not see—it is undeniable—that all the other nations had made efforts to write down their histories and to thereby claim distinction? Our Holy Scriptures abound in powerful references to this: "Write this for a memorial" [Exod 17:14]; "Now, come, write it on a tablet, inscribe it in a book, that it may be with them in future days, forever" [Isa 30:8]; "And now write for yourselves this song" [Deut 31:19]. Also Job, peace be upon him, relished writing of his experiences, and listing his afflictions, and making a case through his words, as it is written: "O, that my words be written . . ." [Job 19:23]. The need arises to commit history to writing and teach it to future generations, in accord with the scriptural dictums [of Deut 4:9]: "You will make them known to your children, and to your children's children," and [Ps 78:3]: "things we have heard and know." Our kings who ruled wrote their chronicles, as it is written: "Are they not written in the book of the chronicles of the kings of Judah and the kings of Israel" [1 Kgs 15:7]. And it is said: "They are written in the words of Nathan the prophet" [1 Chr 29:29] and "in the prophecy of Ahijah the Shilonite . . . and in the vision of Jedo the seer" [2 Chr 9:29]. The same in reference to other nations: "in the chronicles of the kings of Persia and Media" [Esth 10:2].

Because of the persistence of the exile and its long duration, the Hebrew language was progressively lost, was cut off, or nearly cut off, as the early rabbinic sages said: "The Galileans who were not careful about their language did not retain their learning" [*b. 'Erubin* 53a]. Nothing remains of the Hebrew language except the twenty-four books of the Bible, which contain only those parts of the language for which there was a need. From this the nation took all the material for [composing] prayers, petitions, chastisements, praises, songs, laments, eulogies, and all other forms of literary and rhetorical discourse. They were aided also by the language of the Mishna, for it is pure Hebrew. Even though it goes against a few of the rules of [biblical] grammar, nevertheless, one must rely on those who handed it down, for they lived in a time closer to that of the [biblical Hebrew] language. One must try to explain their expressions that depart from the rules of grammar, as did Abu al-Walid ibn Janaḥ and other great grammarians to the extent that they were able.

Chapter 8

In chapter 8 ibn Ezra lists a number of tropes and figures, illustrating each by citations from Arabic poetry, medieval Hebrew poetry, and biblical prose and poetry.

Beware of juxtaposing words [in which the first ends and the second begins] with similar letters—letters with the same point of articulation—for this is ugly in poetry and in the opinion of men of music. . . . even though the Hebrew language permits it, and does not refrain from it, as in *bin nun* [Exod 33:11]; *yaruṣ ṣaddiq* [Prov 18:10]; *we'ozel lo* [Prov 20:14]; *me'ereṣ zikram* [Ps 34:17]; *ki yeš šeber* [Gen 42:1]. Likewise the juxtaposition of similar letters [within a word]: *'al pešaṭṭem* [1 Sam 27:10]; *ušhaṭṭem* [1 Sam 14:34]; *wehim'aṭṭim* [Ezek 29:15]. All that the Bible permits is permissible. However, since in poetry especially we follow Arabic practice, it is incumbent upon us to do as they do as far as we are able.[9]. . .

In our language repetition of the same idea is permissible as long as the words are different. In fact, one of the greatest scholars of language [Jonah ibn Janah] considers such usage to be elegant and eloquent. For example, "Who has made and done" [Isa 41:4]; "I created him, I fashioned him, indeed I made him" [Isa 43:7]; "So that they may see and know and consider and comprehend" [Isa 41:20]. There is one among the scholars who believes that "I created him" [in Isa 43:7] refers to insemination, and "I fashioned him" to the development of limbs and veins, and "I made him" to the skin. But this is reading too much into it. The real intent [of the repetition] is to provide emphasis. Other examples are "tired and weary" [Deut 25:18], "he expired and died" [Gen 25:8]. "He expired" and "he died" are redundant. [In Lev 17:15 the phrase] "and he is impure until evening" renders "and he is pure" redundant. But "your wives will become widows and your children orphans" [Exod 22:23] is not of this type, contrary to the opinion that "your wives will become widows" renders the mention of "your children orphans" redundant. For there can be childless widows [lit.: a mother without children] and motherless orphans.[10]

Some of these same words occur alone [i.e., not paired with others of similar meaning], and the sense is unambiguous. For example, the word *tired* (*'ayep*) [which was illustrated above as occurring with *weary*] signifies "thirsty" in "you do not give water to the *'ayep*" [Job 22:7]. In other cases it signifies "hungry," as in "[Give me some of that red stuff] for I am *'ayep*" [Gen 25:30]. In "and the wine is for the *'ayep* in the wilderness to drink" [2 Sam 16:2] it signifies "thirsty" or perhaps "hungry," since wine counteracts hunger. [Another illustration of *'ayep* meaning "hungry" is] "Please give loaves of bread to the people who are following me, for they are *'ayepim*" [Jud 8:5]. The word *expired* occurs alone in "for Aaron expired" [Num 20:29].

There are cases of even more extensive repetition, such as "The Lord is my allotted share and my cupful; you control my destiny" [Ps 16:5].

There is a fourfold repetition if one adds the first-person possessive suffix to "allotted" [yielding "my lot, my share, my cupful, my destiny"]. . . .

There are instances when the language is clear and when it is terse. It is written "hewers of trees and drawers of water" [Josh 9:23]; "from your hewers of trees to your drawers of water" [Deut 29:10]. The meaning would be clear had it said only "hewers" and "drawers," without "of trees" and "of water," as it is in "and behold I have allocated to the hewers" [2 Chr 2:9], and in "when the drawers came out" [Gen 24:11]; "she drew for all his camels" [Gen 24:20]; "from where the young men draw" [Ruth 2:9].

Metaphor is close to this, for example "a garden [*gan*] locked . . . a fountain [*gal*] locked, a sealed-up spring" [Song 4:12], provided that the *nun* in *gan* is in place of a *lamed*, it being the singular of *gallim* ["fountains"].[11]

At times this repetition is found in Hebrew not in this manner, for example, "Most blessed of women be Yael, wife of Heber the Kenite, of women in tents most blessed" [Jud 5:24], and "The Lord remembered us, he will bless us, he will bless the house of Israel, he will bless" [Ps 115:12]. First come the general statements and then the specific. In "the heaven is the heaven of the Lord" [Ps 115:16] the first "heaven" is the subject and the second is descriptive, as though it is a place or seat for the Lord, as it is written "he who sits in heaven" [Ps 123:1]. In "Lord, Lord, merciful and compassionate God" [Exod 34:6] the first "Lord" is a [proper] name and the second is an attribute.[12] . . .

But the interpreter errs who says that "from your land, and from your birth-place, and from your father's house" [Gen 12:1] is [three] synonyms with the same meaning. For "your land" is the land of Cutha [Assyria], that is Ur of the Chaldeans, and "your birth-place" is his city, and "your father's house" is his home and family. . . .

Chapter 8, Part I

Metaphor: 'Isti'āra

This trope is among the most excellent of literary tropes and among the most pleasing features of prose and poetry. In poetry—because it is constructed on a single rhyme and meter which one is obliged to follow, and some of its syllables are metrically short and others long—a poet would not use a short syllable [in creating a metaphor] in place of a long, but would use what is appropriate in order to preserve the [metrical] structure which he chose.

Know that besides this explanation[13] of that which a poet is obliged to use and through the use of which prose works may be enhanced, metaphor is one of the most aesthetically pleasing devices for the needs of both genres; and even though literal expression is fundamentally more reliable, whereas metaphor is aggrandizing, but it is suffused in beauty. A literary composition, when it is clothed in metaphor [and ornamented with circumlocution and subtlety],[14] its silken texture and delicate glaze become beautiful.[15] The difference between ornamented language and unornamented [lit. naked] language is like the difference between incoherent speech and eloquent speech,[16] even though some poets of both peoples [Jews and Arabs] forswore it—because of what they heard it became despised and was considered ugly, but that is on account of overuse. But any knowledgeable person of our time who rejects metaphor disregards what his own eyes see and leads himself astray, for metaphor is so frequent in our scriptural [lit. prophetic] books that it cannot easily be counted. And there is no detriment in this; indeed, one cannot do without it. Because they understood this well, Arab poets imitated that which is found in the prophetic books. Here I cite for you just a few of many examples . . . :[17] "fork [lit. mother] of the road" [Ezek 21:26]; "the dark [lit. pupil of the eye] of night" [Prov 7:9]; "shafts [lit. sons] of his quiver" [Lam 3:13]; "on the [lit. wings of the] heights of the town" [Prov 9:3]; "your neck is an iron sinew" [Isa 48:4]; "the doors of his face" [Job 41:6]; "grain of heaven" [Ps 78:24]; "sounding of the mountains" [Ezek 7:7]; "tumult of your innards" [Isa 63:15]; "from the profusion / protrusion of her honor" [Isa 66:11]; "the burning of the famine" [Lam 5:10]; "the fat of the land" [Gen 45:18]; "the dew of your youth" [Ps 110:3]; "the navel of the land" [Jud 9:37]; "offspring of the day" [Prov 27:1]; "wine of violence" [Prov 4:17]; "helmet of salvation" [Isa 59:17]; "wings of dawn" [Ps 139:9]; "bread of laziness" [Prov 31:27]; "tongue of gold" [Josh 7:24]; "cloak of righteousness" [Isa 61:10]; "staff of bread" [Lev 26:26]; "bottles of the sky" [Job 38:37]; "my night of desire" [Isa 21:4]; "joy of your help" [Ps 51:14]; "lip of the curtain" [Exod 26:4]; "eyelids of dawn" [Job 3:9]; "cords of love" [Hos 11:4]; "fruit of your thoughts" [Jer 6:19]; "face of the war" [2 Sam 10:9]; "the point of a diamond" [Jer 17:1]; "his strides of iniquity" [Job 18:7]; "horn of his anointed one" [1 Sam 2:10]; "spider's webs" [Isa 59:5]; "wind/spirit of jealousy" [Num 5:14]; "sparks of the bow" [Ps 76:4]; "rod of his anger" [Isa 10:4]; "sun of righteousness" [Mal 3:20]; "teaching of faithfulness" [Prov 31:26]; "pillars of smoke" [Joel 3:3].

The Arabs spoke clearly about the benefit of this type of language. They praised it widely and considered it an enhancement to writers of elevated discourse. They accord honor to those who suit it to their needs in their poems, as occurs in their Qur'an [he cites examples].

By having said this, and having cited the Qur'an of the Arabs, I have not heeded the widespread repugnance [to metaphor] felt nowadays by our nation's "expert" jurists, for I have observed that the leading jurists and greatest scholastics, R. Saadia [Gaon] and R. Hai [Gaon] and others, made recourse [to metaphors] in their interpretation of enigmatic scriptural passages. So, too, even in Christian commentaries, with all of their weaknesses. Yet, today members of the aforementioned group [opposed to metaphor] prick up their ears, today, and train their eyes on the trifles of other people's behavior, but they are blind to their own inadequacies.[18] . . .

Let us return to our topic. Metaphor is a term from a known entity [applied] to an unknown entity, and that is all. If you would only examine it rationally, and weigh it on the scales of investigation, its merit would become obvious to you.

There are obvious metaphors and concealed metaphors. The obvious are like those that I cited above, and the concealed are like "The heavens declare the glory of God" [Ps 19:2]. It becomes clear that this is figurative language, not literal, from the words "there is no speech . . ." [Ps 19:3]. A few sages think that *'omer* is discourse in general and *debarim* are things and individual words. "Day to day utters speech" is metaphorical language, referring to the effect created when the sun shines forth from the east every twenty-four hours as it completes its circuit. "And from the edge of the heavens is its rising-place" refers to its distinctive movement from east to west along the plane of the zodiac, by which [movement] the span of the year is divided into the four seasons.

Gather for yourselves from the verses of the Bible however much you like and find pleasing. And when you read attentively the poems of the famous poets of both nations, you will discern the breadth of their aspiration, you will increase ease from them, and through them joy. As for me, in every speech that I gave, and in every letter that I wrote, and in every poem that I composed, I followed this course when I found it in the Holy Scriptures. Therefore, I did not create my own metaphors, for it [the Bible] contains enough for the most part; except if its path was not apparent to me and its procedure was not clear to me. . . .

Chapter 8, Part 2

Oblique Reference: 'Ishāra

Oblique reference is something hinted at but not expressed. . . . In Hebrew oblique reference comes in a diversity of many types. One of these is "Arise, north, and come, south" [Song 4:16]. "North" means "north wind," and "south" means "south wind." Afterward, both winds will act together. and it says "Blow upon my garden," and mentions the purpose, which is "that its perfume may diffuse." After that it describes the ultimate purpose: "my lover will come to his garden and eat his luscious fruits." One of the great commentators explained the verse "I will say to the north, give back; and to the south, do not withhold" [Isa 43:6] in this way. He said: "He turned to inquire of these two winds."[19] But this is incorrect. "North" here refers to Iraq and "south" to Byzantium, that each of the two domains should restore those exiled in its midst. It is sufficient [for Song 4:16] to designate the direction, without the word *wind*. Similarly it is written "and pursues the east" [Hos 12:2]—that is, "the east wind." This is equivalent to "the east wind carried the locust" [Exod 10:12].

There is another kind of oblique reference, as in "set firm like a garment" [Job 38:14]. A garment cannot be firm except on a body, and therefore neither the body nor the garment exists. Similarly, "I will escape with the skin of my teeth" [Job 19:20]. Teeth have no skin, and therefore [the meaning is] he will not escape with anything. Another example is "he will receive a donkey's burial" [Jer 22:19]. A donkey has no burial except "dragged out and left lying." But those who analyze "a refuge from winds" [Isa 32:2] and "like the eminences of a wild ox" [Num 23:22; 24:8] in this manner are mistaken. . . .

Among the oblique references in the Bible are "Before Ephraim and Manasseh rouse your might" [Ps 80:3], which refers to the Ark of the Covenant which traveled[20] in this position, as you can see in the order of the standards.[21] The early sages found oblique references that were in the category of esoteric interpretations, such as "he mustered his retainers" [Gen 14:14], which refers to Eliezer, and the oblique reference is to him alone, and no one else. Also "Go down there" [Gen 42:2], which refers [by *gematria*] to the dwelling of the people in Egypt for 210 years.[22] "We will worship and we will return to you" [Gen 22:5] hints that they will return in peace. "For the goodness of the land of Egypt is yours" [Gen 45:20] hints at "and they despoiled Egypt" [Exod 12:36]. . . .

Chapter 8, Part 3

Antithesis: Muṭâbaqa

Ibn Ezra discusses a trope called muṭābaqa, *which involves the pairing of opposites. It is so common in Arabic and Judeo-Arabic poetics that he does not formally define it, but a definition can be extracted from his examples: a word in the* delet *finds its antithesis in the* soger. *Often a double or triple antithesis is present. In fact, the ideal seems to be that every term in the* delet *be mirrored in the* soger. *This trope is not to be confused with Lowth's "antithetic parallelism." In* muṭābaqa, *the* delet *as a whole need not be antithetic to the* soger *as a whole. The parallelism may be synonymous but achieved through the use of antithetical terms. Compare the trope of* muqābala *in part 6.*

The pairing of opposites . . . in Hebrew is common, e.g., "The pursuers of intrigue *draw near*; they are *far* from your teaching" [Ps 119:150]; "Let every *valley* be *raised*; every *hill and mountain made low*" [Isa 40:4]; "who sits *on high*, to see *below*" [Ps 113:5–6], which means "to sit in heaven to see on earth."[20] Among the most refined of paired opposites is "*A hot-tempered man provokes a quarrel; a patient man calms strife*" [Prov. 15:18]. Another example of paired opposites is "*baseness is exalted* among men" [Ps 12:9]. . . .

Every word in the *delet* [of one of Ibn Ezra's own poems that he cites here] parallels every word in the *soger* and is antithetical to it. There is in the Bible a similar example: "*at daybreak it sprouts and flourishes; at evening it withers and dries up*" [Ps 90:6].

Chapter 8, Part 4

Paronomasia: Mujānasa

Ibn Ezra divides paronomasia into several categories. In the first presented here, the word play involves a proper name and a word with similar phonemes. In the second, it involves words with different meanings, and often from different parts of speech, which share at least two root letters. Other categories not translated here involve verbs derived from nouns, words derived from parts of the body, elliptical expressions, and words derived from numerals.

This section deals with similar [sounding] words with different meanings, and among the rhetoricians it is called "resemblance." It is considered beautiful among most scholars of language since it is one of the instruments of rhetoric. In Hebrew there are many examples: "In Beth-le-'aphrah cover yourself with dust ['*apar*]" [Mic 1:10]; "the houses of Achzib are a disappointment ['*akzab*]" [Mic 1:14]; "a dispossessor [*yoreš*] I will bring you, O dweller of Mareshah" [Mic 1:15]; "Now scourge yourself [*hitgodedi*], O daughter Gedud" [Mic 4:14]; the city will spread down [*tišpal*] into the Shephelah [Isa 32:19];[21] "and 'Ekron will be uprooted [*te'ager*]" [Zeph 2:4]; "in Heshbon they planned [*ḥašebu*] against it evil" [Jer 48:2]; "Tyre [*ṣor*] has built a fortress [*maṣor*] for itself" [Zech 9:3]; "O [city named] Madmen, you too will be silenced [*tiddomi*]" [Jer 48:2].

Besides this type of matching there is "The knave [*kelay*] his instruments [*kelayw*] are wicked" [Isa 32:7]; "for they are more numerous [*rabbu*] than locusts ['*arbeh*]" [Jer 46:23]; "My kidneys [*kilyotai*] perish [*kalu*]" [Job 19:27]; "He who goes with wise men [*ḥakamim*] will become wise [*yeḥkam*]; he who shepherds [*ro'eh*] fools will suffer ill [*yeroa'*]" [Prov 13:20]; "you have not bought [*qanita*] for me a reed [*qaneh*] with silver" [Isa 43:24]; "may the Lord enlarge [*yapt*] Japheth [*yepet*]" [Gen 9:27]; "and you will be noted [*nipqadta*] when your seat will be noted [*yippaqed*]" [1 Sam 20:18]; "of my wandering [*nodi*] you have taken account [*saparta*]; put my tears into your waterskin [*no'deka*], into your accounts [*siprateka*]" [Ps 56:9].

Chapter 8, Part 6

Correspondence (Parallelism): Muqābala

The trope called muqābala *is difficult to distinguish from* muṭābaqa, *presented in part 3. Both seem to involve the paralleling of opposites. J. Dana (*Happo'eṭiqa, *132–35) suggests that in* muṭābaqa *the notion of parallelism dominates, while in* muqābala *the emphasis is on antithesis or contrast. In the latter, the antithesis may occur* within *the* delet *or the* soger*; in the former it involves a word in the* delet *contrasted with a word in the* soger, *thereby giving more weight to the structure that we know as parallelism. The terminology is therefore confusing in that* parallelism, *the term used to render* muqābala, *is better applied* to muṭābaqa. *Note also that the notion of parallelism contained in* muṭābaqa *is more limited than ours, since it refers only to cases containing antithetical terms.*

This section deals with the parallelism of opposites . . . and in the Bible there are many examples, such as "His talk was smoother than butter, but war was in his heart; his words were more soothing than oil, but they were drawn swords" [Ps 55:22]. . . . "Seedtime and harvest, cold and heat, summer and winter,[25] day and night" [Gen 8:22]. . . . "Who makes him dumb or deaf or seeing or blind" [Exod 4:11]. The word *seeing* [*piqqeaḥ*] relates to the two defects [deafness and blindness] and is placed between them; or he was afflicted with both of them. I saw this explanation in a work by the elder Abu al-Faraj [Abu al-Faraj Harun ibn al-Faraj = Aaron ben Jeshua], of Jerusalem, may God have mercy on him, a Karaite.[26] . . . "You have sowed much and brought in little; you eat without being satisfied; you drink without getting your fill; you clothe yourselves, but are not warm; and he who earns anything, earns it for a leaky purse" [Hag 1:6].

Chapter 8, Part 8

Repetition (Anaphora): Tardīd

Most of the examples contain anaphora, but the requirement that the repetition occur at the beginning of the half-lines is not made explicit. Compare the trope in part 9.

This section deals with [the trope in which] the poet uses a certain word in the *delet* and then repeats it in the *soger* in the same form. This does not spoil [the line]; on the contrary, it increases its beauty. The Bible is full of examples, such as "Your right hand, O Lord, is glorious in power; Your right hand, O Lord, shatters the foe" [Exod 15:6]; "Ascribe to the Lord, O divine beings; Ascribe to the Lord glory and strength" [Ps 29:1]; "Mountain, mighty one, Mount Bashan; Mountain, jagged one, Mount Bashan" [Ps 68:16]; "Would that I were brought to the bastion; Would that I were led to Edom" [Ps 60:11 = 108:11]; "He consumes the tendons under his skin; he consumes his tendons, does Death's first-born" [Job 18:13]; "The Lord is a man of war; The Lord is his name" [Exod 15:3]. In this verse there is repetition and advancement; after he calls him "a man of war" he goes on to say "The Lord is his name."

Chapter 8, Part 9

Inclusio: Taṣdīr

This section deals with [the trope in which] the poet begins the verse with a word and ends it with exactly the same word; this enhances the beauty of the verse. It is similar to the trope discussed in the previous section; the difference between them is that the repetition is in [the beginning of] the *soger* [in *tardīd*] or at the edges [of the verse in *taṣdīr*]. In the Bible: "Fear the Lord, you his holy ones; for there is no lack to his fearers" [Ps 34:10]. [This is a case of *taṣdīr*] even though one [of the repeated words] is an imperative and the second is an adjective. The word *for* here explains the purpose. . . . The Masora Magna lists the verses in which the opening and closing words are the same, and they number, according to it, thirty-eight; for example, "All of us went astray like sheep, each going his own way; and the Lord visited upon him the guilt of all of us" [Isa 53:6]; "Jephthah the Gileadite was an able warrior, and he was the son of a prostitute, and Gilead begat Jephthah" [Jud 11:1]; "Vanity of vanities, said Qoheleth, vanity of vanities, all is vanity" [Ecc 1:2]; "To their mothers they say, where is bread and wine, as they languish like wounded in the town squares; as their life runs out in the bosom of their mothers" [Lam 2:12], and so forth.

Toward the end of chapter 8 ibn Ezra discusses proverbs and riddles. In the course of the discussion he notes the use of numbers, both in proverbs and elsewhere.

Proverbs in the form of numbers are Prov 30:18; 30:21; 30:24; 6:16. These numbers are to be understood in their real sense, for so they are explained; they are not exaggerations. For there is a custom in Hebrew to use numbers not in their real sense but to signify "many," as in "On one stone seven eyes" [Zech 3:9], "and break it into seven streams" [Isa 11:15], "ten women shall bake" [Lev 26:26], "if a man would beget a hundred" [Ecc 6:3], "even if he lived a thousand years twice over" [Ecc 6:6]. There are other cases in which the numbers are meant literally—as in "he changed my wages ten times" [Gen 31:7], "he will deliver you from six troubles" [Job 5:19], "ten times you humiliate me" [Job 19:3]—for indeed there were exegetes who counted them. The word *sevenfold* always means "seven"—it is not dual or plural —as in "and the light of the sun shall become sevenfold, like the light of the seven days" [Isa 30:26].

*Ibn Ezra discusses the insertion of Qur'anic citations in Arabic poetry and biblical citations in Hebrew poetry. These, of course, had to fit the metrical requirements of the poems. If an entire hemistich (*delet *or* soger*) or complete verse (*bayit*) was made up of a biblical citation, the implication was that the Bible contained metered verses or parts of verses.*

Our poets are also able to do this, more or less, with entire [biblical] verses or with parts of them, that occur in different types of metered poems, with slight additions or subtractions or without them.[27] Most are in the *rajaz*-meter poetry of Psalms, Job, and Proverbs, e.g.,
[Prov 21:13] אוטם אזנו מזעקת דל גם הוא יקרא ולא יענה,
with the elimination of the *waw*,
[Prov 25:28] עיר פרוצה אין חומה;
[Prov 21:22] עיר גבורים עלה חכם וירד [לו] עו מבטחה,
with the addition of *lo*;
[Ps 69:13] ישיחו כי יושבי שער ונגינות [כל] שותי שכר,
with the addition of *kol*;
[Prov 18:13] משיב דבר בטרם ישמע;
[Prov 14:19] שחו רשעים לפני טובים;
[Prov 26:25] גלה חציר נראה דשא.
And in short meter is
[Prov 18:23] ותחנונים ידבר רש ועשיר יענה עזות,
with the addition of *waw*.[28]

And in other metrical patterns there are fragments of biblical verses; if you seek them you will find that they exist.

NOTES

1. Cf. Pagis, *Širat Haḥol*, 13, 17.
2. The Arabic word for poem is *shiʿr*, remarkably close in sound to the

Hebrew *šir*, and it would seem that this resemblance suggested an equivalence in meaning. See above, chapter 4, and Kugel, *The Idea of Biblical Poetry*, 185.

3. Dana (*Happo'eṭiqa*, 262, note 33) suggests that the term *rajaz* be understood as a general designation for poetry, not the specific form of Arabic poetry called *rajaz*. *Rajaz* is the lowest form of Arabic poetry, with considerable leeway permitted in the pattern of long and short syllables. This may account for its use as a general term. Or, ibn Ezra may have used it here because the feature to which he is calling attention in his three biblical examples is the rhyming of the two hemistiches of a verse (according to the definition of rhyme in medieval poetry). This is found in older *rajaz* poems, as opposed to later *rajaz* and *qaṣīdas* in which the rhyme runs throughout the poem and occurs only in the second hemistich of each verse. There is nothing to suggest that ibn Ezra found meter in these biblical examples.

Allony has pointed out that ibn Ezra borrowed this idea from Saadia's *'Egron* (or from a fragment that Allony has identified as belonging to the *'Egron*). The text in question cites as examples Job 28:16; Job 21:4; and Isa 49:1. Ibn Ezra, however, was evidently not prepared to include Isaiah under this rubric, as he found only the books of Proverbs, Psalms, and Job to contain poetry. He substituted Job 33:17 to complete his three examples. See Allony, *Ha'egron*, 80, 112, 386–87, and Kugel, *The Idea of Biblical Poetry*, 238 with note 77.

4. All of these are written stichographically in the masoretic scribal tradition.

5. The Mekilta, Tractate Širta, and the Targum to Song of Songs enumerates ten songs, but the last is to be sung in the future, so ibn Ezra considers that there are only nine. On the enumeration of biblical songs see Kugel, "Is There but One Song."

6. Simon suggests that ibn Ezra may be referring especially to Isaac ibn Ghiyyat in his comment to Ecc 2:8 (cf. Simon, *'Arba' Gišot*, 152, note 80).

7. In Judeo-Arabic, a dotted *gimel* usually represents Arabic *jim*, and an undotted *gimel* generally represents Arabic *ghayn*. Ibn Ezra writes Gozan and Guzana with an undotted *gimel*, not, apparently, to suggest *ghayn*, but perhaps to represent the hard pronunciation of *g*, as it sounds in Hebrew. (But cf. Halkin's note to line 52 on pg. 49.)

8. See Zucker, "Fragments of the *Kitāb Taḥṣīl al-Sharā'i' al-Samā'iyah.*"

9. A similar sentiment is expressed later in chapter 8 (Halkin, 203): "In the Bible there are many examples of this [the use of an adjective without its noun]. What you find there you may use, and if you do not find it, do not create analogous forms. Go where the language leads you and stop where it stops."

10. Ibn Ezra is showing that the two phrases are not redundant—that is, that the "family" referred to in the first part of the phrase (a childless woman) is not necessarily the same "family" referred to in the second (a motherless child, who technically is not an orphan while the father is alive).

11. Unlike the ancient versions and several modern commentaries, ibn Ezra does not want to read *gan* in both phrases but rather *gal*, "fountain." There would then be threefold repetition. For him this reading might have had the additional merit of avoiding the juxtaposition of similar letters, in *gan na'ul*, which, as he discussed above, is to be avoided.

12. Cf. the NEB translation: "Jehovah, the Lord."

13. The explanation in the preceding paragraph that metaphor may be used for technical purposes, to fill the needs of rhyme and meter. (Cf. Dana, *Happo'eṭiqa*, 60.)

14. A variant adds this phrase.

15. Note how ibn Ezra uses metaphor when speaking of metaphor.

16. Metaphorical speech is eloquent, while speech lacking metaphor cannot express things adequately.

17. The list comprises forty metaphorical expressions, of two- or three-word combinations, listed in alphabetical order.

18. Cf. Brann, *The Compunctious Poet*, 79.

19. So Rashi and Abraham ibn Ezra.

20. For this reading see Halkin, *Kitāb al-Muḥāḍara*, 232, note to line 75.

21. According to Numbers 10, the Ark traveled before the Ephraim-division ("standard"), which included the tribes of Ephraim, Manasseh, and Benjamin. Cf. also Numbers 2 and the comment of Abraham ibn Ezra on Ps 80:3.

22. The letters of "go down," *r.d.w.*, are numerically equivalent to 200 + 4 + 6 = 210.

23. This is understood by modern interpreters to mean that God is enthroned above all and looks down upon heaven and earth.

24. This understanding of the verse differs from modern opinion, which is itself divided; cf. RSV: "and the city will be utterly laid low," and NEB: "and cities shall lie peaceful in the plain."

25. Ibn Ezra understands these as "spring and fall."

26. A similar interpretation is given by Abraham ibn Ezra in his comment to Exod 4:11: " 'Dumb' contrasts with giving a mouth [in 'who gave man a mouth'], and 'blind' contrasts with 'seeing,' and that leaves 'deaf' alone, without a contrasting term. But really the word *piqqeaḥ* [lit.: 'open'] contrasts with 'deaf' and 'blind,' as in 'opening eyes' [Isa 42:7] and 'open of ears' [Isa 42:20]."

27. That is, with slight adjustments in order to make the biblical verses conform to the metrical schemes of medieval poetry.

28. Ibn Ezra is trying to show that with a few adjustments, these verses scan as poetry—i.e., that the two hemistiches have the same metrical pattern. Dana, *Happo'eṭiqa*, 182, offers the scansion, but he does not seem to take into account ibn Ezra's additions and omissions.

SOLOMON IBN PARḤON

Solomon ben Abraham ibn Parḥon (twelfth century), a lexicographer, was born in Qal'a, Spain. He was the student of Judah Halevi, whose influence is apparent in the excerpt which follows, and of Abraham ibn Ezra. He later emigrated to Italy, where he wrote his only extant work, Maḥberet He'aruk.

Maḥberet He'aruk *[A Lexical Notebook[1]] was written in Salerno, Italy, in 1160–61. It is a biblical lexicon on the model of earlier such works, and in fact draws heavily on* Seper Haššorašim *[Book of Roots] of ibn Janaḥ, as well as on other works of ibn Janaḥ and ibn Ḥayyuj. Despite this, however, the book is not totally derivative. For one thing, it was originally written in Hebrew, unlike most of its predecessors, which were written in Arabic, and so helped to spread the linguistic learning from Arabic-speaking countries to other parts of Europe, as its author intended. Furthermore, it does contain new material, including original explanations of biblical passages.*

The introduction of the book consists of a summary of biblical Hebrew grammar and concludes with a brief excursus on Hebrew prosody, which is translated below. Here, as elsewhere, we see the close connection between grammar and prosody.

Ibn Parḥon adopted the views of Judah Halevi that metrical poetry is not native to Hebrew and that its imposition on Hebrew does harm to the language. He uses Halevi's arguments and examples to show that metrical poetry is not found in the Bible, and speaks even more forcefully against the view that metrical poetry is an improvement over biblical discourse. The excerpt presented here is found on pp. 4–5 of the Stern edition. Following that in the Stern edition (but originally located later in the work) is a section entitled "Biblical Matters about Which One Must Remove Doubt." This section deals with a number of linguistic and rhetorical usages in the Bible, and shows its author to have been sensitive to the nuances of language and a good interpreter of the literal sense of the Bible.

Edition: Solomon ben Abraham ibn Parḥon, Maḥberet He'aruk, *ed. S. G. Stern (Pressburg, 1844).*

Maḥberet He'aruk

. . . For this reason [because of the phonetic exigencies of Hebrew, in which there cannot usually be three fully vocalized consonants in a row]

Israel never practiced—before it mingled with the Arabs and learned their ways [cf. Ps 106:35]—the art of poetry [Heb.: *piyyuṭ*],[2] and rhyme and meter, for the holy tongue is not like other languages. Other languages can put a mobile *shwa* after any consonant, but Hebrew [lit.: Israel] cannot put a mobile *shwa* except after *'alep*, *he*, *ḥet*, and *'ayin*, and after a doubled consonant,[3] as we have stated. Know that if you count the syllables of the word *pa'al*, you will find two syllables in three consonants. In other languages [i.e., Arabic], each consonant takes a full vowel and therefore forms its own syllable.

If poetry and rhyme and meter were good, the sons of Korah, and David, king of Israel, and Solomon would have used it, for they were poets [or: singers] who composed songs and melodies—songs such as Psalm 88, Psalm 5, Psalm 46, Psalm 9, Psalm 4.[4] Our rabbis said that Ben Arza knew about song but did not want to teach it.[5] There were poets [singers] of high repute in the Temple; why did they not compose their songs in rhyme and their poems in meter like the Arabs? How is it that we, with our limited knowledge, are able to compose metered and rhymed poems and they did not know how? Surely because after we were exiled we saw the Arabs composing rhyme and metered poems, and we imitated them, thereby corrupting the holy tongue and using it in a way that it was not meant to be used. Now David, about whom the Creator said "he knows how to play" [1 Sam 16:16], and he praised him, and praised Solomon by saying "he listened to and sought out and set in order many *mešalim*" [Ecc 12:9], and "his songs were one thousand and five" [1 Kgs 5:12], and said "he was wiser than any person" [1 Kgs 5:11]—after all this, he, in everything that he wrote, did not write one rhyme or one metered poem. How can we say that he did not know how to do as we do? If we dribble nonsense that pleases us, doesn't this show lack of understanding? For we know of the holy tongue only what is in the Bible, while they, who were wise men and prophets and poets [or: singers], spoke before the Creator in all kinds of melodies except poetry, rhyme, and meter. For they said "to him who alone does great wonders" [Ps 136:4], now this is long; and they said "to him who made the heavens with discerning" [Ps 136:5], and this is short. And furthermore "the moon and the stars to rule the night" [Ps 136:9], which is long; and to balance it they said "the sun to rule the day" [Ps 136:8], which is short. But certainly if the holy tongue were not exceptional, they would have done this before all the other nations of the world![6]

R. Judah Halevi, of blessed memory, said that the poet who employs meter uses *sámti* instead of *samtí*, and *'omér* instead of *'ómer*,[7] and this is altogether bad, so he repented before his death and forswore poetry.[8] Indeed, this is an Arabic practice, and their language is designed for it, but we have other interests in our language, namely, that the reader will understand surprise, rebuke, pleading, confusion, interrogatives, and every nuance. The interrogative is [in the grammatical form of] "Is the Lord in our midst or not" [Exod 17:7]; but the confusion of "and he procrastinated" [Gen 19:16] is in the [masoretic] accents.[9] Pleading is in "Why do you do this to your servants" [Exod 5:15], and rebuke is in "would he speak and not act" [Num 23:19]. You can understand all of these from their accents, as though the prophet stands in front of you, speaking to you face to face. This essential element would be lost in the interest of meter and rhyme. There is no greater proof in the world than this. How are we, in the impoverishment of our knowledge, able to do what they did not know how to do? [Because] surely this is not a trait [of Hebrew]; it is a trait of the Arabs.

Following this is a section clarifying a number of linguistic and rhetorical usages in the Bible. Since the discussion is lengthy, it is summarized below, and not all of the examples are cited. Among others, ibn Parḥon points out the following usages:

ABBREVIATION. *Ruth 4:15: "six barleys" = "six measures of barley"; Isa 42:2: "he will not raise" = "he will not raise his voice"; the same in Job 21:12; Prov 9:12: "you will bear" = "you will bear sin"; Job 22:24: "Ophir" = "the gold of Ophir."*

Related to this are cases in which the word 'ašer, *"which," is omitted, and words written in abbreviated forms, in which letters assimilate. There are also cases in which prepositions are omitted, as in Gen 27:3: "the field" = "to the field," and Lam 1:7: "the days of her affliction" = "in the days of her affliction."*

ADDITIONS OR REDUNDANCIES. *Num 16:3:* "All *the community,* all of them *are holy"; Lev 25:46: "As for your Israelite brothers, a man over his brother"; 1 Sam 17:13: "And the three oldest sons of Jesse went, they went after Saul" (and many other examples).*

Ibn Parḥon also brings examples of the repetition of a pronoun (which we would understand as emphasis) and various substitutions of words.

NUMBERS NOT TO BE TAKEN LITERALLY.[10] *There are quite a few instances where ibn Parḥon does not take a number literally, e.g., 1 Sam 1:8: "better than ten sons"; Job 19:2: "ten times"; Ecc 6:3: "if a man beget a hundred," etc. He does, however, take Prov 9:1, "her pillars are seven," literally, for he then enumerates them.*

Various other idiomatic expressions are pointed out. For instance, in addition to metathesis of letters there is metathesis of ideas, as in Ps 104:6: "on mountains stood water," which ibn Parḥon understands as "on water stood mountains," the land being sunk beneath the water; Lev 14:3: "the leprosy was healed from the leper" = "the leper was healed of the leprosy." Related to this are cases of hysteron proteron as in Exod 14:21: "he made the sea into dry land, and he split the water."

NOTES

1. The term *'aruk*, "arranged, ordered," was often used for lexical works.

2. Ibn Parḥon uses the term *piyyuṭ* to designate rhymed, metered poetry and the term *šir* to designate biblical song or poetry.

3. He is referring to words such as *ribebot* [Num 10:36] and *qilelat* [Jud 9:57], which are different in respect to the quality of the *shwa* (and hence in construction) from such seemingly similar forms as *ṣidqat* and *birkat*.

4. These psalms contain terms understood as musical terminology in their opening verses.

5. According to the Mishna (*Tamid* 7:3 and *Šeqalim* 5:1), Ben Arza was in charge of the cymbals, which served as a cue for the Levitical chorus.

6. That is, since Hebrew was the first language in the world, its poets would have been the first to use rhyme and meter had Hebrew been like other languages.

7. Cf. *Kuzari* 2.87.

8. On the topic of poets repenting, see Brann, *The Compunctious Poet.*

9. The masoretic accent on this word is a *šalšelet*, indicating that the word is to be recited in a long, drawn-out manner. Ibn Parḥon's following examples are a matter not so much of accents but of his understanding of the rhetorical context of the passages.

10. Compare the discussion of numbers in Moshe ibn Ezra's *Kitāb al-Muḥāḍara.*

SAMUEL IBN TIBBON AND MOSHE IBN TIBBON

The ibn Tibbon family produced four generations of famous translators of Arabic works into Hebrew. The family originated in Granada but settled in Provence —a non-Arabic-speaking area where their translations were extremely influential in preserving and transmitting important Arabic texts. Judah ibn Tibbon (ca. 1120–1190), known as "the father of translators," translated, among other things, Judah Halevi's Kuzari, *Saadia's* 'Emunot wede'ot, *and ibn Janaḥ's* Seper Hariqma *and* Seper Haššorašim. *His son, Samuel ben Judah ibn Tibbon (ca. 1160–1230), is best known for his translation of Maimonides's* Guide of the Perplexed *and a number of other works by Maimonides. He also wrote a commentary on Ecclesiastes. Samuel's son, Moshe ben Samuel ibn Tibbon (thirteenth century), produced a number of translations of philosophical, mathematical, and medical texts, including al-Farabi and Averroes's commentaries on Aristotle. He also wrote his own commentary on the Pentateuch and on Song of Songs. The fourth member of the family was Jacob ben Machir ibn Tibbon (ca. 1236–1307), grandson of Samuel, who translated works on philosophy, mathematics, and astronomy. There was possibly a fifth ibn Tibbon translator, Abraham ibn Tibbon, about whom little is known.*

The influence of these translators should not be underestimated. Not only were they important in developing the style and terminology of medieval Hebrew prose, but they are responsible, in large measure, for the preservation and spread of major Arabic works (both Jewish and Islamic). In fact, the two most important medieval Jewish works, The Kuzari *and* The Guide of the Perplexed, *were better known in their Hebrew translations than in their Judeo-Arabic originals. It also stands to reason that men involved in translation would hold opinions about language, although these opinions need not be original. Indeed, we do find that both Samuel and Moshe ibn Tibbon expressed their views on poetry, including biblical poetry.*

The excerpt of Samuel ibn Tibbon's discussion of poetry is found in his commentary on Ecclesiastes, no longer extant but preserved in Judah Moscato's citation of it in his commentary on The Kuzari, *entitled* Qol Yehuda [*The Voice of Judah, a reference to the author's name*]. *The following excerpt is from the explanation of* The Kuzari *2.70 (pp. 160–61 of the Vilna, 1904, edition). The first part was translated into Latin by Johannes Buxtorf II in the appendix to his* Liber Cosri. *He speaks of the superiority of biblical poetry to later metrical poetry, and of the superiority of the spoken word to the written word.*

Judah Moscato's Citation of Samuel ibn Tibbon's Commentary on Ecclesiastes

How apt are the words coming from the mouth of R. Samuel ibn Tibbon at the beginning of his commentary on Ecclesiastes. He said: "The art of poetry has different conventions, some are generally held and others differ from nation to nation. Aristotle mentioned them in his book on Poetics. He mentioned that some nations did not make their poems equal in respect to final letters [i.e., rhyme], but that they were equal only when they were read aloud. He says that some nations did not make their poems with uniform meter by means of vocalization, that is, cords and pegs which were of the same pattern and number, but that the lack would be filled in by the melody. There is no doubt that they had an order therein, for not every lack could be filled in.[1] I wrote this for you because it seems that in the generation of David and Solomon, peace be upon them, their poems were like this, for they do not have meter or rhyme. It must be said that those poems had a superiority over the poems being produced today, for their manner was not foreign, and they [the authors] were able to express their thoughts completely. But in these [current] generations, [authors] accepted many conventions regarding what to do and what not to do, and they imposed many limitations on themselves from which they could not deviate to the right or left. This led to forcing and constriction and omission and the permitting of nonsense. And with all of this, the meaning was lost, or at least became difficult to understand. I spoke at length about this to give honor to the poems of David and Solomon and to have this accounted to their merit."

On Kuzari *2.72, the idea that the spoken word is better than the written word:*

Isn't that what R. Samuel ibn Tibbon said in the introduction to his commentary on Ecclesiastes: "There are many ways that a wise teacher can turn and twist words so that perceptive students will understand their meaning, even without explaining or commenting on them—something that is impossible to do when writing a book. Just as a person can say to his neighbor, 'You did well by doing that,' and the person spoken to will understand that he [the speaker] did not like what he did. One does not understand this from the words themselves, for the speaker intends the opposite of what the words say; rather, he understands it from the character of the speech and from the events that accompany it—the speaker's face may redden, or may turn green in anger—or from the tone of his voice—that is, he may not have spoken calmly, as one does when he intends his words to be taken literally, but rather in a tone of disapproval—or from other words in connection with it. . . ."

The following excerpt is from Moshe ibn Tibbon's Commentary on Song of Songs. *He viewed Song of Songs, as did many of his day, as an allegory of the relations between man and his soul. This work influenced Immanuel of Rome, who repeated much of Moshe ibn Tibbon's interpretation in his own commentary to Song of Songs.*

Our interest in the commentary is not in its explanation of the allegorical meaning of the Song, but in the statements it contains about poetry, which are found in the introduction. Basing himself on the superscription "The Song of Songs which is Solomon's," ibn Tibbon begins with a discussion of all the literary works of Solomon, and of the meaning of the term song. *Solomon is credited with authorship of Ecclesiastes, Proverbs, and Song of Songs. Ibn Tibbon assigns each of these to a different form of discourse: Ecclesiastes is literal discourse; Proverbs is* mašal *discourse (i.e., allegorical); and Song of Songs is poetic discourse.*[2] *Ibn Tibbon finds support for this in the opening words of each of the books: "words of Ecclesiastes," "proverbs of Solomon," and "song."*

Then the focus is narrowed to poetic discourse, which is subdivided into three types: (1) metrical expressions not set to music, (2) expressions set to music although they are not metrical or rhymed, (3) expressions employing exaggeration and imagery, that is, metaphorical expression. Only the last type is true poetry, according to Aristotle.

At this point the discussion becomes somewhat confusing, although it is not contradictory, as it may at first appear. Ibn Tibbon says of the first and second types of poetry (which are not true poetry) that they may employ literal or mašal *forms of discourse. This would seem to mean that a metrical or sung work is not necessarily "poetic" in the Aristotelian sense, but may be taken literally or as a* mašal. *Thus, as he will suggest below, Proverbs may employ* mašal *discourse but be poetry of type one or two. As for the third type, true poetry, it is not necessarily metrical but is metaphorical. Ibn Tibbon cites a number of short biblical examples of this type of language; many are the same as those of Moshe ibn Ezra.*

He continues with an Aristotelian-type analysis, discussing five genera of syllogisms. The fifth is poetry, on which Aristotle wrote his Poetics. *Again ibn Tibbon applies this to the Bible, assigning various books to one of the three types of poetry (defined above). Ecclesiastes and Proverbs, and perhaps Job and Psalms, belong to the first type, metrical expression—because they have divided verses like the* batim *of medieval Hebrew poems, even though the verse halves are not metrically equivalent. The stichographic writing of Job, Proverbs, and Psalms and the tradition of considering these books poetic (by virtue of the masoretic system of accents) would seem to be the factors influencing ibn Tibbon. But it is not clear why he included Ecclesiastes, unless it was because, as he mentioned earlier, it was, like Solomon's other books, composed through the Holy Spirit, and was therefore poetry of one type or another.*

In the second type of poetry—words set to music—ibn Tibbon includes the "songs" [širot], *which belong to this type by virtue of their stichographic form of log over brick and brick over log. Again, ibn Tibbon relies on tradition here. But at this point he has some second thoughts about Job, Proverbs, and Psalms and suggests that perhaps they, too, belong to the second type of poetry since ancient poets were concerned primarily with meaning, not with meter; and besides, these books are not really metrical.*

Song of Songs is the third type of poetry: metaphorical. There is no question of its being metrical or set to music. It is not written stichographically. Its language is full of imagery, not to be taken literally and not to be taken as mešalim. *Poetry of type three, it would seem, can employ only poetic discourse, not literal or* mašal *discourse. It is poetry by virtue of its form of discourse, not by virtue of its formal patterning (meter) or melody. Ibn Tibbon goes on to make a sharp distinction between the discourse in Proverbs (*mašal *discourse) and the poetic, metaphorical discourse in the Song. Yet he admits that the Song does contain some allegorical passages, and indeed, he explains the general content as a philosophical allegory.*

Edition: R. Moshe ibn Tibbon, Peruš 'al Šir Hašširim *(Lyck, 1874). Several sections are found in Israel Adler,* Hebrew Writings concerning Music in Manuscripts and Printed Books from Geonic Times up to 1800 *(Munich, 1975), pp. 186–90.*[3]

Introduction to the *Commentary on Song of Songs*

It is known that King Solomon, peace be upon him, composed the scroll [Song of Songs] through the Holy Spirit, like the rest of the books termed "Writings," for he was not a prophet. . . . To be sure, he spoke through the Holy Spirit, and wrote his books in a wise and scientific manner, for so Scripture attests about him when it says "I have given you a wise and discerning heart. There never was anyone like you and there never will be" [1 Kgs 3:12], and when it says "He was wiser than any man" [1 Kgs 5:11]. Therefore his books were written in the same manner as the other books written through the Holy Spirit. We find that he spoke in *mašal* discourse, and in poetic discourse [the discourse of *šir*], and in ordinary [literal] discourse, as it says: "He spoke three thousand *mašal*, and his songs [*šir*] were one thousand and five, and he spoke about the trees . . . and about the animals, and the birds, and the creeping things, and the fish" [1 Kgs 5:12–13]. The last is really literal discourse on natural science, but nothing remains for us of his words and wisdom except three books.

It appears that he composed each of these books in a different form of discourse. The first form is literal discourse, like most of the "Writings." In this form he wrote most of Ecclesiastes, and to indicate which form of discourse it is, he began it with "the words of Ecclesiastes." The second form is *mašal* discourse. One can make good sense of the literal meaning, but there is some comparison and similarity to the *nimšal* in all the mysteries of Scripture.[4] In this form he wrote [the Book of] Proverbs, and to indicate which form of discourse it is written in, it opens with "The proverbs [*mišlê*] of Solomon." The third form is poetic discourse, and it has three subtypes or a combination of them.

The first subtype is metered expression, not recited to a melody. The second subtype is expressions recited to a melody, even though their parts do not have equal meter and they lack rhyme. These two subtypes may be literal or *mašal* discourse. These two subtypes are not true poetry, as Aristotle wrote in his Book of Poetics. The third subtype is expressions in poetic rhetoric, using exaggeration and hyperbole, and comparison and imitation and simile and substitution in praise or in denigration of a subject, to arouse the hearts and reverse the qualities and to reinforce the subject and to affirm its truth with many words and stories and many descriptions and with *mešalim* [metaphors]—not to be taken literally and not to be taken as a parable [*mašal*] for anything that resembles or is comparable to it.[5] This subtype is true poetry. It is found in Scripture, e.g., "fork [lit.: mother] of the road" [Ezek 21:26]; "helmet of salvation" [Isa 59:17]; "cloak of righteousness" [Isa 61:10]; "wings of dawn" [Ps 139:9]; "the dark [lit.: pupil of the eye] of night" [Prov 7:9]; "shafts [lit.: sons] of his quiver" [Lam 3:13]; "I will make my arrows drunk with blood" [Deut 32:42], and many such in Scriptures.[6] This subtype, the more it goes to extremes—in understatement and hyperbole—the better and more praiseworthy, as the Sage's saying goes: The best of poetry is its falseness. This is one of the ways of deluding with which no wise man would occupy himself except to heal the sick of heart and weak of mind, to reverse bad qualities, to gladden the sad, and to strengthen the hearts of the weak, and to arouse the sleeping hearts and draw them out. For [human] nature is drawn to hyperbolic poetry and sweet melody. It is potent magic that kills the healthy and cures the sick. To this subtype belong all the types of melody, that is, the science of music.

Know that things are divided into three categories, according to their essence: totally true, totally false, and a combination of true and false.

The last is further subdivided into three: mostly true, mostly false, and equal in truth and falsity. . . .

He goes on to assign five genera of syllogisms, about which Aristotle wrote separate books, to these categories. Poetry is considered totally false. He then presents each of the five genera, according to Aristotle, and names the book which deals with them. Since his interest here is poetry, as it relates to the interpretation of Song of Songs, he applies the definitions and categories to biblical poetry.

The fifth genus is poetry. Its postulates are postulates that convey images into the hearts of its listeners; this image brings them close to love or hate something, even though they know that there is no reality in those expressions. This is called the Book of Poetics.[7]

Belonging to the first type of poetry are all the poems of Solomon —Ecclesiastes and Proverbs and the like.[8] Perhaps Proverbs and Job and most of Psalms are of this type, for they have divided verses [*pesuqim*], like verses [*batim*] [in medieval poetry], although the parts are not equal in full vowels and *shwas* [i.e., by the standards of quantitative meter], and therefore they are written log over log and brick over brick, like verses [*batim*].

Belonging to the second type are the "songs" [*širot*][9] because they are recited to a melody, even though they do not have meter or rhyme. Rather, what is missing [in the meter] can be filled in by the melody. Therefore they are written log over brick and brick over log, like the *piyyuṭim* with refrains. Or perhaps Proverbs, Job, and Psalms are a combination of the first and second types, and therefore the three of them were made equal [in the length of their verses] by melody and accents [i.e., the special system of masoretic accents used for these three books], and by being written log over log and brick over brick, like the "permission" *piyyuṭim*.[10] Indeed, the early [poets] were primarily concerned in their poems with forthright expression and truth of meaning, and they did not adopt types of poetry except the "melody" type alone,[11] in order to arouse slumbering hearts and to awaken them from their idle sleep, so as to make them attend to the sweetness of the melody; then they would hear the mighty deeds of God, and that which began for other reasons would be done for its own sake.[12] They minimized meter and rhyme in order to improve the [content of the] composition, and they did not find it necessary to add or subtract anything that would detract from the contents. Later poets limited themselves with meter and rhyme, with mobile and quiescent *shwas*, and with metrical feet such that they found it necessary to add and subtract and to insert ungrammatical words which detract from the composition. They gave primary consideration to the power of the meter and the rhetoric, to the [poetic] pattern and rhetorical correctness. . . .

Ibn Tibbon continues his comparison of earlier and later poetry, the first being of true meaning, if lacking somewhat in poetic eloquence. This permits these poems to be put into different words, or even translated into different languages, without losing their value, which is in their contents. Later poetry, however, in which form is the essence, and which is filled with falsities (as true poetry should be), cannot be paraphrased without losing its essence.

He composed Song of Songs in the third type of poetry. He began with "song of songs" to escape from [taking literally the] concrete descriptions by which the lover is described, when it says "Where will you pasture . . . beside the flocks of your fellows" [Song 1:7]; also "his locks are curled, black as a raven" [5:11], "his eyes," "his cheeks," "his hands," "his thighs," etc.—just as it says "To whom can you liken me; to whom can I be compared" [Isa 40:25], and "What form can you compare him to" [Isa 40:18]. As they said, "The power of the prophets is great in that they compare a form to its creator." And [he began with "song of songs"] to make it known that most of his words were expressed in poetic rhetoric, with exaggeration and hyperbole, not for the most part realistic at all. . . . [He expands on the metaphorical language of Song of Songs.]

It is not called "song" because it is metrical, like *Ben Mišlê* [the poems of Samuel Hanagid], or close to metrical, like Proverbs, Job, and Psalms; and not because it is recited to a melody, like the *širot* [i.e., passages labeled *šira*]; hence it is not written log over log and brick over brick like Proverbs, Job, and Psalms—and does not resemble them in melody[13] —and not log over brick and brick over log like the *širot*. Rather, it is called "song of songs" solely because it is expressed in poetic rhetoric, albeit it does contain some *mešalim* [parables or allegories].

NOTES

1. That is, even nonmetrical poetry must have some limits, for it is impossible to fit an infinite number of words into a given melody.

2. On the different forms of discourse see also Joseph ibn Kaspi.

3. I have followed this edition when possible, it being superior to the earlier one. I have not indicated all of the variants, only some of the more interesting ones.

4. That is, a *mašal* can be explained literally, but the mysteries of Scripture make more sense if explained allegorically.

5. The last part of the sentence defines the second sense of the word *mašal*—meaning "metaphor or figurative language"; not to be confused with the earlier sense in which *mašal* was used immediately preceding—meaning "parable, allegory."

6. Compare Moshe ibn Ezra's similar list of metaphors in *Kitāb al-Muḥāḍara*, chapter 8, part 1.

7. Ibn Tibbon probably knew this work through Averroes's *Middle Commentary on Aristotle's Poetics*.

8. This does not contradict his earlier statement in which he distinguished between the forms of discourse in these books. Ecclesiastes and Proverbs are not metaphorical (i.e., poetic discourse) although they may be quasi-metrical, and hence poetry of type one or two.

9. Those passages labeled *šir*, such as Exodus 15 and Deuteronomy 32.

10. "Permission" *piyyuṭim* or "introductory" *piyyuṭim* were composed as introductions to certain prayers in the liturgy.

Variant adds: "Aristotle wrote that some nations did not make the last letters of their poems equal, but that they were equal when recited. He also mentioned that some nations did not observe the convention of unified meter by means of vocalization, that is, full vowels and *shwas* [cords and pegs], which were arranged in the same pattern and number. Rather the lack was filled in by the melody. There is no doubt that they had some arrangement, for not every lack could be filled in by a melody."

11. Variant: "they did not adopt from the types of poetry meter and melody."

12. That is, the listeners would first be drawn to the praise of God because of the melody, and then would come to appreciate the contents.

13. It does not have the same system of masoretic accents as Psalms, Proverbs, and Job.

QUNṬRES BEDIQDUQ SEPAT 'EBER

*This anonymous thirteenth-century grammar (*Notes on the Grammar of the Language of Eber*) ends with the following observations on biblical poetry. They are of the same nature as a number of others, namely, that biblical poetry has meter and rhyme. Yet they strike us as weaker than most, because the examples are forced and unconvincing, and because no distinction is made between what we would consider textual phenomena and interpretive strategies.*

Edition: Qunṭres Bediqduq Sepat 'Eber, *ed. Samuel Poznanski (Berlin, 1891).*

[The Bible] lacks none of the marvelous sciences, even the art of poetry [*šir*] and the art of *piyyuṭ* [i.e., rhymed, metrical poetry]. There are traces of everything in it, just as you see the eightfold acrostic[1] [Psalm 119]—that is, all twenty-two letters are arranged in it eight times. Likewise, as the *payyṭanim* do–each putting his name [in an acrostic] in his *piyyuṭ*–you will find traces of this in the words of the biblical writers [lit.: prophets].[2] For example [Hos 14:4], **אשר בך ירוחם יתום**, which is the name **אביי** in the beginning of the words; and also [Song 8:1] **מי יתנך כאח לי**, which is the name **מיכאל**; and also the Tetragrammaton in the Song of Asaph [1 Chr 16:31], **ישמחו השמים ותגל הארץ**.[3]

Likewise, one finds rhyme, as in [1 Kgs 8:57]:

> יהי ה' אלינו עמנו כאשר היה עם אבותינו
> אל יעזבנו ואל יטשנו

and also [Isa 63:17]:

> למה תתענו ה' מדרכיך תקשיח לבנו מיראתך
> שוב למען עבדיך שבטי נחלתך

and countless others.

Likewise, *gemaṭriot*, such as **שדה זרע** [Ezek 17:5], which is a *gemaṭria* for **ירושלם**.[4] And also **רחם תזכור** [Hab 3:2], in which the word **רחם**, by *noṭariqon*,[5] equals our father Abraham. Also **ששך** [Jer 25:26; 51:41], which is **בבל** by *'atbaš*.[6] Likewise you will find meter, as in [Gen 43:10]:

כי לולא התמהמהנו כי / עתה שבנו זה פעמים,
and also [Exod 21:21]:

[אך] אם יום או יומיים יע / מד לא יקם כי כספו הוא.[7]

These are in the Torah, but in Psalms [we find, Ps 102:5]:

אויה לי כי גרתי משך / שכנתי עם אהלי קדר,

and in Proverbs [30:8]:

רש ועשיר אל תתן לי / הטריפני לחם חקי.

And thus with the rest of the mysterious and secret things. There is not one science missing or lacking from it [the Bible].

NOTES

1. See *b. Berakot* 4b.
2. That is, a proper name in an acrostic, though not the author's name.
3. The attribution to Asaph comes from 1 Chr 16:7.
4. The sum of the letters of each word adds up to 586.
5. *Noṭariqon* is the method of interpreting the letters of a word as abbreviations for other words—a kind of acronym or the like. The author of the *Qunṭres* has used the term mistakenly; he means *gemaṭria*, for the sum of the letters of רחם and the sum of the letters of אברהם are each 248.
6. *'Atbaš* is the substituting of the first letter of the alphabet for the last, the second for the second from last, and so forth, such that *'alep* = *taw*, *bet* = *šin*, etc. This interpretation of *Šišaq* = *Babel* is found in the Targum on Jer 25:26 and in *Numbers Rabbah* 18.
7. Each verse half has eight syllables. To arrive at this pattern he must divide the verse in the middle of a phrase or even in the middle of a word. This was done at times in medieval Hebrew poetry. More surprising is the fact that his examples are taken from nonpoetic passages. Perhaps he did so in order to find meter in the Torah, as well as elsewhere in the Bible; but could he not have found a metrical verse in one of the "songs"?

SHEM TOV IBN FALAQUERA

Shem Tov ibn Falaquera (ca. 1225–1295), a Spanish philosopher, poet, translator, and perhaps physician, was a member of an aristocratic family from Tudela. Little is known of his personal life, including the place of his birth and the exact dates of his birth and death. All that is certain is that he lived in northern Spain and, although this area had already been reconquered by Christians, he received an education typical of Spanish Jews under Muslim rule—including science, philosophy, and Arabic literature, as well as classical Jewish texts. Although a prolific writer—mostly of philosophical and ethical works and poetry (and apparently a Bible commentary which is not extant)—Falaquera is not considered to have been an original thinker. Rather, his views are representative of Jewish thought of his time (and therein lies the benefit to a modern reader in studying him). He drew heavily on Maimonides, whom he defended, and on numerous Arabic and Greek philosophers.

Seper Hammebaqqeš *[The Book of the Seeker] was written circa 1260. It is a didactic work, written in rhymed prose*[1] *with various rhetorical flourishes and interspersed poems, and draws on material from Falaquera's earlier work* Re'šit Ḥokma. *The Seeker, a youth, sets out to discover the best walk of life to follow. He encounters representatives of a number of life-styles, professions, or disciplines, arranged in an Aristotelian-like order: a wealthy man, a soldier, an artisan, a physician, a pietist, a grammarian, a poet, a believer, a Torah scholar, a mathematician, an optician, an astrologer, a musician, a logician, a natural scientist, and a philosopher. With each he debates the merits of his calling, in a formulaic manner: first the Seeker challenges, then the advocate defends his vocation, then the Seeker interrogates further. Thus the reader is presented with the pros and cons of each vocation in a manner reminiscent of, but falling short of, a disputation.*[2] *The section of interest to us is the dialogue with the Poet, which concludes the first part of the work. It expresses the view that the Bible contains poetry, although it does not address the question of what makes it poetry, except, perhaps, to suggest that it is by virtue of its subject matter, which is of the highest value. It distinguishes levels, or degrees, of poetry: the highest being that composed by prophets, the second by biblical poets through the Holy Spirit,*[3] *and the lowest by postbiblical (i.e., Spanish) poets.*

Editions and Translations: Seper Hammebaqqeš, *ed. M. Tama (The Hague, 1772; Warsaw, 1924; reprint, Jerusalem, 1970). H. Schirmann,* Haššira Ha'ibrit Biseparad Ubiprovans, *II (Jerusalem/Tel Aviv, 1956), pp.*

334–42 (partial excerpt). M. H. Levine, Falaquera's Book of the Seeker *(New York, 1976).*

Seper Hammebaqqeš

In order to understand *mašal* and *meliṣa*, the words of the wise and their riddles [Prov 1:6],[4] to know the teachings and the chastisements of the prophets of poetry, the Seeker searched for a poet with tenfold talent, a master of melodies and an expert in love songs, one trained from his youth to speak honor of the honorable of the land. The Seeker found a poet of rare rhetoric and glorious expression, with poetic vision in his heart. . . .

The attributes of the Poet are extolled at length. Then the Seeker, complimenting the Poet's skill, asks why such an intelligent man would occupy himself with poetry, given that poetry falsifies and deceives. The Poet rebukes the Seeker and, as part of his defense of poetry, observes that such great men as Moses resorted to it.

Arise, Seeker, listen and heed my testimony. Scoffer, listen to a rebuke; Fool, understand wisdom. See that praises to God are recited in poetry, which people of old sang—Moses and the Israelites [Exodus 15]. The Ha'azinu Song, which contains all the principles of the Torah, is expressed entirely in poetic form. Many of the poets were righteous and upright men, speaking in the Holy Spirit. The Book of Psalms was written through the Holy Spirit, and it is all hymns. Our sages called Song of Songs the "holy of holies," since it tells of the attachment of the soul to its source and its love and desire for its creator.

The Poet continues to defend poetry. In the course of so doing he tells a story of a king whose son did not possess royal virtues and was not fit to succeed his father. No amount of instruction helped, until an Arab came forth and taught him the art of poetry.[5] *Then the young prince became successful, and his fame spread throughout the land. After this parable, the Seeker continues to question the Poet.*

The Seeker said to the Poet: I ask that you clarify for me four questions concerning poetry, for none of the poets whom I have met have explained them to me satisfactorily.

The Poet replied: Ask as deep as you can [Isa 7:11], for I have an answer for every question.

The first question: Can you tell me the basic definition of poetry? What is it that makes poetry admirable?

The reply: The definition of a poem is a mimetic composition—that is, composed of metaphors—divided into equal periods of articulation —in other words, metrical. This is a requirement for poetry to exist. However, a poem is superior when its subject is inherently valuable, and when the poet beautifies his material with the gold of eloquence.

The second question: Why has it been said that the art of poetry has a strong effect on the masses and that a poetic rebuke affects them deeply? And why are the exhortations and hymns of the prophets, of blessed memory, couched in poetic language?[6]

The reply: The reason is that poetry is based on comparison, and the masses are attracted to comparisons. Indeed, poetic language is used by leaders when they speak to a man whom they wish to accustom gradually to performing certain actions. Such a man, because of his limitations, may lack understanding of his actions. Hence, his imagination must be stimulated so that he will act in the desired manner. In his case, imagination takes the place of understanding. For this reason compositions which embellish and adorn are used.

The third question: Why do poets use metrical language?

The reply: This is to increase their metaphorical power and elegance, to feed man's imagining soul which yearns to see beautiful things. In similar fashion, an artisan draws a figure with a compass and decorates it with various colors and gold.

The fourth question: Why has it been said that poetry causes a man to err so that he mistakes an imaginary object for the real thing? This is especially true when a person's imaginative faculties are weak.

The reply: I do not know.

Then the Seeker said to him: Can you tell me who are the poets whose poems are sweet and verses pleasant?

Replied the Poet: Poems fall into three levels. Some poems are conveyed through prophecy, like Ha'azinu and the Song of Moses; these are of the highest level. Some poems are composed through the Holy Spirit, like the songs of David and others in Psalms, Proverbs, and the Song of Songs; these are of the second level. Some poems extolling God and his wondrous deeds have been composed by skilled poets. These are of the lowest level.

However, poems written in praise or reproof of the deeds of human beings are silvery dross upon a pot of clay, and are like a wooden image which the artisan has covered up with gold. Wise men refrain from reciting such poetry except for immediate and temporary purposes. "Ever since the daily offering has been stopped" [Dan 12:11], and we were exiled, the Holy Spirit has been taken from us and we have suffered; we have committed folly, we have been struck dumb, silenced, made mute, while our pain increased. How, then, can we sing the Lord's song in a foreign land [Ps 137:4]? Some of the poets of the lowest level were of Spanish origin, such as Solomon ibn Gabirol, of blessed memory, R. Samuel Hanagid, of blessed memory, R. Judah Halevi, R. Moshe ibn Ezra, R. Abraham ibn Ezra, R. Isaac ibn Ghiyyat, the sage R. Moshe ibn Kimḥi, of blessed memory, R. Judah ben Ghiyyat, and Joseph ibn Abitur, of blessed memory. There were many other poets in Spain, Catalonia, and Provence. But only a few of their hymns, not all, should be chanted during sacred services. It is proper to praise and extol God only with the psalms of David. For in truth, silence is a hymn to him [Ps 65:2].

NOTES

1. The book is often referred to as a *maqama*, but Brann, *The Compunctious Poet*, 214, note 37, observes that this is not strictly accurate.

2. For further information on the style of *Seper Hammebaqqeš* and its literary analogues, see Brann, *The Compunctious Poet*, chapter 5.

3. This type of distinction is Maimonidean, where it is used to distinguish degrees of prophecy (*Guide of the Perplexed*, 2:45). Abravanel also distinguishes between discourse composed through the power of prophecy and through the Holy Spirit, but considers only the latter to be poetry.

4. S. Harvey, Falaquera's Epistle of the Debate, 129, note 6, sees a double entendre in the use of *mašal* and *meliṣa*: (1) a reference to the art of poetry, and (2) a Maimonidean reference to the parables of the prophets and sages (cf. *Guide of the Perplexed* [Pines translation, 11]). Maimonides differentiates between the parables of the prophets, which, if properly understood, lead one to the truth, and the parables of poets, which deceive and lead one astray.

5. Another reflection of the idea that the Arabs are the true masters of poetry.

6. This does not anticipate Lowth's observation, accepted by modern scholars, that prophetic speech is in poetic form. Rather, it refers to the use of metaphorical language and allegory by biblical authors (cf. Kugel, *The Idea of Biblical Poetry*, 186, note 33).

JOSEPH IBN KASPI

Joseph ben Abba Mari ben Joseph ben Jacob ibn Kaspi (1279–1340) was born in southern France, in Argentière (= "silver," hence the name Kaspi).[1] *Argentière was a center of free thought, from which ibn Kaspi seems to have drawn, and his quest for knowledge led him far and wide—to various Spanish cities and even to Egypt to study the works of Maimonides from the mouths of the grandsons of the great philosopher (but this turned out to be a major disappointment). He returned to Provence during the time of the Persecution of the Shepherds, was almost killed, but then continued his intellectual odyssey by going to Fez where, according to his information,* The Guide of the Perplexed *was being studied in Muslim philosophical schools.*

Ibn Kaspi was a prolific writer, producing more than thirty works, including a dictionary and a grammar, a commentary on Abraham ibn Ezra's commentary, Maimonides's Guide of the Perplexed, *and most of the books of the Bible. His views were inconsistent: on one hand he liked reason and logic (he was a great admirer of Maimonides), but on the other hand he held some mystical ideas and wrote some mystical works. It is perhaps not surprising, then, that the responses to his work were mixed, some considering it praiseworthy and others heretical. The excerpts presented here show ibn Kaspi largely in his rational mode, but with hints of the mystical (especially at the end of his Commentary on Song of Songs). In general, he opposed the allegorical interpretation of the Bible, and the literary approach which he espoused is, in some ways, amazingly modern; yet he clearly accepts the allegorical interpretation of Song of Songs so common in the Middle Ages.*

Among his ideas which modern literary critics will find of interest are his concern with the original intention of the author, the proper generic identification of a text, and his fourfold classification of the semantic relationship between verse halves in Proverbs. He appears to hold contradictory views on the first point, insisting in his Commentary on Proverbs that we have only the written text, and should not go beyond its surface meaning to guess at the author's hidden intentions (shades of New Criticism and the intentional fallacy); yet in his Commentary on Song of Songs he criticizes those who are not true to the author's intent and purpose. In the matter of the relationship between verse halves, he anticipates the system of Lowth, whom he predated by five centuries, although he did not recognize the phenomenon of parallelism per se. Ibn Kaspi's categories are (1) verses in which the entire verse continues the same idea (roughly equal to synonymous parallelism); (2) verses in which the second half contains antonyms of the first, such that the meanings of both halves accord (this is roughly equivalent to antithetic parallelism); (3) verses similar to the second type but containing ellipsis; (4) verses in which the first part is the mašal *(metaphor, parable, or "vehicle") and the second part is the* nimšal *(explanation of the metaphor, "tenor"). He offers some further refinements on his second type.*

Edition: "Ḥaṣoṣrot Kesep"[2] *in* 'Asara Kelê Kesep, *ed. Isaac Last (Pressburg, 1903), 83–85, 183–84. A slightly different text of the commentary on Song of Songs, with English translation, is found in C. D. Ginsburg,* The Song of Songs and Coheleth *(1857; reprint, New York, 1970), 47–49.*

Introduction to the Second Commentary on Proverbs

Said Joseph the Kaspi, author of *Hassod*: This book is like the ethical books of the philosophers. There is nothing in it, in my opinion, obscure or mysterious, in reference either to a married woman or to any other matter. Rather, the whole is according to its literal and obvious sense. Indeed, the book is called *Mišlê*,[3] because most of its principles are illustrated by one example but apply, by comparison and analogy [*mašal*], to many cases, as it is common in philosophical books to make analogies. This is the way to interpret "Listen, my son, to the teaching of your father" [Prov 1:8]—this applies just as well to the teaching of one's rabbi and the like. Also, "A son of an intellectual gathers in the summer" [Prov 10:5]—this applies to any person from whatever occupation,[4] for one must labor at the appropriate time in order to sustain life at a future time. This is like the [rabbinic] proverb "Whoever works before [lit.: on the eve of] the sabbath will eat on the sabbath" [*b. 'Aboda Zara* 3a]. Hence I say this.

When it says "To save you from a strange woman" [Prov 2:16], and "Here comes a woman to meet him" [Prov 7:10], and all that follows this, Solomon did not intend to refer throughout this whole book to matter and form[5]—not that I can prove the contrary in every case; but if this were so, we could say the same for many books of the Torah and of the rest of the Bible. Indeed, I say this, for whence did the spirit of God pass over us to inform us that such was his intention, his inner purpose? We do not have anything except the written text; we have only the writing as it is, in its apparent [sense]—how good and honored it is. Why are we not satisfied with the obvious [meaning of the] words, for necessity led him to reprove us in what follows concerning "a strange woman, an alien woman whose talk is smooth" [Prov 2:16; 7:5], and no man among us can ever escape from this, even if he is different, more or less. Why couldn't Solomon be like one of the philosophers, like Aristotle and his comrades, who wrote profusely about this? In general, I do not understand the way of the exegetes who preceded me, and I already told you in *Seper Hassod*[6] that all the words of the Torah and the Bible are, as far as I am concerned, [to be understood] in their literal sense, like Aristotle's books on logic and nature, except when the meaning cannot be taken literally.

The point is, this book is aptly called *Mišlê* for many reasons: there are in this book metaphors [*mešalim*] of one thing for other things, as is also the custom of philosophers. For example, "they are a graceful garland for your head" [Prov 1:8], and "in vain a net is spread" [Prov 1:17], and also "like vinegar to the teeth, like smoke to the eyes" [Prov 10:26], and also "a gold ring in a pig's nose" [Prov 11:22]. All the books of the philosophers are filled with these kinds of comparisons and metaphors, and how much more so are there similar usages in this book. They are fashioned with clear and eloquent language, constructed with the art of poetry. When it says "Wisdom cries aloud in the streets" [Prov 1:20] and "wisdom of women" [Prov 14:1], and the entire pericope, all these are poetic expressions [lit.: words of the art of poetry] and the *meliṣa* of the poets in their poems. But the sense of the matter is literal, self-explanatory. Many of the books of the sages are of this type, and there is no need to speak about it at length.

There are also in this book a few questions of language. When it says "he who sows injustice" [Prov 22:8], the issue is not sowing and reaping and winnowing; there are many such cases in this book —indeed, all of the prophetic [i.e., biblical] books are like this. In general, for several reasons Solomon saw fit to call this book *Mišlě*, just as he called his first book Song of Songs. All of these matters are explained; there are no mysteries of wisdom here, only ethical teachings and reproofs, as is appropriate and fitting of all sages.

Having established this, I say that in this book there are many types of phrases and verses. There is a type in which they [the phrases in a verse] continue one idea, that is, the entire verse continues one idea, as in "Wisdom cries aloud in the streets, in the squares she raises her voice" [Prov 1:20]; and also "Happy is the man who finds wisdom, and the man who gets understanding" [Prov 3:13]; and also "The blessing of the Lord enriches, and he adds no sorrow with it" [Prov 10:22]; and also "Pleasant words are a honey-comb, sweet to the soul and a balm to the bones" [Prov 16:24]. There are many such in this book.

There is a second type in which one part of the verse is the reverse of the other part; that is, one statement is the opposite of another statement in respect to both subject and predicate, or in another manner, in such a way that both are in accord. Examples are "For an abomination to the Lord is the devious man, but the righteous are in his confidence"

[Prov 3:32]; and also "The wise shall inherit honor, but fools shall get disgrace" [Prov 3:35]; and also "A wise son gladdens his father, but a foolish son is the sorrow of his mother" [Prov 10:1], and many like this.

There is yet a third type, in which the verse has but one subject but the predicates are opposites, and both together are in accord.[7] Examples are "When the righteous prosper, the city exults; and when the wicked perish—joy" [Prov 11:10]; and also "Doing mischief is like sport to the fool, and wisdom to the man of understanding" [Prov 10:23]; and also "The doing of justice is a joy to the righteous, but it is a downfall to the doers of iniquity" [Prov 21:15], for "the doing of justice" is the subject of both.

There is yet a fourth type, in which one part of the verse is the *mašal* and the other part is the *nimšal.* Examples are "Like vinegar to the teeth, like smoke to the eyes, so is the lazy man to those who commission him" [Prov 10:26]; and also "Like golden apples in silver ornaments is a word well spoken" [Prov 25:11].

These are the types that this book comprises, even if some of them are in the form of imperatives and negative imperatives, which are not inflected expressions, and some of them in the form of inflected expressions.

Of the second type that we mentioned, in which a part of a verse is the reverse or opposite of the other part, there are cases in which the phrases themselves are opposites, as in "The son of an intellectual gathers in the summer, but the son who brings shame sleeps in the harvest" [Prov 10:5]; and also "A wise son gladdens his father, but a foolish son is the sorrow of his mother" [Prov 10:1]. And there are cases in which the phrases themselves are not opposites but the thing that is the correlative of one is opposite of the other,[8] as in "Blessings are on the head of the righteous, but the mouth of the wicked conceals violence" [Prov 10:6]. For "righteous" and "wicked" are opposites, while "blessings" and "concealing violence" are not opposites; however, the correlative of "concealing violence"—that is, "curses"—is the opposite of "blessings." Also, "The labor of the righteous leads to life, the produce of the wicked leads to sin" [Prov 10:16], for the correlative of "sin" is "death" [and it is the opposite of "life"]. Also, "Deceit is in the hearts of the planners of evil; for the counselors of peace there is joy" [Prov 12:20], for "deceit" and "joy" are not opposites, but rather the correlative or corollary of "joy" is the opposite of "deceit"—that is, "belief." Or [a different explanation], the correlative of "deceit"—that is, "sorrow"—is the opposite of "joy." Also, "Better a poor man who walks in his blamelessness than one who speaks perversely and is a fool" [Prov 19:1]; and elsewhere [Prov 28:6] it is "the rich"[9]—for the correlative of foolishness is wealth.[10] Also, "A prince lacking understanding is very oppressive; he who despises gain will lengthen his days" [Prov 28:16], for the correlative of "a prince lacking understanding" is that he will shorten his days, as we will explain.

These are the types which this book comprises, and it is proper that each and every type be investigated well, and each categorized. And it is proper that we be careful not to exchange one type for another, lest we exchange the living and the dead. May God save us from this.

Commentary on Song of Songs

Said Joseph ibn Kaspi: Having commented earlier on Ecclesiastes and Proverbs, which Solomon, peace be upon him, composed in his wisdom, it is fitting that we write a few words of commentary on Song of Songs, which Solomon, peace be upon him, also wrote. I have no need to explain the words, for they have been explained well already; therefore I will speak only of the meaning of this book in general, and will make suggestive remarks about the particulars. Even the general meaning is not my own [original interpretation], for the Luminary who enlightens the earth [Maimonides] enlightened our eyes when he dealt with this specifically in [*The Guide of the Perplexed*] part III, chapter 51.[11] His allusion there is sufficient for us. Therefore I say that I have no doubt that this book belongs to the second type of *mešalim* that the Teacher [Maimonides], of blessed memory, mentioned at the beginning of his book [*The Guide of the Perplexed*], in which not every word in the *mašal* applies to the *nimšal*.[12]

Ibn Kaspi goes on to discuss the philosophic allegory of the Song of Songs—the union of the active intellect with the receptive intellect.

Having explained the general idea, we have no need to explain the specific expressions. Only a few of them attest to the meaning. Most are but decorative refinements in the style of poetic art and rhetorical science. This Solomon, peace be upon him, informs us at the beginning of his book by calling it "Song of Songs."

Another general point: Solomon, peace be upon him, composed three books which we possess, corresponding to the three types of discourse which the prophets, peace be upon them [i.e., authors of scriptural books], used. The first is entirely open and literal, with nothing beyond this—this is called "all silver." The second is entirely hidden, with nothing revealed, having only metaphors and imagery—this is "all gold." The third has both hidden and revealed [i.e., literal and figurative meanings]—this is called "apples of gold." So Solomon, peace be upon him, composed the three books: Ecclesiastes is of the first type, Song of Songs is of the second type, and Proverbs is of the third type. Remember this and apply it to the Torah, the Writings, and the Prophets. Indeed, in every passage we are in danger of exchanging one type for another, until we exchange the living for the dead. For this leads us to one of two errors: [either we mistake the literal for the figurative or the figurative for the literal]. If we put into the composition something false and lying, something not intended by the author, this, then, is not an interpretation. It is a new and original work. I call an "interpretation" only that which calls forth the intent of the author. Each type [of discourse] is indicated[13] to a person of clear mind and sound judgment; we cannot give complete proof for this. It suffices to say that the truth is self-evident.

Another important matter. In it [Song of Songs] are references to the meaning of Moses, peace be upon him, as he [Solomon?] has in his other books. Indeed, all the prophets, peace be upon them [i.e., authors of Scripture], explain words and synonyms that occur in the Torah of Moses, especially on what is written in the Torah in reference to Ma'aseh Bere'šit and Ma'aseh Merkaba[14]—these being the essence of the Torah. Heed the exaggerated strategies of the prophets, peace be upon them, and after them of the sages of blessed memory, for when they want to make many deep allusions, they do not use the same word that occurs in the Torah, but rather they change to a different word that is like a synonym of the first, for instance, "wine" and "drink of the grape." From this arose the wonderful exaggerations in the words of the rabbis of blessed memory, for wisdom was not hidden from them, but we do not recognize it.

These remarks are sufficient to explain this book according to our intention. Praise be to God, and blessed be his name. Amen.

NOTES

1. He was also known as Bonafoux del' Argentière.
2. This title is used for the Commentary on Proverbs and the Commentary on Song of Songs.
3. That is, the plural construct of the word *mašal*.
4. Ibn Kaspi understands the word *maskil* to indicate the member of a class or profession, not, as we would, simply as a designation for the wise or prudent.
5. That is, to an esoteric thought disguised as a commonplace.
6. This was ibn Kaspi's first work, a commentary on the Torah.
7. This is like the second type but contains ellipsis.

8. In this type there are two terms which are not exactly opposites but which are, in ibn Kaspi's analysis, one step removed from opposites. He finds a correlative—that is, a semantically related idea—of one that is the opposite of the other.

9. Prov 28:6: "Better a poor man who walks in his blamelessness than one who perverts his ways and is rich."

10. Using the equivalence of the first parts of Prov 19:1 and 28:6, ibn Kaspi draws the equivalence between "fool" and "rich" in their second parts.

11. See the end of that chapter: "In this dictum the Sages, of blessed memory, followed the generally accepted poetical way of expression that calls the apprehension that is achieved in a state of intense and passionate love for Him, may He be exalted, a *kiss*, in accordance with its dictum: *Let him kiss me with the kisses of his mouth* [Song 1:2]" (Pines, 628).

12. Introduction to part I: "Know that the prophetic parables are of two kinds. In some of these parables each word has a meaning, while in others the parable as a whole indicates the whole of the intended meaning" (Pines, 12). Maimonides was often called *Hammoreh*, "the Teacher, Guide"—a play on the title of his *Moreh Nebukim*, *The Guide of the Perplexed.*

13. Variant: the text itself [lit.: the face of the book] proves . . .

14. The Account of Creation and the Account of the Chariot (in Ezekiel's vision), the two central foci in mysticism, the first referring to cosmology and the second to mystical speculation or theosophy.

PROFIAT DURAN

Profiat (Isaac ben Moshe Halevi) Duran (ca. 1350–1414), also known as Ha'ephodi after his "signature" '. p. d.,[1] *was a scholar and a physician. He was probably born in Perpignan (southern France) and later resided in Catalonia (northern Spain). He experienced the persecutions against the Jews of Spain in 1391 and was forcibly converted to Christianity. It is unclear whether he later reverted to the practice of Judaism or remained outwardly a Christian (under the name Honoratus de Bonafide), but it is clear that he continued his Hebrew philosophic and linguistic writing on behalf of the Jewish community. He is best known for his anti-Christian polemics* 'Al Tehi Ka'aboteka *[Be Not like Your Fathers] and* Kelimmat Haggoyim *[The Shame of the Gentiles].*

No less important is his work on Hebrew grammar, Ma'aseh 'Epod *[Work of the Ephod, from Exod 28:15; 39:8], whose title reflects its author's cognomen, written in 1403. Not only does it demonstrate the author's extensive knowledge of Semitic and romance languages, and Greek, as well as familiarity with earlier Hebrew linguistic literature, but it approaches grammar through a logical analysis of linguistic principles and an objective critique of earlier grammatical works. This marks a new stage in the history of grammatical study. In some ways* Ma'aseh 'Epod *is quite modern: in its system of analysis of verbal conjugations, in its theory of articulation and pronunciation, and in its emphasis on the social function of language. Presented here are Duran's summary of the vicissitudes of the Hebrew language, which is representative but more thorough than most, his discussion of poetry, which he mentions only briefly in the context of the tripartite division of language into grammar, rhetoric, and poetry, and an interesting note on why the Hebrew language is called* lašon haqqodeš, *"the holy tongue." In the last he demonstrates his acute analytic abilities in linguistic matters. His sentiments on the importance of the study of the Bible are strongly felt and expressed. Bible study is advocated not only for its intrinsic religious merit, but also because it is the repository for and model of the Hebrew language in its most advanced form.*

Edition: Y. T. Friedlander and Y. Hacohen, Ma'aseh 'Epod *(Vienna, 1865).*

Ma'aseh 'Epod

Chapter Seven

. . . What happened to the Hebrew language is what happened to its speakers; that is, it became weak when they became weak, and it diminished when they diminished, and it was forgotten in their exile and wanderings. Just as it had been before the most perfect of languages, the most ample and most replete of all of them, as was necessitated by the nature of its usage, it became like its speakers—the most constricted of languages, inadequate for discourse in both nouns and verbs in many respects if not most of them. Maimonides wrote [*Guide of the Perplexed*, part I, chapter 61] in reference to the Tetragrammaton, "and it is possible that it signifies in the language which today we have only a small part of." He wrote furthermore in part I, chapter 67 that we today are ignorant of our language; thus he already demonstrated the constriction of the Hebrew language today and its diminution. And the sage [Judah Halevi], author of *The Kuzari*, also wrote [*Kuzari*, 2.68]: "It had the same fate as its bearers; it became impoverished when they became impoverished, and it became constricted when they became fewer. But in respect to its form, it is the noblest of languages, as we know from tradition and from logic."

He [Judah Halevi] gave as the reason for its weakening and diminishing the weakening and diminishing of its speakers, and this is because after its people were exiled and scattered here and there among the nations of the lands, they contented themselves with the languages of those nations, and set aside their special language and forgot it, as it says: "They mingled among the nations and learned their ways" [Ps 106:35]. In the seventy years of the Babylonian exile, close to half of the people forgot their language, as it says: "half of their children speak Ashdodite and do not know how to speak Judean, like the language of each people" [Neh 13:24]. The meaning of the verse is "half their children speak Ashdodite, like the vernacular of each people, and do not know how to speak Judean." Now if at that time this constricting happened to them, what about this [present] long exile during which the evil men of foolish nations destroyed our books and compositions and destroyed much of our nation's wisdom? All this is the reason for the constriction and diminution of the Hebrew language.

Furthermore, another important factor, besides this one, was that those who strove after the wisdom of the Torah, that is, the authors of the Talmud, set aside that special language and wrote in Aramaic, which is, to be sure, a corrupted form of the holy tongue. Perhaps they did not do this from choice but from necessity, for the [Hebrew] language had already been forgotten when the Talmud was written, since it was more than 430 years after the destruction and exile of the people. . . . Thus I provide an excuse for the early sages. But also in these times I see that the later talmudic sages are following in the footsteps of the early sages in their discussions in their academies. When they are occupied in study they do not speak only Hebrew, but they combine the vernacular with it. They do not wish to distinguish between the holy and the secular. I would apply to them the verse "Half their children speak Ashdodite." Do not read[2] *benêhem*, "their children," but rather *bana'êhem*, "their cultured ones." Moreover, the teachers of young children, not surprisingly, follow their ways, and to them the verse applies in its literal sense [i.e., literally, "half their children"]. For this main reason the language was forgotten and almost lost, except for what was preserved of it in the Holy Scriptures, which—through the Lord's solicitude for that language and for its [or: His] people—remained complete and perfect in form and content. About this there is no disagreement among Jews anywhere in the world [lit.: from India to Ethiopia—cf. Esth 1:1].

During those same seventy years of Babylonian exile, lack and confusion already had begun to overtake them, and people began to despair. Because he discerned their falling away, the head of the scribes, Ezra the Priest and the Scribe, took counter measures and exerted every effort to correct the perverted, and thus did all the scribes who came after him. Those scribes corrected as best they could, and they kept [the text] exact by counting the sections [*parašiyyot*], verses, words, letters, plene and defective spelling, the exceptional and the common linguistic usages, and similar things. This is called "scribes" [*soperim*], and they made compositions about this—they are the books of the Masora. In places where lack and confusion overtook them, they indicate *qere* and *ketib*, in order to show there is some doubt.

Now it appears that even in the time of the First Temple this lack had already begun to diminish the people's care and attention. It is written concerning the Torah scroll that Hilkiah the priest found it by accident. It says: "When they brought out the silver that was brought to the temple . . . and he said to Shaphan, "I found a Torah scroll in the temple" [2 Chr 34:14–15], as if he found it by accident. Look how he fulfilled [the dictum in Josh 1:8] "you should meditate on it day and night"; that is what is meant by "And Torah they seek from his mouth" [Mal 2:7]. Moreover, Josiah, who was one of the pious kings of Judah, found it unfamiliar. It is written regarding the king: "And he will read from it all the days of his life" [Deut 17:19], but he [Josiah] did not read it; rather Shaphan read it for him, and when he heard its words he tore his garment. It appears that this was something new to him.

When Ezra the Scribe saw the people's negligence and laziness in studying Scripture, he thought that perhaps this laziness and negligence came from the difficulty of reading the books, so he was wise enough to invent vocalization in order to make the reading easier for everyone. In addition, he invented the accents so as to give sweetness to the reading, to arouse in the hearts of men the pleasure of sweet song that the accents give to the Bible. Also, so that the Bible would have stability and permanence and would be fixed in the memory, for it is known that song and melody lead to memorization, for by means of them memory and recall are made easier. These are the two reasons for the invention of the accents, besides the primary reason that I stated before.

Such was the wisdom of Ezra to leave those books forever in exact and complete form, and to bring desire to the hearts of men to study them diligently, and to render them [i.e., the people] perfect by means of the rectitude of those books which enlighten the darkness of the world. But all this did not prevent the lessening of men's heeding of the truth when they read them. They did not turn after it [the truth] because of negligence in studying the Holy Scripture; rather, they rejected it. Also in the preservation of the Hebrew language they were not careful, and this was the reason that they forgot the Torah and the commandments. The [talmudic] sages testify to this when they say [*b. 'Erubin* 53a]: "The people of Judah, who were careful about their language, retained their learning, but the people of the Galilee, who were not careful about their language, did not retain their learning." Now see how great is the damage and loss that derives from laziness and negligence in preserving the Hebrew language; while care for it [the language] prevents the disappearance of diligent study of Scripture and thorough investigation of it. I say that this led to the destruction of Israel by sword, and to the scattering of its remnant, and to their subjugation and low state, and to the changing [i.e., incorrect reading] of the Torah, for the stupidity of the people and their lack of expertise in the language and the text brought them to turn aside from the Torah. The rest you already know. And perhaps this is the meaning of "The people of the Galilee who were not careful, etc."—for those people were contemptible [*galilim*], and we want nothing to do with them.

Even in our own times I see that the sages and great men of Israel neglect the Bible. It is sufficient, in their view, to read the weekly portion "twice in the original and once in the Aramaic translation" [*b. Berakot*

8b], and if you ask them about a certain verse, they will not know where it is from. Moreover, they think it foolish that one should spend his time on the Bible, for the Talmud is the essential thing. This disease is very severe in the Franco-German community especially in our generation and the preceding one, but it was not so in previous generations, for we see the crown of glory of the talmudic sages, who shed light on its mysteries; the great rabbi Rashi, of blessed memory, penetrated deeply into the meaning of the Bible and wrote his excellent commentaries on it, and also wrote fine things about grammar and language. This should serve as an example to all who are below him in wisdom. . . .

Menaḥem ibn Saruq wrote to Dunash ibn Labrat: "If we had not been exiled from our land, and our language in its entirety were in our hands as in months of old and years gone by, and we rested secure in peaceful dwellings, then we would know all the fine points of our language and its various effects, and we would know its metrical system, and would abide by it. For every people has a metrical system and a grammar, only we have lost ours on account of [our] many sins, and it has disappeared on account of [our] great guilt, from the day on which we went into exile. And after having been ample and vigorous, it [the language] became constricted and hidden, and disappeared."[3]

Here, then, he [Menaḥem ibn Saruq] has demonstrated by these words the constrictedness of the Hebrew language today, and its disappearance from us; and the reason for all this is that it was set aside. Indeed, its superiority over all the languages becomes clear from the ways and modes in which it is used. The sage [Judah Halevi], author of *The Kuzari*, wrote on this [*Kuzari* 2.68]: "The Hebrew language alone was far superior to others. Its superiority [is proven] by logical inference, corresponding to the degree of superiority required by the people who used it. They had a need not only for eloquence [or: rhetoric] but, what's more, for prophecy, which was widespread among them, and also for exhortations, songs, and hymns. Is it conceivable that their leaders, Moses, Joshua, David, and Solomon, lacked eloquence when they needed it to speak, as we lack it here today, because the language is lost to us? Look at the Torah, in describing the Tabernacle, the ephod, and the breastplate, and the like, when it requires uncommon terms, how it finds exactly the right ones. How well composed the narrative is. The same for the names of peoples, species of birds, and stones. And [the same goes for] the hymns of David, the complaints of Job and his exhortations to his friends, Isaiah's prophecies of doom and comfort, and similar passages."

Chapter Eight

The science of language includes grammar, rhetoric [*meliṣa*], and poetry [*šir*]. It is therefore appropriate to present a definition that includes all three, and afterward to distinguish each according to its distinctive features. . . .

When discourse has sweetness, beauty, enhancement, and ornament, in simple or complex [forms], it is then called rhetoric [*meliṣa*], which derives from "How pleasing [*nimleṣu*] is your word to my palate" [Ps 119:103], that is, how mellifluous and sweet. . . . If it [discourse] has all this and also meter, it is called a poem [*šir*]. . . . I mean by meter the equivalence in the parts of the composition in respect to [length of] vowels, as you already know. Indeed, this is called *šir* ["song"] because by means of the meter it is possible to sing it aloud. The term *šir* has, in addition, already been applied to anything that is explained allegorically [lit.: in the manner of *mašal*], such as Song of Songs and the like. The rhetoric and poetry of Israel already had a unique feature which I have not found among other nations. The rhetoricians and the poets of Israel gave to their work sweetness, beauty, and enhancement by incorporating into it biblical and rabbinic passages, and by attempting to make these fit into their work, whether in their original biblical sense or in a new nuance which they give them in the work.[4] This is the real praiseworthy and glorious aspect of [Hebrew] rhetoric, and of the rhetoricians, who fashion their works well and provide them with sweetness by the divine word [i.e., by using scriptural allusions]. Indeed, this is so because the Hebrew language is now deficient, as was explained, and therefore anyone who wants a sweet and beautiful composition must enhance and beautify it with rhetorical discourse that already exists. Thus their loss is outweighed by their gain, and their impairment is their remedy. . . .

Chapter Thirty-three

Duran inquires into why Hebrew is called lašon haqqodeš, *"the holy tongue." He cites Maimonides, who says that it is because Hebrew has no words for the genital or excretory parts of the body, and can express these matters only indirectly; then he cites the refutation of Nachmanides. He concludes that even if Maimonides were correct, this would not explain the term* holy *in connection with Hebrew. At best, Hebrew would be called "the euphemistic tongue." He then cites with somewhat more approval the idea that Hebrew is holy because it is the language of the Holy Scriptures, the language that God spoke. But even this is not a totally satisfactory explanation for the term:*

It is not the way of men to name a language after a composition or book written in it. Moreover, I do not find anywhere in the Bible that the Torah or Prophets are called "holy," albeit they are the holy of holies. In the Bible a language is designated by reference to the people who speak it or to the land in which it is spoken. Designation by reference to people is "teach them the language and the writings of the Chaldeans" [Dan 1:4]; "to the Jews in their own script and language" [Esth 8:9]; "the language of various peoples" [Neh 13:24]. Designation in reference to land is "half your children speak Ashdodite" [Neh 13:24], this being the language of Ashdod. Therefore, I think that the Hebrew language is called "the holy tongue" because it is the language of the people called "holy," as it says "Israel is holy to the Lord" [Jer 2:3]. They are also called "a holy seed." And it is spoken in a land called "holy"—"in my holy mountain" [Ezek 20:40]; "the beautiful holy mountain" [Dan 11:45]; "your holy cities" [Isa 64:9]. Therefore this language is called "the holy tongue." This is an expression composed of a rectus and a construct, as was explained. [That is, it means "the tongue of the holy (people or place)."] It would be correct to call it "the tongue of [the people of] Israel" or "the tongue of the land of Israel." Since the word *holy* includes both, it was called just "the tongue of the holy."

NOTES

1. Several explanations of this acronym have been offered: (1) *'ani propiat dur'an* ("I am Profiat Duran"), (2) *'amar propiat dur'an* ("Profiat Duran said"), (3) *'en propiat dur'an* (*En* is a Castilian title of nobility). In addition, the word *'epod*, "ephod, breastplate of the priests," also connotes, according to Duran's interpretation, atonement for idolatry; and by taking this name Duran may have admitted shame or sought repentance for his conversion to Christianity. Cf. Anne D. Berlin, "Shame of the Gentiles of Profiat Duran," 6 with notes 20 and 21.

2. Duran is employing the hermeneutic device of *'al tiqrê*.

3. This citation can be found, with minor variations, in *Tešubot Talmidê Menaḥem ben Ya'aqob 'ibn Saruq*, 27–28. Ibn Saruq was arguing against the propriety of using Arabic meters in Hebrew poetry—his reason being that they were not native to Hebrew and that they led to grammatical corruptions. Duran cites ibn Saruq's words for another purpose: to support the idea that the Hebrew language had undergone a decline.

4. For the ways in which biblical allusions were employed in medieval poetry, see Pagis, *Ḥidduš Umasoret*, 70–77; and Brann, *The Compunctious Poet*, chapter 2.

MOSHE IBN ḤABIB

Moshe ben Shem Tov ibn Ḥabib (fifteenth century), grammarian, poet, and translator, was born in Lisbon but lived much of his life in southern Italy. It was there, in Bitonto in 1486, that he completed Darkê No'am *[Paths of Pleasantness, from Prov 3:17], a short work on the structure and forms of Hebrew metrical poetry. This work was probably written as a companion volume to his Hebrew grammar* Marpe' Lašon *[Healing of the Tongue, cf. Prov 12:18].*

Ibn Ḥabib categorizes metrical poetry into three types: syllabic meter, something approaching syllabic meter, and quantitative meter. He locates biblical poetry in the first and second types. That is, he finds that most poetic verses in the Bible contain two verse halves which are equal or almost equal in the number of syllables, although these syllables may be either long or short. Ibn Ḥabib's system of analyzing biblical meter, according to which a mobile shwa *counts as a full vowel, differs from the canons of Spanish Hebrew poetics, and appears to have been influenced by the syllabic meter that came into use for the first time in Italian Hebrew poetry just shortly before the writing of his book.*[1] *Although they arose in different circumstances and for different reasons, his method and results are oddly similar to those of at least one school of modern biblical scholars —those who count syllables and find that lines often match, or fall within certain limits, in respect to their number of syllables.*[2] *There does not seem to have been a direct line of descent from ibn Ḥabib to scholars such as F. M. Cross and D. N. Freedman, but, as James Kugel has shown, ibn Ḥabib did have an influence on later scholars who read (and misread) him.*[3]

Ibn Ḥabib is most famous for his story of the putative eighth-century B.C.E. *poetic epitaph on a Judean grave in Murviedro, Spain. Ibn Ḥabib recounts it in order to document the existence of Spanish-Hebrew–style metrical poetry (i.e., poetry with quantitative meter and rhyme) among the ancient Judeans (although not in biblical writings), so as to prove that this type of poetry was a native Jewish phenomenon and not a technique borrowed from the Arabs. Those who later cite this story, Azariah de' Rossi and Immanuel Frances, do so for equally chauvinistic purposes, often to counteract the opinion of Judah Halevi, who acknowledged that the Jews* did *learn the technique from the Arabs. However, de' Rossi and Frances agree with Halevi that* biblical *poetry lacks meter; they do not, like ibn Ḥabib, indulge in attempts to find syllabic meter in the Bible.*

The tombstone inscription which ibn Ḥabib describes actually exists, but it does not date from First Temple times, nor does it contain exactly the words that he quotes.[4] *It is a fourteenth-century inscription which was misread, in conformity with and support of the Spanish Jewish myth that the Jewish community in Spain was ancient (and therefore the Jews were not parvenus), that these Jews were descendants of the Judean aristocracy (hence their cultural elitism), and that the Jews of Spain were far distant from Palestine at the time of Jesus (and so had no hand in his crucifixion).*

Edition: W. Heidenheim, Darkê No'am 'im Marpe' Lašon *(Rodelheim, 1806). The book was first published in Constantinople, ca. 1510, then in Venice in 1546 and 1564. See also Kugel,* The Idea of Biblical Poetry, *198–99, 236–37, and Kugel, "The Influence of Moses ibn Ḥabib's* Darkhei No'am."

Darkê No'am

Pages 5–7. Ibn Ḥabib begins by citing distinctions in types of poetry made by Aristotle and al-Farabi. He then discusses three classes of Hebrew poetry: (1) poems intended for the improvement of the intellect, (2) poems intended for the restoration of equilibrium when "accidents of the soul," such as anger and pride, threaten to overcome it, and (3) poems intended for the elevation of the soul from "lesser accidents," such as fear, pain, and cowardice.

These three classes are very praiseworthy, even though they are interchangeable, more or less. Upon them are based all of the Book of Proverbs, its revealed and hidden parts, most of the Book of Ecclesiastes, most of the Psalms of David, and some of the words of the prophets. Indeed, there are three other classes which are the opposite of the first three, and which undo all that the first three achieve. Heaven forbid that any bit of these be found in the prophetic books or in [the books written in] the Holy Spirit.

Now, according to metrical criteria, poems can be divided into three types:

The first is metrical poetry in respect to the number of syllables in its two half-verses,[5] the first verse half agreeing with the second. [It does] not [agree] in its subparts, or at its end [i.e., it does not have metrical feet or rhyme], except by chance, not intentionally.

The second is similar to the first except that sometimes the first verse half does not agree with the second, even in the number of syllables, but the deficit is filled by the melody or the vocal articulation, or the extra is absorbed by the melody. Psalms, Proverbs, and Job are of these two types. In Psalms, the first type is Ps 119:145 [8 + 8]: *qe-ra'-ti-ka ho-ši-'e-ni / we-'eš-me-ra 'e-do-te-ka,* Ps 146:9 [9 + 9]: *ya-tom we-'al-ma-na ye-'o-ded / we-de-rek re-ša-'im ye-'a-wet,* and many others in which the first half of the verse agrees with the second half only in the number of syllables. Likewise in Proverbs, Prov 1:8 [9 + 9]: *še-ma' be-ni mu-sar 'a-bi-ka / we-'al ti-ṭoš to-rat 'i-me-ka,* Prov 10:5 [8 + 8]: *'o-ger baq-qa-yiṣ ben mas-kil / nir-dam baq-qa-ṣir ben me-biš.* And likewise in Job 5:20 [8 + 8]: *be-ra-'ab pod-ka mim-ma-wet / ub-mil-ḥa-ma mi-dê ḥa-reb.* There are many others. But in fact, most are of the second type; that is, the two halves of the verse do not agree in the number of syllables. Belonging to the second type are the Song of the Sea, the Ha'azinu Song, the Song of David, and the Song of Deborah,[6] for the lacking or extra [syllables] will be filled in or absorbed, as we explained. But we will not deal with these two types.

The third is metrical poetry which agrees in all its aspects: in the number of cords, and with the same rhyme in every verse. Not only this, but the poets are very careful about full vowels and semivowels. They put only a semivowel under a semivowel and a full vowel under a full vowel.[7] These are alternated in patterns, as we will explain, with God's help. The Hebrew language is superior in this to all other languages, because in the others it is impossible to fulfill this condition. Along with this, the [Hebrew] poets employ biblical verses, whether in their literal sense or in a homonymous or metaphorical manner,[8] and there is no language that can attain this superiority. Any poem that is not metered in respect to full vowels and semivowels will be despised by the guild of poets, and shame, trouble, and injury will come to its author. In my opinion, this manner of metrical poetry is very ancient. I swear by heaven and earth that when I was in the kingdom of Valencia, in the community of Murviedro, all the people at the gate and the elders told me that the tombstone of the army officer of Amaziah, king of Judah, was there. When I heard this I made haste, I did not tarry, to see his tombstone, a stone monument on the top of a mountain. After much toil and trouble I read the inscription; there was a verse[9] engraved on it, and these are its words:

> שאו קינה בקול מרה לשר גדול לקחו יה
>
> *se'u qina beqol mara / lesar gadol leqaḥo yah / /*
>
> Raise a lament in a bitter voice / for the great officer whom the Lord has taken / /.

We could not read further for it was effaced, but the second verse[10] ended with לאמציה, "to Amaziah."[11] Then I believed that this manner of metrical poetry was from the time that our forefathers were in their land.

NOTES

1. See Pagis, "Hamṣa'at Ha'iambus Ha'ibri Utemurot Bameṭriqa Ha'ibrit Be'iṭalia," 686.

2. Although, to be sure, the manner in which syllables are counted is not always identical.

3. "The Influence of Moses ibn Ḥabib's *Darkhei No'am.*"

4. See Cantera [Burgos] and Millas, *Las Inscripciones hebraicas de España*, 294–303; and Cantera y Burgos, "Espana Medieval: Arqueologia," 46–47. The inscription reads

. . . לשר גדול לקחו יה והוא נתן . . .
. . . אמצים (?) ר' יהודה בן רבע

[. . . Raise a lament] for the great prince whom the Lord has taken, and he gave
[. . .] *'mṣym* R. Judah son of Reba'.

A similar inscription, said to read "This is the sepulcher of Adoniram, treasurer of King Solomon, who came to collect the taxes and died," actually says: "This is the sepulcher of R. Judah, son of Solomon Shemtov, of blessed memory, who departed to his eternal place in Tishre, year 74 [= September–October, 1313]." (See *Las Inscripciones*, 304–308.)

5. Counting a mobile *shwa* as equivalent to a full vowel.

6. Kugel, *The Idea of Biblical Poetry*, 199, note 61, notes that these are the four songs listed in the tractate *Soperim.*

7. That is, not only is the total number of syllables the same, but the type of syllable—cord or peg—must fit the metrical pattern.

8. Biblical allusions could be straightforward and easily recognized, or extremely subtle and applied metaphorically to a totally new entity.

9. Or "poem," but see the following note.

10. Hebrew: *šir.* Kugel ("The Influence of Moses ibn Ḥabib's *Darkhei No'am,*" 322, note 16) notes that the word *šir* here means "a line of verse." This is confirmed by Immanuel Frances's term *bayit,* "verse of poetry," at this point in his version of the tale. I have also translated the previous occurrence of *šir,* two sentences earlier, by "verse."

11. As Kugel points out ("The Influence," 310), this inscription consists of one complete line (*delet* plus *soger*), composed in the quantitative meter known as *marnin* : ˘ — — — ˘ — — — / ˘ — — — ˘ — — — //. Furthermore, the last word of the otherwise effaced second line rhymes with the last word of the first line: *yah-ya* —a rhyme which conforms with the dictates of medieval poetic form in which the final consonant-vowel-(consonant) of each verse must agree. One problem, however: if לאמציה is vocalized in its classical form, לְאֲמַצְיָה, it breaks the metrical pattern. (But divergences are often permitted at the ends of lines.)

DON ISAAC ABRAVANEL

Don[1] Isaac Abravanel (1437–1508) was a statesman, philosopher, and biblical exegete. Born in Lisbon, whence his family had come from Seville (Castile, Spain) shortly after the persecutions of 1391, he was educated in the Latin classics as well as in traditional Jewish texts and Jewish philosophy, along with its Greek and Arabic forerunners. He also took an interest in Portuguese national literature. His life reflects the dislocations common to Jews of that time. In 1483, forced to flee Portugal, he made his way to Castile, where a year later he was called to the court of Ferdinand and Isabella. After the expulsion of the Jews from Spain in 1492, Abravanel went to Italy—first to Naples, then to Messina, Corfu, Monopoli, and finally Venice.

Despite these many dislocations, Abravanel produced commentaries on large sections of the Bible and a number of philosophical works, all of which reflect his apocalyptic views. Although he was exposed to Renaissance thought, his own work bears the stamp of medieval scholasticism. His writings gained popularity in later Christian and Jewish circles. Christian interest is attributable, in general, to the Reformation emphasis on the Bible and on Hebraic scholarship; and, more specifically, to Abravanel's lucid engagement with both Jewish and Christian interpretations. Abravanel's strong messianic views struck a chord in both Christians and Jews—in the former because of his refutation of Christianity and its doctrine of the Messiah; and in the latter because of growing mystical and messianic movements.

Abravanel's commentaries do not follow the familiar line-by-line format. His usual procedure was to divide the biblical text into sections or chapters and introduce each with a set of questions. These often pose problems of a literary nature—concerning authorship, the purpose of the pericope, and its structure, arrangement, and location—and are frequently more interesting than the answers. This is followed by a brief summary of the chapter's contents and purpose, and a discursive exposition (sometimes verbose and repetitive) in which the initial questions are answered. The passages translated below are taken from Abravanel's introduction to his commentary on Exodus 15 (which does not contain questions) and his commentary on Isaiah 5. The commentary on Exodus, which is presented here first, was actually written after the commentary on Isaiah. The commentary on Isaiah was begun in Corfu in 1495 and completed in Monopoli on August 19, 1498. The commentary on Exodus was completed in Venice on September 29, 1505. Some of the material on poetic theory is repeated in both.

In his commentaries on Exodus 15 and on Isaiah 5, Abravanel, following the tradition reflected in Moshe ibn Tibbon's Commentary on Song of Songs, *distinguishes three types of poetry. The first type is metrical poetry of the kind composed in medieval Hebrew. He finds no evidence of this type in the Bible. The second type consists of nonmetrical poems which were once sung. The rhythm of the poems is a result of the melody to which they were set. Examples are the biblical passages which observe the masoretic convention of stichographic writing. Abravanel sees in this convention proof that these poems were divided into lines which conformed to musical phrases. The third type consists of poems which employ figurative language. Following a tradition which had been traced back to Aristotle, and was perpetuated by a number of Jewish sages and poets, poetry is equated with metaphoric language.*

Having presented the three types, Abravanel, in the commentary on Exodus, proceeds to classify Exodus 15; he finds in it evidence of the second and third types. It fits the second because it is written stichographically, and had, therefore, presumably been set to music. It fits the third type because it employs figurative language.

Abravanel then goes on to discuss the problem of whether all figurative usages constitute poetry. More specifically, he is concerned with the prophetic use of allegory and parable. These are not, ipso facto, *to be considered poetry. This, in turn, raises the issue of the difference between composing through the medium of prophecy and through the Holy Spirit (the means through which poetry was composed). Building on and departing from Maimonides's views on the degrees of prophecy, Abravanel differentiates the two as follows: Prophecy is a state in which the prophet loses control and initiative, and speaks the words of God. When composing through the Holy Spirit, the author has conscious control over his words. A biblical prophet was capable of experiencing both states, and hence of producing both prophetic messages and poetry. Generally speaking, the two can be easily distinguished because in the first the words are attributed to God, and in the second they are attributed to a human author.*

This distinction has another implication: that the Torah and the Prophets—i.e., sections of the Bible considered to be the words of God, and having a higher degree of sanctity than the Writings—contain at least two levels of discourse: the words of God and the words of man. How did poetry—the words of man—come to be included in the Torah and the Prophets? Abravanel answers that it is because God accepted these words and delighted in them, and commanded that they be written therein.

Editions and Translations: The Commentary on the Latter Prophets *was first published in Pesaro in 1520, and the* Commentary on the Pentateuch *in Venice in 1579. Both have been reissued a number of times; recent editions are* Commentary on the Pentateuch *(Jerusalem, 1963) and* Commentary on the Latter Prophets *(Jerusalem, 1955). Part of the Commentary on Exodus 15 is contained in I. Adler,* Hebrew Writings concerning Music in Manuscripts and Printed Books from Geonic Times up to 1800, *1–5. J. Buxtorf included a Latin translation of the introduction to the Exodus 15 commentary in his* Liber Cosri, *pp. 407–15. J. Kugel,* The Idea of Biblical Poetry, *193–94, contains a short excerpt and discussion.*

Commentary on Exodus 15

Before we explain the words of this song, it is proper to clarify it in respect to poetry [in respect to the types of poems, in order that we may know whether its words conform to one type or a combination of different types].[2] I say that the people of Israel have three types of poems. The first type is discourses constructed with specific line length, meter, and rhyme,[3] even though they were recited without a melody, their poetic aspect being in the agreement of the words—their similarity or equivalence at the end of the discourses. That is, at the end of poetic verses [*batim*] they resemble each other in the three final letters, or in the two final [letters], in accord with their vocalization and pronunciation.[4] They observe quantitative meter, clear language, and allusions to scriptural verses. These poems are called *ḥaruzim* ["strings of beads"] because they are ordered rows—from the phrase *ṣawwa'rek baḥaruzim*, "your neck in strings of beads" [Song 1:10], which are precious stones and pearls pierced through and strung together and arranged in an ordered formation. In a similar vein, in the words of our sages of blessed memory, "*maḥarozot* of fish" [*b. Baba Meṣi'a* 21a], which are strings of fish attached one after another in sequence, tied by their noses with hemp. By analogy, poems of this type were called *ḥaruzim*, because their lines are [metrically] equal and connected together; for the words in this type of poem are metered in respect to full vowels and semivowels in the system of vocalization. This art in this type of metrical poetry is praiseworthy,[5] and they [the poems] are sweeter than honey and the honeycomb. They are composed in our holy Hebrew tongue with greater perfection than in any other language.

It is true, though, that we do not find any examples of this type of poetry in the words of the prophets [i.e., the Bible] or among the sages of the Mishna and the Talmud, for its origin was in the diaspora, among the sages of Israel who were in Arab lands, who learned from them [the Arabs] this poetic art. They employed it with skill in our sanctified tongue, surpassing in dignity and honor what the Arabs did in their language; moreover, also among the sages of Rome, in the Latin language, and in other foreign languages are found metrical poems, but not with the same distinctive perfection as they were composed in the Hebrew language. Afterward this precious art was copied by the sages of our people who were in Provence and Catalonia, and also in the kingdom of Aragon and the kingdom of Castile. And they spoke divinely, with all wisdom and knowledge, doubly wise. "What is sweeter than honey and what is stronger than a lion."[6] This type of poetry was an innovation of the diaspora; new things came from nearby. Our prophets and early sages of blessed memory did not conceive of them. Therefore there is no need to speak of them here since the Song of the Sea is not one of them.

The second type of poetry is the type whose words are set to a melody, even though they have neither meter nor rhyme. These are called poems only by virtue of their song and melody. Some sages have already noted that poems like these are different from the rest of scriptural prose in two ways: in substance and in form.

By substance I mean that they deal with metaphysical matters which indicate exaltation, glorification, and praise, grasped from the deeds of the Lord, firmly fixed in the mouths of the righteous and the enlightened, as it says: "The sound of song and salvation in the tents of the righteous" [Ps 118:15], "Sing, O righteous, to the Lord; praise is fitting to the upright" [Ps 33:1], "With paeans to God in their throats" [Ps 149:6], and many other citations. This is in order that their mouths would be trained to ever arouse them to metaphysical knowledge. They would always sing them with tunes and sweet voices or with sweet-sounding instruments, and the voices and tunes would be arranged with wisdom and in good order so as to arouse the hearts of the listeners so that they would pay heed to understand their deepest meanings. In reference to this our sages of blessed memory said that all songs are holy.[7]

By form I mean the form of arrangement that determines the order of the recitation [of its words] and their melodic arrangement. That is what our sages meant by "brick over log, log over brick; log over log, brick over brick." The meaning of this is that the composers of these ancient songs required that the enumeration of the words be arranged in accord with the arrangement of the melody which they established for singing them; to make the order of their form in the measurement[8] of the order of their syllables. In this measured order they set them to musical arrangements. There are musical arrangements in which the first [part] corresponds to the third, and the second to the fourth, equal to a long musical line or a short one. The long musical line is called "brick." The short one is called "log"; it is one-half the length of a brick. This arranged measurement in which the first corresponds to the third and the second to the fourth is called "log over log and brick over brick." The Ha'azinu Song [Deuteronomy 32], the dialogues of Job, and Proverbs were set in this manner: long over long and short over short. The recitation of the song is arranged in accord with the arrangement of its meaning. In this form is [Deuteronomy 32]:

line 1 May my discourse come down like rain
line 2 My speech distill as the dew
line 3 Like showers on young growth
line 4 Like droplets on the grass

These poems are preferable to prose or ordinary [i.e., unpoetic] discourse because most people forget the ordinary prose even if they repeat them [the words] day and night. But if they are set to music, sung or played, they will always be remembered by means of their melodies, as it is said, "This poem shall confront him as a witness, for it will never be forgotten from the mouth of his offspring" [Deut 31:21]. About this our sages of blessed memory said [*b. Megilla* 32a], "Anyone who reads [the Bible] without the cantillation or recites [the Mishna] without the proper intonation, Scripture says of him, 'Also I gave you laws which are not good, etc. [Ezek 20:25].'"[9] This is to say, that it will not stick in their minds.

The poems that are brick over log, and the reverse, are many and varied in type, like the Song of Deborah, 2 Samuel 22, and the whole Book of Psalms. In a few carefully written books you also will find many of the dialogues of Job and the words of the Book of Proverbs written this way. The composers of these poems, each and every one, had as their purpose to measure the words so that they would correspond exactly to their musical arrangement. And when the musical arrangements change, the measurement of the words changes. There is no doubt that there were known melodies, but they were forgotten because of the passage of time and the length of the exile. Everything was in accord with the modes of different musical instruments, the number of their strings, cords, and holes: lyre, pipe, timbrel, flute, lute, cymbals, *neginot, gittit, šeminit,* ten-stringed harp, harp, and their like. Accordingly, they changed the musical arrangements known by names such as *menaṣṣeaḥ, mizmor, maskil, miktam, šir,* and their like. The measurement of the words of these poems changed as the melodies changed. Indeed, wonderful things were contained in this wisdom through divine insight. This, then, is the second type of poetry.

The third type of poetry is that which employs exaggeration and hyperbole and metaphor and forms to praise or denigrate a subject, either in an ode or a lament or a eulogy. Everything of this sort is called poetry, and it is intended to stir the heart, to alter the inner thoughts, and to reinforce the desired subject in its veracity through extended discourse, narrative, much description, and figurative language not to be taken literally as it is in real life. This type is the essence of poetry.

On this Aristotle wrote a Book of Poetics among the Books on Logic.[10] He wrote there that the unique feature and description of poetry is that there should be praise and denigration of a thing, and so forth, such that the more a poet extends his metaphors with hyperbole and exaggeration and impossibilities, the better his poetry will be. And about this the Sage wrote that the best of poetry is its falseness. By falseness is meant to falsify the literal sense. No wise man would occupy himself with this except to cure the sick of heart and the weak of mind, to reverse depression, to cheer the sad, and to awaken the sleeping and draw them out. For human nature is drawn to the hyperbolic poem and is activated by its strangeness; it is like strong drugs that can kill the living or cure the sick of chronic illness. An example of this type of poetry in the Torah is "Then Israel sang this song: Spring up, Well, sing to it. The well which the princes dug, which the nobles of the people started with engraving instruments and staffs" [Num 21:17–18]. It is well known that the princes did not dig the well with writing implements, but this is said in a poetic way. The Book of Song of Songs is also of this type, in that the yearning lover is an allegory for the Holy One Blessed Be He, and the bride for the rational soul. And in reference to this our sages of blessed memory said: "All the songs[11] are holy, and the Song of Songs is holy of holies."

It is said of Solomon that he spoke three thousand proverbs and that his poems numbered one thousand and five [1 Kgs 5:12]; for a poem is one of the types of proverbs [*mešalim*] mentioned.[12] So also the words of Isaiah [5:1]: "Let me sing to my beloved a song of my lover to his vineyard." This song also contains a parable [*mašal*], comparing the congregation of Israel to a vineyard. Likewise it is said [Isa 26:1]: "On that day this song will be sung in the land of Judah: 'We have a strong city.'" Here divine providence is likened to a city and tower of strength.

Having presented these types of poems, it is now appropriate to clarify which type the Song of the Sea [Exodus 15] is, which Moses our Teacher, peace be upon him, composed, or whether it contains several types. Clearly it is not the first type—metrical poems—but is rather the second type and also the third type. It is the second type because it is connected and measured on eight melodic arrangements of which two are very short, two are very long, and four are of medium length. The first [line] corresponds to the ninth and the eighth, these being short. The second corresponds to the tenth, and the third to the eleventh. These four [2, 3, 10, 11] are medium. The fourth corresponds to the twelfth, and the fifth to the thirteenth. These four [4, 5, 12, 13] are long. The sixth corresponds to the fourteenth, and the seventh to the fifteenth. This is its form.

1. He hurled into the sea.

2. The Lord is my strength and might.
3. He is become my salvation.
4. This is my God and I will glorify Him.
5. The God of my father and I will exalt Him.
6. The Lord is a man of war.
7. Lord is His name.
8. The chariots of Pharaoh.
9. And his army.
10. He cast into the sea.
11. And the choicest of his officers.
12. Are drowned in the Reed Sea.
13. The deeps covered them.
14. They went down into the depths like a stone.
15. Your right hand, Lord, glorious in power.
16. Your right hand, Lord.

This arrangement and measurement repeats again, in accord with the melody which was arranged for it.[13] Every song was set to known musical arrangements, and you will find evidence for this in this song, because for the sake of the measurement [or rhythm], the words were contracted, and it was necessary in many places to lengthen and to add a letter in order to align the measurement [of the words] and the melody. In other places it was necessary to omit a letter or letters for this reason. The letters which were added in this song are the two *yods* and the *waw* of *yekasyumu* ["covered them"], since it would have been sufficient to say *kissam*; the *yod* of *ne'dari* ["glorious"]; the *waw* of *to'kelemo*[14] ["it consumes them"]; the *waw* of *torišemo* ["shall subdue them"]; the *waw* of *kissamo* ["covered them"]; the *waw* of *tibla'emo* ["swallowed them"]; the *waw* of *yo'ḥazemo* ["grips them"]; the *taw* of *'emata* ["dread"]; the *waw* of *tebi'emo* ["you will bring them"]; the *waw* of *tiṭṭa'emo* ["you will plant them"]. The omitted letters are *yod* of *wezimrat[i] yah* ["my might"]; also *timla'emo* instead of *timmale' mehem* ["will be filled with them"]; *waw* of *nehalta be'ozka* ["you guide with your strength"], which should have been *nehalto* ["you guide it"]; also the word *lebab* ["heart"] in the phrase "[the heart of] all the inhabitants of Canaan melted." Don't think that the master prophet [Moses] erred in grammar or spelling; rather, the subject of the poem and the requirements of the melody and the tune necessitated this. It thus becomes clear that this song belongs to the second type of poetry which I discussed.

In fact, it is also of the third type—the figurative type—as is clear from the phrase "The Lord is a man of war." This is a figurative expression, for God is not a man, and he is not a warrior. Likewise, "Your right hand, Lord, is wondrous in strength; your right hand, Lord, shatters the foe"—for God has neither a right nor a left hand. Likewise,

"With the blast of your nostrils," "You make your wind blow," "You put out your right hand," "A place for your dwelling," "Your hands established." These are all poetic expressions referring to God, figurative language, and the imagery is not realistic, as will be clarified in the exposition of the verses of the song below.

Now the question arises: If everything expressed figuratively and in elegant language is considered poetry, then does this mean that prophetic visions that were in the form of parables [*mešalim*] and riddles are poetry? Isaiah made many parables about Israel and about the [other] nations, as when he said [7:18]: "On that day, the Lord will whistle to the flies at the ends of the water-channels of Egypt and to the bees in the land of Assyria"—which was a parable referring to Pharaoh and Sennacherib. Likewise he compared Hezekiah to the waters of Siloam which flow slowly [8:6], and he compared the king of Assyria to the waters of mighty rivers[15] [8:7], and the Messiah he compared to a shoot from the stock of Jesse and a twig from his roots [11:1]. There are many other cases like this in his [Isaiah's] words, and also in the words of the other prophets; but their figurative discourses were not called poetry on this account. Rather, I would respond to this in the terms of Maimonides, that there is a great difference between the prophecy that comes to prophets from God, and the Holy Spirit through which the true believers of Israel speak.[16] For prophecy is the effluence that flows into the intellect and imagination of the prophets; at the time of his prophecy the prophet's faculties are asleep and his senses lost, and his soul is occupied with providence, and he tells people what he saw or heard without its being within his control. He introduces what he saw by "And he prophesied," and like the expression of Isaiah [21:10]: "That which I heard from the Lord of Hosts I told you," or, as Amos said several times, "Thus the Lord showed me" [7:1, 7; 8:1].

The Holy Spirit is not like this, for it does not have visual images and parables, and when it comes one does not fall into a trance or lose one's senses. Rather, the prophet [when speaking through the Holy Spirit as opposed to prophecy] wills and chooses to speak as he wishes: words of wisdom, praise, warning, and so forth. And because the divine spirit accompanies him and helps him to compose, this level is called the Holy Spirit. It is a preparation for full-fledged prophecy. Maimonides has already written in *The Guide of the Perplexed*, part II, chapter 45, when he discusses the degrees of prophecy, that prophecy can come once in its highest degree, and on another occasion it can come in a different, lower degree. For just as a prophet does not prophesy all of his life continuously, but prophesies for a time and then prophecy leaves him for a time, so he may prophesy one time in the form of the highest degree of prophecy and another time in a lower degree, or through the Holy Spirit only.

From this you will know and understand that all poetry that you find in prophetic speech is something which they [the prophets] arrange themselves through the Holy Spirit—not something they saw through prophecy. This is not so regarding the rest of the visions, for all visions are full-fledged prophecy, and they are not on the level of the Holy Spirit as Maimonides would have it. But each and every poem is through the Holy Spirit—through the workings of the prophet who arranged it through will and choice; for it is not involuntary. As I mentioned, the prophets, while sometimes they achieve true prophetic visions, when they are awake and are not prophesying, they speak words through the Holy Spirit in beautiful elevated style and elegant language. Look at the prophet Samuel, who wrote the books of Samuel and Judges through prophecy, and therefore his books were included among the prophetic books; nevertheless, this did not prevent him from writing the Book of Ruth through the Holy Spirit, without prophecy. And therefore it is included in the Writings. Likewise Jeremiah wrote, through prophecy, his own book and the Book of Kings; and through the Holy Spirit he wrote the Book of Lamentations. Therefore his books [Jeremiah and Kings] were included in the Prophets, and Lamentations was included in the Writings.

When it comes to poetry, the prophet writes and arranges it through the Holy Spirit that is in him; it is not a vision that appears to him through prophecy. For this reason Scripture always attributes it to the prophet who authored it [i.e., does not attribute it to God], as it says in the Song of the Well [Num 21:17]: "Then Israel sang"; [Jud 5:1]: "And Deborah sang, and Barak, son of Avinoam"; [Song 1:1]: "Song of songs which is Solomon's"; [Isa 5:1]: "Let me sing for my beloved"—thereby ascribing the song to the one who arranged it. The same for the Song of the Sea, where it says [Exod 15:1]: "Then Moses, and the children of Israel, sang this song and they said, 'Let me sing to the Lord' "—since they themselves arranged and sang it. Therefore at the end of it they prayed over their success [vv. 16, 17]: "Terror and dread descended upon them. . . . You will bring them and plant them. . . ."

Now don't let the Ha'azinu Song appear problematic for you, for God gave it to Moses and Joshua, for he commanded Moses to say it as if he himself had arranged it, as if the words were from his mouth and not from the mouth of God. He said: "Now write for them this song" [Deut 31:19], and the style of the words demonstrates it: "Give ear, Heavens, and let me speak. . . . for the name of Lord I proclaim." The rest of the words, too, are all in the language of Moses our Teacher, the speaker. And at the end he said: "Take to heart all the words with which I have warned you this day. . . . For this is not a trifling thing for you. . . ." [Deut 32:46–47]. All this shows that Moses spoke this song as if he had arranged it himself.

And this being so, the parables that occur in his full-fledged prophecy are not called poetry, since they are not from the intentional workings of the prophet, through the Holy Spirit, but rather he saw them through full-fledged prophecy. However, the parables that the prophets made and arranged by themselves, and wrote through the Holy Spirit, these are called poetry. Such is the case of the Song of the Sea, in that Moses arranged it to praise and glorify God, who answered him in the time of trouble. So, too, Miriam, his sister, made a song with drums and dancing, as will be explained. That these songs were written in the Torah and the Prophets is due to the fact that God accepted them and delighted in them, and commanded that they be written therein. So, then, the arranging of this song [Exodus 15] was done by Moses, and its writing in the Torah was at the command of God.

Commentary on Isaiah 5

*Abravanel poses six questions on the chapter before offering his comments. These are (1) Why is this called a "song"? It is not written stichographically, like the other songs in the Bible. And merely the fact that it is a parable (*mašal*) does not qualify it as a song or poem, for there are many parables in the prophetic books that are not songs. (2) Is this prophecy or the Holy Spirit? That is, did God write it, or did Isaiah? (3) Not all elements of the parable are explained in the interpretation of the parable. Why is there a lack of symmetry and completeness in the composition? (4) Why are there five "woe" pericopes, and why are they selective about the sins that they mention? (5) Why are words of comfort inserted in the "woe" passages? (6) Are verses 21–22 redundant? Why was verse 23 not constructed as a "woe" passage?*

The fourth prophecy: from Isa 5:1 to 6:1. There are seven pericopes in it.

1. 5:1–7
2. 5:8–10
3. 5:11–17
4. 5:18–19
5. 5:20
6. 5:21–23
7. 5:24

I pose the following six questions about this prophecy:

THE FIRST QUESTION. Why is this prophecy called a "song"? There is nothing songlike [or poetic] in its form or content; it is not written brick over log.[17] And if one says that it is called a song because it is a parable of the vineyard, well, don't we find in the words of this same prophet many parables about Israel and about the nations, yet none of them is called a song. For example, "On that day, the Lord will whistle to the flies at the ends of the water-channels of Egypt and to the bees in the land of Assyria" [7:18], which is a parable of Pharaoh and Sennacherib. Likewise he compared Hezekiah to the waters of Siloam that flow slowly [8:6], and he compared the king of Assyria to the mighty waters of the [Euphrates] River [8:7], and once he compared him to the rod of his anger, as it is said, "Ha, Assyria, rod of my anger" [10:5]. He also compared the Messiah to a shoot from the stock of Jesse [11:1]. Now, none of these *mešalim* are called song, and the same is true for the *mešalim* of the other prophets, of which there are many: the great eagle for Nebuchadnezzar [Ezekiel 17], and the fig for Israel [Jeremiah 24], and many others; these were not called song. Therefore it is appropriate that we should investigate the nature of this song, for it is a major component of prophetic speech, although the commentaries do not discuss it.

THE SECOND QUESTION. "A song of my lover to his vineyard." We cannot avoid difficulties whether we say that the prophet arranged and composed this song himself or whether we say that it was told to him by God through prophecy, like the rest of the prophecies. If the prophet composed it, his saying "a song of my lover to his vineyard" is a problem, for the song of the prophet is not the song of his lover.[18] But if God made the song and gave it to the prophet, then "Let me sing to my beloved" is a problem, for it shows that he [Isaiah] sang and composed it himself.[19] [If God had composed it] it would have been more appropriate to say "The song which Isaiah son of Amoz saw," as it is stated in other prophecies. Rashi interprets *lididi* as "*for* my beloved," as in the phrase "The Lord will fight for you" [Exod 14:14], i.e., "on your behalf."[20] [It says] "A song of my lover" because he [the lover, God] sings it for his people, about the matter of his vineyard.[21] In my opinion this song was the counterpart of the prophecies which God arranged and put into the mouth of the prophet; but we do not find in any of them that the prophet says "Let me speak this prophecy" in reference to "my beloved," for it is accepted that what a prophet sees he tells, and what he hears he speaks. Now to Moses our Teacher, God said about the Ha'azinu Song, "Now write down this song and teach it to the children of Israel" [Deut 31:19]; but he did not say about it "Let me sing for my beloved" as Isaiah said.

THE THIRD QUESTION. You will see in this song [several] parts. One part speaks about the perfection of the vineyard in terms of the nature of its location, as it says, "My beloved had a vineyard on a fruitful hill." Another part speaks of the perfection in terms of labor—in the expressions "he broke the ground, cleared the stones, planted it with choice vines, built a watchtower inside it, hewed a winepress in it." Another part recounts the sins: "He hoped it would yield grapes, but instead it yielded wild grapes." Another part recounts the punishment: "I will remove its hedge, that it may be ravaged. I will break down its wall," etc. And of these parts of the parable that we mentioned, you will not find counterparts in the interpretation [*nimšal*] except for two: "For the vineyard of the Lord of Hosts is the house of Israel; and the seedlings he lovingly tended are the men of Judah," which is the interpretation of the first part of the parable; and "He hoped for justice, but behold, injustice; for equity, but behold, iniquity," the counterpart of the third part of the parable.[22] There is, therefore, a problem: why are the other parts of the parable, referring to the favors he showed them and to the punishments that he will pour upon them, not mentioned in the interpretation?

THE FOURTH QUESTION. What motivated the prophet to compose five pericopes, each beginning with "Woe"? The first is in 5:8, the second in 5:11, the third in 5:18, the fourth in 5:20, and the fifth in 5:21.[23] These five sins alone which he mentions sufficed in his lament; he did not mention the rest of the sins of which he accused them earlier, whether it was thievery, as in 3:14, or whether it was evil conduct and pride.

THE FIFTH QUESTION. In his second "woe" pericope the following expression occurs: "And the Lord of Hosts is exalted by judgment. . . . Then lambs shall graze as in their meadows . . ." [vv. 16–17]. Now this constitutes consolation. Wherefore, then, was it included in the lament? If he had wished to comfort and console them regarding what would happen after their redemption, it would have been more appropriate for him to mention this after the evils which he mentioned five times in the "woe" pericopes, and not in the middle of them.

THE SIXTH QUESTION. In respect to verses 21–22: "Woe, those who are wise in their own eyes. . . . Woe, those who are such doughty winedrinkers"—look, he himself forgot what he said just before, in verse 20: "Woe, those who call evil good and good evil"; for in their foolishness they could not render true verbal judgment. And if these two laments were intended to say the same thing, then one is superfluous. Indeed, it has been said that "those who are such doughty winedrinkers" is altogether similar to "those who rise early to chase liquor" [v. 11]. This being so, this expression [vv. 21–22] is therefore redundant. There is also a question as to why he did not say "woe" in 5:23: "those who vindicate the one in the wrong in return for a bribe and deny vindication to those in the right." For this is an independent expression.[24] It is harsher, more bitter, and stronger than the expressions in which he used "woe."

*After presenting his six questions, and a brief statement that the general sense of the chapter is to explain the destruction and exile of the Northern Kingdom to the Judeans, Abravanel adds two discourses bearing on the matter of poetry within prophetic speech. In the first he presents the three-part categorization of poetry, in words almost identical to those in his commentary on Exodus 15 (which was written after the Isaiah commentary). He makes clear that in the case of the first two types, "it makes no difference whether figurative or literal language is used; they are deemed poetry solely on the basis of their written form or melody." The third type, of course, is marked by the use of figurative language (*mašal*), but as to why all instances of* mašal *are not automatically poetry, he does not immediately explain. The explanation is implicit in the second discourse, namely, that the manner of composition—the Holy Spirit versus prophecy—is the determining factor.*

The second discourse takes up in greater detail the matter of prophecy versus the Holy Spirit, also found in the commentary on Exodus 15. Abravanel concludes that all "songs" so labeled in the Bible were composed through the Holy Spirit and are therefore poetry (as opposed to prophecy). Hence the answers to the first two questions: Isaiah 5 is called a "song" because it belongs to the third type of poetry; it uses figurative language, and was composed through the Holy Spirit, in the manner of poetry.

The subsequent commentary provides the answers to the remaining questions. Abravanel resolves the problems of structure and symmetry (questions 3 and 4) in the following way. He divides the parable into eight parts:

1. *My beloved had a vineyard*
2. *On a fruitful hill*
3. *He broke the ground, cleared it of stones*
4. *He planted it with choice vines*
5. *He built a watchtower inside it*
6. *He even hewed a wine press in it*
7. *He hoped it would yield grapes, but it yielded wild grapes*
8. *Remove its hedge so that it will be ravaged. . . .*

The counterpart of part 1 is verse 7a, "For the vineyard of the Lord of Hosts is the House of Israel . . . ," and the counterpart of part 7 is verse 7b, "He hoped for justice, but behold, injustice. . . ." The prophet saw fit to place the counterparts of the first and seventh parts next to each other because these parts frame the parable of the vineyard and its building—i.e., they form the beginning and end. What follows is the story of the punishment. Part 2 is echoed in the first "woe" pericope, part 3 in the second "woe" pericope, part 4 in the third "woe" pericope, part 5 in the fourth "woe" pericope, part 6 in the fifth "woe" pericope, and part 8 finds its counterpart in verse 24, "Indeed, as straw is consumed. . . ." There is, then, balance between the parable and its interpretation, and the number of "woe" pericopes is accounted for.

Abravanel refutes the idea that the image of shepherding flocks in verses 16–17 conveys a message of comfort; he sees in it a picture of desolation, thereby obviating the problem raised in his question 5.

Abravanel links "Woe, those who are wise," "Woe, those who are valiant," and "Woe, those who vindicate the one in the wrong" into one thought which is not redundant with "Woe, those who call evil good and good evil." Those who think they are wise and those who look heroic by drinking to excess are the very ones who, as a result of these actions, vindicate the wrongdoers. Therefore, there was no need for the word "woe" before "those who vindicate." Question 6 is thus answered.

NOTES

1. "Don" is an honorific title.
2. These bracketed words are supplied by the editor of the Hebrew edition.
3. The wording of this phrase contains an allusion to Lev 19:35.
4. Abravanel refers here to the rhyme of medieval Hebrew poetry, in which the final consonant-vowel-consonant (not merely vowel-consonant, as in English rhyme) must agree.
5. Variant: "is the Lord's art."
6. This is a pastiche of Ps 78:19; Job 11:6; Jud 14:18. It is followed in the next sentence by a reference to Deut 32:17.
7. Cf. *m. Yadayim* 3:5 and *Song of Songs Rabbah* 1:10: "All the *ketubim* [Writings or Scriptures] are holy, but the Song of Songs is holy of holies."
8. The word is *miškal*, "meter, measurement, rhythm." I have translated it by "measurement" to distinguish it from the metrical poems of the first type.
9. Variant: "All who read the Torah without cantillation, it is as if the Torah wears sackcloth" [*b. Sanhedrin* 101a].
10. This reflects the long tradition in which poetics and rhetoric were considered branches of logic; more specifically, Aristotle's *Poetics* was included as the eighth section of the *Organon*, preceded by the *Rhetoric*. Cf. Dahiyat, *Avicenna's Commentary on the* Poetics *of Aristotle*, 12, and Weinberg, *A History of Literary Criticism in the Italian Renaissance*, 2. Abravanel was most probably familiar with Aristotle's *Poetics* through Averroes's *Middle Commentary*.
11. The statement in *Song of Songs Rabbah* 1.10 and *m. Yadayim* 3:5 reads "All the *ketubim* [Writings or Scriptures] are holy. . . ."
12. Abravanel considers Solomon's poems to be a subset of his *mešalim*. Compare Moshe ibn Ezra, who said that Solomon's three thousand *mešalim* refers to prose.
13. It is not clear on what basis Abravanel arrived at this division of lines. Although this poem is written "brick over log" in masoretic Bibles, the stichography there does not conform to Abravanel's. Kugel (*The Idea of Biblical Poetry*, 194) notes that "the classification is complicated and (so one must conclude after repeated attempts at making it consistent) somewhat arbitrary."

One may hazard the guess that the eight melodic arrangements refer to the eight melodic modes known in medieval musicology. See Werner and Sonne, "The Philosophy and Theory of Music in Judeo-Arabic Literature." On p. 303 they state: "We may conclude that, though it has at times been overlooked, musical and metrical theories in Hebrew literature are closely interwoven and can hardly be separated from each other." According to the chart of modes on p. 302, two of the modes are long, two are short, and four are of medium length. This corresponds to Abravanel's statement. What remains puzzling is the criterion for dividing the words into the sixteen "lines" as Abravanel has done. Why, for instance, is "Your right hand, Lord, glorious in power" all one line, while the following line contains only "Your right hand, Lord"? The answer may be that he began with the musical arrangement and simply divided up the words to fit the music. That is what he suggests happened originally; the songs were set to music, and for the sake of the measurement, or rhythm, the words were contracted or lengthened. In other words, the phrasing was adjusted to fit the music.

14. It should be *yo'kelemo*.

15. Text should read "river," i.e., the Euphrates. Cf. the commentary on Isaiah 5, where it is correct.

16. Abravanel's views on prophecy are expounded at greater length in his commentary to Maimonides's *Guide of the Perplexed*. Cf. Reines, *Maimonides and Abravanel on Prophecy*, especially 180–98. *The Holy Spirit* is a technical term used by Maimonides to signify a lower level of prophecy and by Abravanel to distinguish true prophecy from the type of inspiration through which poetic parts of the Bible were composed.

17. These are the criteria for identifying the second type of poetry.

18. If the prophet were speaking in the first person, citing his own song, he would say "my song," not "my lover's song." Abravanel argues here that this phraseology suggests that it is God's song which Isaiah is conveying, and therefore it is a product of prophecy, not the divine inspiration through which human authors compose poetry. But see below.

19. Here the first person suggests that it is, indeed, the song of Isaiah.

20. Rashi's interpretation, "*for* my beloved" rather than "*to* my beloved," supports Abravanel's contention that Isaiah sings this song on behalf of God.

21. If this is Isaiah's song, as Abravanel wants to prove and as he demonstrated from the phrase "Let me sing on behalf of my beloved," then why does it say "A song of my lover" instead of "my song"? [Note that the NEB translates "my love-song."] It is the lover's song because further on, in verses 3–6, the lover speaks in the first person, whereas in verse 1 the first person belongs to Isaiah. As Abravanel says a few pages later, "the prophet composed this song which is ascribed and assigned to his beloved, who is God, and to his vineyard, which is Israel." Abravanel is sensitive to the shift in person in the poem and touches upon issues which a modern literary critic would call "persona" or "voice," though he, of course, did not view it in these terms.

22. The link is based on the idea "He hoped for X but got Y."

23. Another "woe" begins 5:22, but Abravanel does not consider this a new pericope. See, however, his sixth question, below.

24. Abravanel apparently views this as unconnected to the idea in verses 21–22.

JUDAH MESSER LEON

Judah ben Yehiel Messer[1] *Leon (ca. 1420–ca. 1497) deserves, like his later compatriot Azariah de' Rossi, the designation of "Renaissance man." Born in "Monticulus," which has been identified most recently with Montecchio Maggiore (a small town in Vicenza Province, near Padua and Mantua),*[2] *he lived for varying amounts of time in most of the important Italian cultural centers, including Ancona, Padua, Venice, Bologna, Mantua, and Naples. Having been well educated, both in Jewish sources and in the secular disciplines of philosophy and medicine, he participated actively in these communities in various capacities; in addition to his role in Jewish religious, communal, and educational affairs, he was empowered to practice and teach medicine. His scholarly writings include a "trivium" consisting of a grammatical treatise,* Libnat Hassapir, *two works on logic,* Miklal Yopi *and* Super-Commentary on Isagoge-Categories–De Interpretatione, *and a treatise on rhetoric,* Nopet Ṣupim; *he also wrote commentaries on other philosophical texts and on the Torah.*

Nopet Ṣupim *[The Honeycomb's Flow, from Ps 19:11], first published in Mantua in 1475–76, was written in Hebrew for an educated Jewish audience, probably medical students. It reflects its author's desire to combine the secular and Jewish worlds of learning. In this case, the worlds are those of classical rhetoric and scriptural study.* Nopet Ṣupim *is, in essence, a study of the rhetoric of the Hebrew Bible based on the model and terminology of the Greek and Latin rhetoricians.*[3] *Messer Leon accepted the tenet that all science and knowledge is contained in the Bible, and he proceeded to demonstrate that the Bible had already put into practice all of the principles expounded in classical rhetorical texts. In this respect,* Nopet Ṣupim *is not unlike Moshe ibn Ezra's* Kitāb al-Muḥāḍara wa-'l-Mudhākara, *which finds that the Bible contains all the figures of Arabic rhetoric.*

The excerpts which follow illustrate Messer Leon's attitude toward the Bible and his interpretive approach. My translation relies heavily on that of Isaac Rabinowitz, with one major exception: I have not called attention to the many biblical allusions which dot Messer Leon's diction.

Editions and Translation: Nopet Ṣupim, *photograph of ms. with introduction by R. Bonfil (Jerusalem, 1981). A. Jellinek,* Nofet Zufim *(Vienna, 1863; reprint, Jerusalem, 1971). I. Rabinowitz,* The Book of the Honeycomb's Flow: Sepher Nopheth Ṣuphim by Judah Messer Leon *(Ithaca and London, 1983).*

Nopet Ṣupim

Book I, Chapter 13

In the days of prophecy, in the months of old, when out of Zion, the perfection of beauty, God shone forth, we used to learn and know from the holy Torah all the sciences and truths of reason, including all that were humanly attained, for everything is in it [the Torah], either latent or clearly stated. What other peoples possessed of these sciences and truths was very little, compared to us, so that the nations that heard the fame of us were wont to say: "Surely this great nation is a wise and discerning people" [Deut 4:6]. But after Providence departed from our midst, because of our many sins, when prophecy and insight ceased, and the science of our wise men was hid, we were no longer able to derive understanding of all scientific developments and attainments from the Torah's words. This condition persists because of our deficiency—our failure to know the Torah in full perfection. Thus the process has been reversed: after we have learned all the sciences, or part of them, we then study the words of the Torah; then our learned eyes are opened to the fact that they [the sciences] are contained in the Torah's words, and we wonder how we could have failed to realize this from the Torah itself to begin with.

This has frequently been our own experience, especially in the science of Rhetoric. For when I studied the words of the Torah in the way common among most people, I had no idea that the science of Rhetoric or any part of it was included therein. But after I had studied and investigated Rhetoric, searched for her as for hidden treasures [Prov 2:4], out of the treatises written by men of nations other than ours, I then came back to see what is said of her in the Torah and the Holy Scriptures. Then my learned eyes were opened, and I saw that it is the Torah which is the giver. Between the Torah's sweet expressions and stylistic elegancies—and, indeed, all the statutes and ordinances of Rhetoric which are included in the Holy Scriptures—and all of the like that other nations possess, there is such a marked difference that to compare them is like comparing the hyssop in the wall with the cedar in Lebanon [1 Kgs 5:13]. Now I marvel how previously the spirit of the Lord passed me by, so that I did not know where her place is. You could apply the same comparison to all other sciences.

Book II, Chapter 4

When you study praise and censure in the Holy Books—the main content of the speeches made by the prophets for the purpose of extolling the virtues and of laying the vices low . . .—you find all the considerations mentioned above with regard to which praise and blame are formulated. This is exemplified in the Davidic psalm entitled "To the Leader. In the mode of Shoshanim, for the sons of Korah" [Ps 45:1].

Before proceeding with the exposition of the verses, it should be understood that this psalm was composed through the Holy Spirit and concerns the Messiah, his deeds, and the qualities for which one should praise him. . . . He [the psalmist] depicts the Messiah as if the Messiah were alive at that time, and he were speaking with him face to face. This discourse, then, belongs in the class of Epideictic and, within this class, in the division of "praise." You should, moreover, note that the *šošan* is, as we think, the flower called "lily." It has six sepals, being etymologically derived from *šeš* ["six"]. "His lips are like lilies" [Song 5:13] means comparable in fragrance, as is attested by the end of the verse, "dropping with flowing myrrh," where, as is obvious, the intended meaning is a comparison in respect to fragrance. So, from fragrant things we come to understand the possessor of fragrance. And so, too, from the qualities and deeds of the Messiah which, through the Holy Spirit, the psalmist had in mind, he came to understand the Messiah and his function. While it is possible to say that *šošanim* was perhaps a musical instrument, or one of the meters of poetry which we no longer know, the psalmist's use of this term in any case also suggests that he would pronounce, on the attributes and qualities of the Messiah, a complete discourse with all its parts—which are six, namely Introduction, Statement of Facts, Partition, Proof, Refutation, and Conclusion, as is well known—parts altogether as sweet and pleasing when they are "sweet to the soul" [Prov 13:19] and captivate hearts, as fragrant things.

It should, furthermore, not go unnoticed that the term *šir* in the holy tongue sometimes refers to a composition which is unclear in meaning and, on the surface, false—in the sense of "The best of poetry is its falseness"—while at times it denotes an utterance set to music, even though its literal sense is factual [lit.: true] and clear. An example of the first [definition of *šir*] is the Song of Songs; an example of the second is "And Miriam sang to them" [Exod 15:21]. It is in this second sense that the term *šir* is to be taken in the passage under consideration. . . .

Book IV, Chapter 46

Metaphor

Metaphor is diction in which certain words are taken as *mašal* and in a transferred sense, because some resemblance obtains between the literal and the transferred meanings which allows this appropriately to be done. For example, "The wilderness and the parched land shall be glad; and the desert shall rejoice, and blossom like the rose" [Isa 35:1][4] Gladness is properly attributable to humans but is used here through resemblance; for the bringing forth of flowers is indicative of a great good in the case of a desert and parched land, just as gladness is indicative of good in the case of humans. . . .

Book IV, Chapter 47

Allegory

Allegory,[5] as it is used here, is diction in which the meaning is something other than that literally indicated by the words. It differs from Metaphor in that Metaphor involves just a few words, while Allegory involves the entire statement. It comes in the form of a comparison—either magnification or minification—or of a contrast.

An example of the first [i.e., comparison]: "My beloved had a vineyard on a fruitful hill. He digged it and cleared it of stones, and planted it with the choicest vines . . ." [Isa 5:1]. The prophet is comparing the subject of Israel to this vineyard, as explained at the end of the passage [v. 7]. . . .

An example in the form of a contrast: "Behold, you are wiser than Daniel; no secret can be hidden from you" [Ezek 28:3]. The actual meaning intended here is contrary to what it appears to mean—that is, that the prince of Tyre was in fact a great fool in comparison to Daniel. . . .

Book IV, Chapter 68

Since the prophets were experts in rhetoric—as by common consent they are without peer among the orators of the nations—it follows that all their words are pure utterances, refined. It also follows that there is no anomaly whatsoever in their words; a construction that may be called anomalous by the grammarian is, to the orator, appropriate to the theme and completely satisfying to the audience. Therefore, as I have studied the Holy Scriptures, I have found in them figures other than those already mentioned; and perhaps they are unique to our language. I cite some of them here. . . .

Messer Leon goes on, in the following chapters, to cite, among others, biblical examples of pleonasm, ellipsis, the inclusive term, anticipation, irony, inversion, euphemism, and strange usage. Some of his examples and explanations are quite convincing, even by modern literary standards. For instance, he notes in chapter

75 that the negative construction in "not clean" [Gen 7:2], "not good" [1 Sam 2:24], and "not good" [Ps 36:5] is euphemistic, that these forms were employed rather than words such as "defile" or "evil." He links this with the statement in Aristotle's Rhetoric, *Book III, that negative epithets and words should be used only when imputing shame or when attempting to suppress a matter. In chapter 76 he discusses "Strange Usage," cases in which grammatically irregular words are found. The purpose of this is to call attention to, enhance, and heighten the strangeness of the subject matter. He cites forms in Ezek 9:8 [*wene'sa'ar*], Ezek 8:16 [*mištaḥawitem*], and Isa 63:3 [*'eg'alti*], and explains that Ezekiel's vision was obviously extremely strange and that the form in Isaiah creates an effect that enhances the theme in a way which could not have been achieved by a regular grammatical form.*

NOTES

1. "Messer" is an honorific title which became part of his name.
2. Rabinowitz, *The Book of the Honeycomb's Flow,* xx.
3. According to Rabinowitz, ibid., lx–lxi, notes 214, 215, this work is the first of its kind, having anticipated similar approaches to the Bible by several hundred years.
4. Judah Messer Leon follows David Kimḥi's interpretation of this verse.
5. The Hebrew is *haš'ala,* literally "metaphorical or figurative use of a word." Messer Leon differentiates this from "metaphor" (*hityaḥasut,* literally "relationship"), which he discussed in the previous chapter.

YOḤANAN ALLEMANNO

Yoḥanan ben Isaac Allemanno (ca. 1435–after 1504), philosopher and exegete, was a descendant of a family expelled from France.[1] *He was raised in Florence, in the home of Yehiel (Vitale) of Pisa (member of a famous Italian Jewish family of bankers), and educated in Greek and Arabic philosophy and Latin literature, both classical and medieval. He taught in various Italian cities, settling for a time in Mantua, where he was a guest of Luigi III Gonzaga. Allemanno returned to Florence in 1488 where, again under the patronage of Yehiel of Pisa, he completed several works which had been in progress and wrote additional ones.*

Allemanno's most important work was Ḥešeq Šelomoh *[Solomon's Desire, from 1 Kgs 9:1 and a reference to the Solomonic authorship of Song of Songs], a philosophical commentary on the Song of Songs, completed at the urging of Giovanni Pico della Mirandola. In it, Allemanno opined that the Song was, in its literal sense, about earthly love, and allegorically about divine love.*

In the excerpt presented here, Allemanno discusses the meaning of the word šir. *He understands it to signify (1) a melody and/or words set to a melody, and (2) a poem, not necessarily sung, which employs metaphor. He places the Song of the Sea and Ha'azinu in the first category, along with the books of Psalms, Proverbs, and Job (traditionally considered poetic because of their special masoretic accents). In the second category he places the Song of the Vineyard in Isaiah 5, clearly metaphorical and not stichographically written, and, for reasons that are not clear, the Song of Deborah, which is stichographically written and which others classify with the Song of the Sea and Ha'azinu.*

Editions: There is no complete edition of Ḥešeq Šelomoh. *Part of its introduction was published by Jacob Barukh, under the title* Ša'ar Haḥešeq *(Livorno, 1790; reprint, Halberstadt, 1862). The present translation is based on the fragments edited by I. Adler in* Hebrew Writings concerning Music in Manuscripts and Printed Books from Geonic Times up to 1800 *(Munich, 1975), pp. 39–45. Moshe Idel and Arthur Lesley will discuss Allemanno in a forthcoming study,* Yohanan Alemanno: A Kabbalist and Humanist in Fifteenth-Century Italy *(New Haven).*

Ḥešeq Šelomoh

The title of the Book [of Song of Songs]: This book is called *šir* ["song"], a multivalent name,[2] because it signifies, first of all, "melody," as in "all the daughters of song" [Ecc 12:4], meaning "all the organs of song." The words arranged to be played by the mouth or by instruments are also called by this name [*šir*], the melody having been composed for them. They are divided into types according to the variations in sounds and in meanings.

Some are metered in sound and rhymed with all the art of pegs,[3] their purpose being sweetness of sound and pleasantness, not only the meaning of the discourse or its essence. Others are not metered or rhymed but are arranged in short or long lines—log over log and brick over brick, or log over brick and brick over log—like the Song of the Sea and the Ha'azinu Song and Psalms, Job, and Proverbs, in which the purpose is the meaning of the discourse etched in the soul, not the melody and the pleasantness alone. Still others are, by virtue of their contents, love songs or victory songs or *mešalim* or wisdom songs or genres like those referred to by the sage [Abraham] ibn Ezra: "All Arabic poems are about love and desire, Latin poems about wars and vengeance, Greek poems about wisdom and craftiness, Hindu[4] poems about proverbs and riddles, and Hebrew [lit.: Israelite][5] poems about songs and praise to the Lord of Hosts."[6] Of the last type are all the poems of David, peace be upon him.

And secondly, this name [*šir*] signifies discourse not set to melody and not composed in the narrative style, like all of Chronicles and the words of Ecclesiastes, and not in the style of *mašal* and *meliṣa,* like all of Proverbs and Ezekiel and those copied by the men of Hezekiah—but, rather, composed in mimetic and imitative style, by comparison to or imitation of something else, in a dream or in real life, for the purpose of bringing the desire of the listener to love or hate the compared thing, even if it is not real. This is called poetry in the Art of Rhetoric. Of this type are the Song of Deborah and the Song[7] of Isaiah [Isaiah 5].

NOTES

1. The name Allemanno is Italian for "Ashkenazi," signifying a member of the Franco-German Jewish community. He was known in Hebrew as Yoḥanan ben Isaac Ashkenazi or Yoḥanan ben Isaac of Paris.
2. Or, "a homonymous noun."
3. That is, in the manner of medieval Hebrew poetry.
4. Variant: Jewish.
5. Variant: Ishmaelite.
6. Cf. Schirmann, *Haššira Ha'ibrit,* I, 578.
7. Variant: songs.

AZARIAH DE' ROSSI

Azariah (Bonaiuto) ben Moshe de' Rossi (Min Ha'adumim) (ca. 1511–ca. 1578), the epitome of a Renaissance man, member of an eminent Italian Jewish family, was born and educated in Mantua. He made his living as a physician, spending most of his adult life in various Italian cities, including Ferrara, where his major work, Me'or 'Ênayim *[The Light/Enlightenment of the Eyes, from Prov 15:30], was written. He returned to Mantua toward the end of his life and died there shortly after supervising the printing of his book.*

Me'or 'Ênayim, *published in 1573, when de' Rossi was over sixty years old, is in many respects an amazing work. It bears testimony to the vast erudition and critical mind of its author. Authorities cited in it include Greek philosophers (which de' Rossi read in Latin translation), classical rhetoricians and historians, Church Fathers, medieval Latin and Italian authors, and Renaissance writers (especially Pico della Mirandola). Of course, Jewish sources (Bible, Talmud, medieval works) are also cited. In fact, de' Rossi took special note of Jewish writings from the Hellenistic period, and he was the first Jew in fifteen hundred years to focus attention on Philo (whom he called by the Hebrew translation of his name, Yedidya the Alexandrian). Through judicious research, de' Rossi was able to show that Philo used the Greek translation of the Bible (Septuagint) and not the Hebrew text.*

Me'or 'Ênayim *contains three parts: "Qol 'Elohim," "Hadrat Zeqenim," and "'Imrê Bina."*[1] *The first describes the earthquake which de' Rossi experienced in Ferrara in 1571, and which prompted the writing of the book. The description of the earthquake and its effect on the population is followed by a discourse on the reason for and significance of earthquakes in a wide range of sources, Jewish and non-Jewish, ancient and medieval. The second part of the book, "Hadrat Zeqenim," is a Hebrew translation of the Letter of Aristeas, which had been unknown to the Jews till that time.*

The third part, "'Imrê Bina," is the longest and most important part of the book. It is a work of Jewish historiography, containing a number of critical innovations, not unlike those in critical histories during the Renaissance. For the period of ancient history, de' Rossi compared the Talmud with classical (both Jewish and non-Jewish) sources, often to the disadvantage of the Talmud. (He did not, however, apply this critical method to the Bible.) In a detailed examination of Jewish chronology, he determined that the Jewish calendar in use in his day, which dated years from the Creation, was of comparatively recent origin, and that its claim to accuracy could not be substantiated from ancient sources. Among other subjects which Me'or 'Ênayim *takes up are archeology, numismatics, the development of the Hebrew language, and biblical poetry.*

The book, innovative as it was in its outlook and methodology, and critical as it was of the historical accuracy of the Talmud, elicited controversy among Jews and was banned in many communities. Even in Mantua, where the book was printed and where the orthodox conduct of the author was known, it was forbidden for a person under twenty-five years of age to read it. As a result, Me'or 'Ênayim *had little influence on Jewish scholarship until it was rediscovered in the period of the Haskalah (Enlightenment) at the end of the eighteenth century. The situation was different among Christians. De' Rossi's work was better accepted by Christians than by Jews. Witness the fact that Johannes Buxtorf II included a Latin translation of chapter 60 of* Me'or 'Ênayim *in his appendix to* Liber Cosri, *whence it came to the attention of Robert Lowth.*

De' Rossi's chapter on poetry is as erudite and sophisticated as the rest of his book. It is, in hindsight, a precursor to modern perceptions of biblical poetry. Certainly it influenced Robert Lowth, and Lowth influenced all who followed him. But a proper understanding of de' Rossi requires an understanding of his context. For, while there is no question that he was innovative, his innovations did not spring ex nihilo, but derive from his predecessors and the thought of his Renaissance contemporaries to an extent not generally appreciated.

De' Rossi begins by citing Judah Halevi and Don Isaac Abravanel, with whom he agrees that biblical poetry lacked quantitative meter (of the medieval Hebrew type). He then cites the earlier views of classical authors—Philo, Josephus, Eusebius, and Jerome—who did find quantitative meter (of the classical type) in biblical poetry. Finally, he refers to Moshe ibn Ḥabib, who claimed to have found evidence of extrabiblical metrical poetry in Hebrew from First Temple times. De' Rossi wished to sort out these conflicting views and ascertain the true nature of biblical poetry. He does this in a most clever way—one that allows him to view the question of meter in biblical poetry in an entirely new light.

*There must be some rhythmic or metrical quality that distinguished poetry from the other discourse in the Bible, reasoned de' Rossi. One could sense it in the recitation of the words, yet no one could analyze it. If these "structures and measures" were not to be found in the number of syllables or feet, they must lie elsewhere. De' Rossi concludes that they are in the "number of ideas" (*mispar ha'inyanim).

Both terms, number (mispar) *and* ideas ('inyanim), *are significant. De' Rossi uses* number *rather frequently, whereas his predecessors use it hardly at all, preferring terms such as* mišqal, *"meter." This would seem to indicate that de' Rossi adopted the Renaissance concept of* numerus *as opposed to* metrum, *as discussed above in chapter 4. That is, he freed himself completely of the notion of quantitative meter in the Bible (and in this sense sided with Halevi and Abravanel).*[2] *But this does not mean that he had to abandon the search for meter, for in the Renaissance the notion of the* number *of syllables, rather than the* type *of syllables, began to serve as the criterion for meter. However, in a move that takes him beyond the normative view of the Renaissance, de' Rossi also rejected the number of* syllables *as the key to biblical meter. The key to biblical meter lay, said de' Rossi, not in the number of syllables but in the number of* ʻinyanim.

The word ʻinyanim *(singular:* ʻinyan*) in de' Rossi's context is usually rendered today as "ideas" or "thought units." In medieval Hebrew it meant, among other things, "sense, meaning." It is the term used to translate Arabic* maʻāni *(singular:* maʻnā*), "theme" or "meaning as opposed to form."*[3] *Although it is doubtful that de' Rossi knew the Arabic background of the term, he must have been familiar with the term* ʻinyan *from Hebrew writings, specifically ibn Tibbon's translation of* The Kuzari *2.72, to which he refers several times. In this passage* ʻinyanim *is used twice: once to mean "meaning" and once to mean "signs": "In the remnant that remains of our language . . . subtle but profound signs [*ʻinyanim*] are embedded to promote the understanding of the meaning [*ʻinyanim*]. . . . These are the [masoretic] accents." Herein lies the view that (1) in biblical poetry meaning takes precedence over meter, and (2) the masoretic accents, which indicate the meaning, are a kind of substitute for meter. This view is repeated in a number of sources (see, e.g., Archivolti), and de' Rossi was undoubtedly aware of it. It would seem that de' Rossi is borrowing this view with an important change.*[4] *For him it is a question not of meaning versus meter (as it was for Halevi) but of meaning as the structuring device of meter. "Ideas" provide the basic building blocks of biblical poetry.*[5] *His innovation is that* ideas can be counted, and that when counted they produce a regular, balanced pattern. *In other words, de' Rossi does find meter in biblical poetry; however, it is not the meter of sounds but rather the meter of ideas.*[6]

Over what length of text does this "meter" operate? The first point to recognize is that de' Rossi does not take the verse as the basic prosodic unit, as most did before him. Here, too, he applies a semantic criterion, dividing verses into "clauses" based on semantic phrasing (and sometimes on grammatical criteria, such as subject and predicate). Clauses are further broken down into "measures." The number of measures may vary, even within one verse, but according to de' Rossi's analysis, a clause with two measures has subjoined to it another with two measures, a clause with three has another with three, and so on. The "metrical pattern" is in the pairing of clauses with the same number of ideas. This may sound to a modern scholar like the discovery of parallelism, but it was not. It remained for Robert Lowth to take that step; de' Rossi was seeking meter. The relationship that he perceived between clauses was mathematical, not grammatical and/or semantic, as in our understanding of parallelism. So intent was de' Rossi on the mathematical precision of his system that he occasionally had to eliminate a word from the count, and even so he was forced to admit that he could not fit all poetic verses to his system.[7]

De' Rossi's system has much to recommend it (although it was largely ignored for many years). For de' Rossi himself, it must have cut the intellectual Gordian knot of the question of meter. It also has certain religious-nationalistic ramifications.

Why does de' Rossi cite numerous classical sources which hold that biblical poetry has meter when he disagrees with this view? There is, I think, a tension here, an ambivalence that did not trouble Judah Halevi (who did not hesitate to say that metrical poetry was a late borrowing into Hebrew from Arabic). De' Rossi wanted very much for biblical poetry to have meter—to have the regular hexameters and such that classical poetry had (he was living, after all, in Renaissance Italy).[8] *"Ought we not believe that all the songs in the Holy Scriptures . . . and the books of Job, Proverbs, and Psalms, all of them, without doubt, observe an arrangement and structure?" Yet he could not fool himself into believing that biblical poetry employed quantitative or syllabic meter. So he discovered a substitute: a "metrical system" which was the equivalent of classical tetrameters, hexameters, and the like. It is no accident that he speaks of "two measures," "four measures," etc.—that is, dimeter, tetrameter, etc. This meant that biblical poetry had the virtue of being metrical, in the manner in which de' Rossi defined it. And it also meant, as de' Rossi points out in the name of his colleague Judah Provenzali, that Hebrew poetry was not a latecomer to the metrical scene (as Halevi had said) but that its metrical system preceded all others. Here, as elsewhere in* Me'or 'Ênayim, *one finds that along with his commitment to rational analysis, de' Rossi maintained his commitment to his tradition. His blending of the two yielded a new perspective on biblical poetry.*

Editions and Translations: Me'or 'Ênayim *(Mantua, 1573); ed. David Cassel (1866; reprint, Jerusalem, 1970).*[9] *Chapter 60 is translated into Latin in the appendix of Johannes Buxtorf's* Liber Cosri. *See also J. Kugel,* The Idea of Biblical Poetry, *200–201. Joanna Weinberg is preparing a complete translation, to be published in the Yale Judaica Series.*

Me'or 'Ênayim

Chapter 60

On Poems Composed in the Holy Tongue

Since I have been speaking of our holy tongue—its letters, vowels, and accents—I would also like to touch upon the poems composed in it, both modern and ancient. I would note that the godly sage [Judah Halevi], author of *The Kuzari*, near the end of his second discourse [2.67ff.], when he shows the superiority of our aforementioned language over all other languages, from tradition and from logic [i.e., from the interpretation of scriptural verses and from logical inference], as it seemed to him, concluded there that the poems which some of our later sages tried to enhance with musical compositions, thereby making them metered in respect to complete and incomplete syllables—that, as far as is known, these are not natural to the Hebrew language but are derived from Arabic. For, on the contrary, Hebrew precludes them since its natural [form of] composition is that which is acquired through the accents which indicate the ideas [or "meanings"; Hebrew: *'inyanim*]. And the fact that the aforementioned sages considered a composition to be [poetic] by virtue of the meter of the syllables, as was stated—to him [Judah Halevi] this is simply a difference of opinion, as he explained at length in the reference that we cited.

Sharing this opinion is the sage Don Isaac [Abravanel] in his commentary on Isa 5:1, for he stated how in our holy tongue there are found three types of poems. The first type is poems metered in terms of syllables and rhymed, customary among us today, not by reason of Holy Scripture but borrowed from Arabic poetry—indeed, more praiseworthy than theirs. The second type is poems which are distinguished from the rest of [biblical] writings not by virtue of the words themselves or any other aspect of them, but by virtue of their euphony and [the fact that] they are sung, such as the Song of the Sea [Exodus 15], Ha'azinu [Deuteronomy 32], [the Song of] Deborah [Judges 5], the Song of David [2 Samuel 22], and others like them. And the third type is poems which are not identifiable as such by virtue of the words or the voice of the singer but only by virtue of their meaning, in that the sense is not literal, but, on the contrary, the best of it is its falseness [i.e., they use metaphorical language], such as the Song of Songs and the aforementioned Song of Isaiah [Isaiah 5]. And that this [the use of metaphorical language] is essentially what constitutes poetry, first and foremost, is what The Philosopher [Aristotle] wrote in his famous Book of Poetics.

Thus, the words of these sages, [the author of] *The Kuzari* and Don Isaac [Abravanel], appear to be indeed correct, since we do not find in all of Scripture even one [poem written] in the manner of those [later] poets [i.e., poems with meter].

However, opposed to this view you will find Yedidya [Philo] of Alexandria, who we said lived before the destruction of the Second Temple, for in the chapter that was described [above], from *De Vita Contemplativa*,[10] when he mentions how there were then among the Jews sects of men and women who separated from worldly passions in order to serve God and seek wisdom, like all the orders of brothers and sisters that are found today among the Christians, he stated: "These people, in addition to giving themselves over to introspection, compose poems of several types of regular feet to sing in divine worship." After several sections in the same chapter he wrote further: "When the president would see that the lessons were finished and the sound of discussion had ceased, then he would rise and recite another hymn in praise of God, be it his original composition or one taken from the compositions of a poet [lit.: prophet] of old. Thus, the ancients had many types of metrical poems, with three measures, and hymns with melodies for singing during the service before the altar."

Likewise Josephus [Flavius], at the end of his second book for the Romans [*Jewish Antiquities* II, 16:4] wrote that the Song of the Sea [Exodus 15] is hexameter, i.e., a poem with six measures, and in book IV, chapter 8 he wrote the same thing about the Ha'azinu Song [Deuteronomy 32]—that it has six measures in the holy tongue.

Also [Eusebius] the Caesarean, who lived about two hundred years after the destruction [of the Second Temple], in his *Praeparatio Evangelica*, book XII, 16,[11] wrote: "Plato said that it is proper for poems recited to honor God to be metrical and euphonious. Now, this lesson that we learn from him [Plato] through words, the Jews show us through deeds. For hymns and metrical poetry for divine worship were not customary among them, except those composed by the prophets [i.e., biblical authors] through the Holy Spirit."

Likewise, the Translator for the Christians [Jerome], in his *Letter to Paula*, wrote that some of the psalms are poems having three measures, and some having four, and such is the Ha'azinu Song and also Proverbs, and the chapters in Lamentations are also poems having measure, but they are each different from the other. For Lamentations 1 and Lamentations 4 [*sic;* should be 2] have three measures included in one verse, and Lamentations 3 has triplets of three [measures in] three [verses], and Lamentations 4 is similar to the first chapters." In his preface to the Book of Job he wrote that its [Job's] beginning and ending are simple prose, but the dialogues are poems with six measures in different forms which he compared to many poems of the Roman sages. Whosoever does not believe his words—that metrical poems are found in the Holy Scriptures—will accept the testimony of Philo and Josephus and Origen and Eusebius. Likewise, in the preface to Eusebius's *Chronicon*, wherein he [Jerome] spoke about the superiority of our holy tongue and the difficulty of conveying its natural beauty in translation into any other language, he said: "What book has as lovely songs as the Book of Psalms, which is comparable to the poetry of the Roman Horace and the poetry of the Greek Pindar? Does it not sometimes move quickly in the manner of iambic and sometimes resound like alcaic and sometimes become inflated like sapphic and sometimes proceed in half-feet? And what song is as beautiful as the Song of Moses in Deuteronomy 32 and the Song of Isaiah in Isaiah 5? Are not these poems worthy of as much honor as the songs of King Solomon and as perfect as those of Job? And all of these which we mentioned have five or six measures, just as Josephus and Origen wrote."[12]

In a small work published with the grammar entitled *Darkê No'am* by [Moshe] ibn Ḥabib you will find these words: "When I was in the kingdom of Valencia in the community of Murviedro all the people at the gate and the elders told me that there was a tombstone of an army officer of Amaziah, king of Judah, and then I hastened to see it. It is a stone monument on the top of a mountain, and after toil and trouble I read the inscription. There was a poem engraved on it and it reads: *se'u qina beqol mara / lesar gadol leqaḥo yah //* ['Raise a lament in a bitter voice / for the great officer whom the Lord has taken //']. I was not able to see more, but the poem[13] concludes 'to Amaziah.' Then I believed that this kind of metrical poetry was customary from the days when our fathers were [dwelling] in their land."

Indeed, according to these sages, our holy tongue in its nature and usage from earliest days does not preclude poems with measure and meter, not only by virtue of the melody in which they were sung, in accord with Don Isaac [Abravanel]'s statement cited above, but by reason of the words themselves.[14] And [according to those same sages] some of these [metrical poems] were found in the Bible. Nevertheless, I inquired of many contemporary sages whether they knew how to find and identify in them [biblical poems] any measure or meter, but no one could. But, while everyone acknowledges that the euphony of the poetry resounds in the recitation, no one could account for the difference between them [the metrical poems] and the rest of the words of the Torah, Prophets, and Writings in respect to the melody.

As my cares welled up within me to resolve these [diverse] opinions and to discover part of what is sought, my heart tells me that there are, without doubt, measures and structures in the aforementioned biblical poems, but they are not dependent on the number of complete or incomplete syllables, as in the poems common among us nowadays, for these are, in the words of *The Kuzari*, practices of Arabic poetry, which represents a corruption of our language. Rather, their structures and measures are in the number of ideas and their parts, from subject to predicate and that which is conjoined to them, in every clause[15] and phrase that is written. There are cases in which a clause contains two measures, and together with the second [clause] attached to it there will be four [measures]. And there are cases containing three, and together with the second there will be six complete measures.

An example of this is *your-right-hand, O-Lord* [Exod 15:6]. This is one independent clause containing two units, or, one could say, two measures. *Glorious in-power*, which is similar to it [in the number of measures], is attached to it, and together they have four [measures]. Likewise the second *your-right-hand O-Lord* has two others, and *shatters the-foe* has two more, and together they have four. In the same manner is *the-foe said / I-will-pursue I-will-overtake / I-will-divide the-spoil / my-desire shall-have-its-fill-of-them / I-will-bare my-sword / my-hand shall-subdue-them / you-make-blow with-your-wind*, and so forth. However, the Ha'azinu Song has 3–3, which make six, e.g., *give-ear O-heavens and-let-me-speak / let-the-earth hear my-words / may-my-discourse come-down like-rain / may-my-speech distill like-dew*, and so forth. Sometimes within a single verse, and even more so throughout an entire song, both of these types of measures will occur—two-two and three-three—according to how the poet [lit.: prophet] was inspired and as the variation suits the meaning. An example of this is [Exod 15:8]: *by-the-breath of-your-nostrils / the-waters piled-up*, which is two-two; *the-flowing-waters stood-erect like-a-wall / the-deep froze in-the-heart-of-the-sea*, which is three-three. Likewise, the Song of the Well [Num 21:17–18]: begins three-three and afterward follows two-two. Similarly, the Prayer of Habakkuk (which is *'al šigyonot* [Hab 3:1], like *šigayon ledawid* [Ps 7:1], and he gave it to the conductor of melodies which were fitting for it, as it says "to the conductor of my melodies" [Hab 3:19]) proceeds in three-three [Hab 3:3]: *God comes from-Teman / the-Holy-One from-Mount-Paran sela / his-majesty covers the-skies / his-splendor fills the-earth.*

In some utterances the intelligent reader must recognize a few words which for some reason are not included in these measures, as in the Ha'azinu Song [Deut 32:20]. The word *wayo'mer* ["he said"] is an independent utterance, and so *I-will-hide my-face from-them* counts as three measures, *I-will-see what is-after-them* as another three, and so forth. And the two occurrences of the Tetragrammaton in the Prayer of Habakkuk [3:2] which signal the vocative are each independent [of the metrical count], and thus the phrases in which they are located are three-three.[16] Hab 3:17 works in a different way: subject and predicate. *For-the-fig-tree* is the subject, and the predicate is *does-not-blossom*; so the whole verse contains twelve utterances which can be resolved into six stopped clauses [*ma'amarim posqim*]. For you should count neither syllables nor words but only the ideas. And in regard to this, often a small word is to be joined to whatever is next to it. So verses in Psalms observe the arrangement which we have described: [Ps 51:3] *favor-me God as-befits-your-faithfulness* is three; [as is] *as-befits-your-great-compassion blot-out my-transgression.* [Ps 56:11]: *in-God whose-word I-praise / in-the-Lord whose-word I-praise.* Also in Proverbs [1:20]: *wisdom cries-aloud in-the-streets / in-the-squares she-raises her-voice.*

It has not escaped my notice that there are many verses which I am unable to fit into the systems described above, and perhaps the exceptions outnumber those that follow the rules. So, then, following my line of argument, may intelligent readers be enlightened and proceed to discover what has escaped me. In any event, ought we not believe that all the songs in the Holy Scriptures—the Song of the Sea, [the Song of] the Well, Ha'azinu, [the Song of] Deborah, and the Song of David—and the books of Job, Proverbs, and Psalms, all of them, without doubt, observe an arrangement and structure, this in one style and that in another, or even one [song] itself having different measures? For, indeed, we sense when we recite them a special quality even if we cannot completely discern their structures; just as we also speak, stand up, and sit down without being aware of which parts of the body perform these actions, for they are instinctive [lit.: by virtue of divine wisdom] to us. Especially regarding the poems of David which were recited before the altar of the Lord there is no doubt, as *The Kuzari* said in the second discourse [2.65], that they used to set them to music, and that there [in biblical Israel] it [music] reached perfection and would arouse the soul with its special quality.

Now do not be surprised by our statement that one poem can have different measures, for if you are familiar with the types of poetry of great poets of other nations, such as Horace, Terence, and others, it will be clear to you that they, too, do likewise—everything being in accord with the appropriateness of the meaning of the subject, and the variations which occur in it due to the motions of the body and the soul.

Know, intelligent reader, that I desired to hear the reaction to this inquiry of a certain notable contemporary authority, especially since he is knowledgeable about matters of poetry. I put my words to the discerning one, the third of the Provenzali brothers—they are luminaries in my country, Mantua—he is Rabbi Judah [Provenzali], author of *Seper Nepuṣot Yehuda*.[17] I presented my essay to him from the beginning of this chapter until here, and according to his words (he being a man who does not deceive), my explanation seemed correct to him. He also added on his own that instead of the statement that our modern [poets] borrowed suitable poetic techniques from the ancients of other nations, we can give honor to our own tongue and people and say the opposite: on the contrary, the ancients of other nations had already borrowed from the ancients of our nation. And you can find support for him from what the Rabbi and Teacher [Maimonides] wrote in [*The Guide of the Perplexed*] part I, chapter 71, and similarly [Abraham ben Shem Tov Bibago], author of *Derek 'Emuna*, section 3, that there was great wisdom in early times in Israel, but when other nations ruled us it came into their hands; and to us, when we then learned something from them, it appeared as though they originated it, but it was the reverse.

Be that as it may, our inquiry thus far has established that the words of *The Kuzari* and Don Isaac [Abravanel] which we cited at the beginning of this chapter—i.e., that they deny the existence of biblical poems with quantitative [lit.: pegs and cords] meter like those customary nowadays—are the words of true and discerning sages. But, this not withstanding, we will not desist from affirming that there are, without doubt, different measures, dependent on ideas, in the manner we discussed; and for this reason they [biblical poems] are superior to those that depend on syllables. If you discern the true meaning of the aforecited words of *The Kuzari*, you will see that it touches on some of what we have written. Your own eyes will see additional superiority in the various poems of the prophets [i.e., biblical authors], for is it not possible to translate some of them into another language and still preserve their meter, or almost so, whereas this is impossible in poems in which the rhythm is dependent on syllables and their number, as is obvious to all who know?[18] Moreover, if the matter of the army officer of Amaziah is true, we will not be able to deny that the [poetic] practice among us today (which according to *The Kuzari* and Don Isaac [Abravanel] is borrowed from Arabic) was current from that time among some common people for ordinary purposes, [but] not among poets [who composed] through the Holy Spirit.[19]

Furthermore, among the things that one should consider in this context, albeit I do not see contemporary poets who are mindful of it, is that among the nations that preserve and organize their wisdom in suitable ways, you will find that every poem observes the meter suitable to its subject: there is a difference between the meter of joyful poems, called by them lyric, and the meter of poems of mourning, called elegy, and the meter of heroic [poems] which they compose to glorify a hero or great king compared to a divine being, and so forth in this manner. We should do likewise in poems composed in meter, such that their structures suit their purpose, and not every meter should be determined by whim. By way of example, the rhythm that you find among the best of the poets and their predecessors in poems of joy or praise or prayer is not appropriate for the meter of lamentations or epitaphs and the like. For the words of the poem must be correct for the voice, just as the voice must be correct for the required occasion. Won't you consider the valid observation that we made above in reference to the Book of Lamentations: that in Lamentations 1 and 2 each verse contains three stopped clauses [*ma'amarim posqim*], and each stopped clause contains subject and predicate with its accompaniments; Lamentations 3 likewise preserves their manner [i.e., has the same structure]—for this reason it is attached to them—but it [each verse] is divided into three sections. But Lamentations 4 does not contain its ideas in each verse, only two-two which are four.[20] Look and you will find, and from this you will know that these were their ways [of composing] lamentations. And thus Josephus wrote for the Romans, [*Jewish Antiquities*] book 10, chapter 6,[21] that Jeremiah lamented over Josiah in a poem composed in a rhythm[22] of mourning and sorrow. Not so Lamentations 5, which is a prayer. You will see that it is constructed in a different style—that is, one-one which are two, similar to the verses in Job, Proverbs, and Psalms which we mentioned.[23] Likewise the Ha'azinu Song and the Song of Deborah preserve a different meter of three-three which are six, like heroic poetry, which is considered by them [the classical poets] the best and noblest. So, I will not belabor the point, for these words of mine are just a small and insignificant part of what could be said. The wise [reader] will understand and add [to them] with discerning sensitivity.

There follow a number of paragraphs dealing with epitaphs and related matters. Azariah provides his own epitaph and one for his grandson. Toward the end of the chapter he returns to the subject of poetry.

So, now let us leave these matters and return to the main point of the chapter. Let us accept this principle: that poems based on the rhythm of pegs and cords—according to their number and rules—are not truly natural to our language, and the sage [Judah Halevi, author of] *The Kuzari* was correct in his statement that they [i.e., those who attempt to impose meter on Hebrew] go against its excellent character in that for the most part they move forward where they should pause and pause where they should move forward [that is, they do not differentiate between mobile and quiescent *shwas*], and they connect what should be separate and separate what should be connected—and other such damage as is caused by one who does not take proper care. But the poems proper to it [Hebrew] are those that preserve their melodies in terms of ideas, in accord with the words of the prophets [biblical poets] that we mentioned. God in his goodness will open our eyes, and we will draw from his Torah wonders galore before his great acts of faithfulness forever. Sela.

There follows a long closure for the book as a whole.

NOTES

1. A response which de' Rossi wrote to his critics, entitled "Maṣrep Lakkesep," is often printed along with the book.

2. All pre-Renaissance authors who discover meter in the Bible are speaking of quantitative meter. Even those who discover what we would call syllabic meter perceive it as a simple form of quantitative meter.

3. This was pointed out to me by Raymond Scheindlin. See also Allony, *Ha'egron*, 153, note 27. The Arabic and Hebrew terms share the same root and are phonetically similar, prompting their equivalence for purposes of translation.

4. De' Rossi twice cites *The Kuzari* to support his own position. Once he says: "If you discern the true meaning of the aforecited words of *The Kuzari*, you will see that it touches on some of what we have written." In summing up his position, near the end of the chapter, de' Rossi again stresses the correctness of Judah Halevi and the closeness of Halevi's position to his own.

5. De' Rossi does not bring the masoretic accents into the discussion.

6. Lowth calls it the "rhythmus of things." "Things" is the English translation for Buxtorf's Latin *rerum*, by which he renders *'inyanim*.

7. He accepts as poetry those passages traditionally considered as such: the "songs" and the books of Job, Proverbs, and Psalms. He does not apply his system to other parts of the Bible, with the exception of Habakkuk 3, which is labeled a "prayer" and contains the term *šigyonot*, also found in Psalms and understood as a musical term.

8. He lauds the fact that the classical poets varied their meters to suit their different poetic genres.

9. For a complete listing of editions, see Weinberg, "*Azariah de' Rossi: Towards a Reappraisal of the Last Years of His Life*," 493, note 1.

10. III and X. Cf. Colson, *Philo*, vol. IX, 128–31, 162–63.

11. The reference appears to be to chapter 22 in our editions. Cf. Gifford, *Eusebius: Preparation for the Gospel*, 645.

12. For Jerome's *Letter to Paula* cf. Migne, *Patrologiae cursus completus. patrum latinorum. patrum graecorum*, 22, 442–43 (Letter XXX); for Job cf. ibid., 28, 1081–82; for the *Preface to the Chronicon* cf. ibid., 27, 36. For a discussion of some of these passages see Kugel, *The Idea of Biblical Poetry*, 152–56.

13. "Poem" or "verse." *Darkê No'am* reads *haššir haššeni*. See note *ad loc.*

14. That is, the poems did not get their meter secondarily, when they were set to music, but their words were written *ab initio* to be metrical.

15. "Clause" is used here loosely, as some do not contain a subject and a predicate.

16. Azariah divides the verse as follows:

> Lord, I have heard your renown and I am afraid
> Renew your deeds in the midst of years.

This is different from the division of the verse in NJPS and NEB. Although Azariah here considers "in the midst of years" [*beqereb šanim*] one word, he must consider it two words in the following phrase.

17. This is Judah ben Abraham Provenzali, brother of David and Moses. The family was one of the prominent families of Mantua. Another contemporary of de' Rossi, Judah Moscato, wrote a book with the same title, *Nepuṣot Yehuda.*

18. Moshe ibn Tibbon makes a similar observation about the translatability of poems in which meaning takes precedence over meter. For a modern view on the translatability of parallelism, see apRoberts, "Old Testament Poetry: The Translatable Structure."

19. That is, the Jews in biblical times utilized quantitative meter for everyday purposes, but not in scriptural writings. The implication is that quantitative meter was not borrowed from the Arabs.

20. This seems to mean that the verses in Lamentations 4 are not made up of three independent sentences, like the preceding chapters, but that they are composed of two pairs of phrases.

21. The reference is in book 10, chapter 5 in our editions. See also Rashi on Lam 4:1.

22. The Cassel edition reads *bemiqṣat* ("a modicum"), but Buxtorf has *bemiqṣab* ("in the rhythm of"), which is preferable.

23. Lowth, *Isaiah,* xxxiii, notes that "the fifth chapter does not at all seem to answer that description. Besides, he says the verses of it are like those of Job, Psalms, and Proverbs, of two of which books he said before that the verses were trimeters. I know not what he means, unless it be that one and one sentences make two, that is, a distich; and that this chapter consists of distiches, of two short lines, as the books of Job, Psalms, and Proverbs, for the most part do; which is true." The last is what de' Rossi apparently meant.

SAMUEL ARCHIVOLTI

Samuel ben Elḥanan Jacob Archivolti (1515–1611), an Italian Jewish poet and grammarian, produced a number of works, among them 'Arugat Habbosem *[The Bed of Spices, from Song 5:13]. This is a grammar, beginning with a discussion of letters and parts of speech, verbal tenses and conjugations, etc., and concluding with an explanation of Hebrew accentuation and poetic form. We present here parts of chapters 31 and 32 containing some of Archivolti's views on language: the relationship between spoken and written discourse; the relationship between melody and words in song and poetry; his use and explanation of Judah Halevi's* Kuzari; *his division of discourse into four types; and his identification of rhyme in the Bible. He also suggests that the Bible employed a simple form of meter.*

Editions and Translations: 'Arugat Habbosem *(Venice, 1602; Amsterdam, 1730). Johannes Buxtorf II translated chapter 31 and the beginning of chapter 32 into Latin in the appendix to* Liber Cosri.

'Arugat Habbosem

CHAPTER 31. [An introductory paragraph precedes.] I will begin by saying that there are three means of acquiring human perfection, and they are the enlightenment of the soul [i.e., philosophical thought], speech, and written composition. We find that the enlightenment of the soul is broader [i.e., less ambiguous] than speech, for speech has limitations—for instance, the word *ḥariput* can be used in reference to odor, to the sword, to intellectual sharpness, and the like, with a different connotation in each—while in the enlightened soul each concept is kept distinct. But, on the other hand, we find that speech is more meritorious than the enlightenment of the soul and the logic of the heart [i.e., thoughts of the mind], since these benefit only those who possess them, while speech benefits others as well. Similarly, written composition has greater power than speech, for speech benefits only the listeners, the contemporaries of the speaker, while written composition benefits the contemporaries of the writer and future generations. On this Job said: "O that my words be written" [Job 19:23].

However, in another respect speech is less circumscribed than written composition, for speech is aided by the gestures of the speaker—he winks his eyes, points his fingers, or makes other movements to tell one what his discourse is about, until the logic of his heart is reproduced in the mind of the listeners. On this they say: "From the mouth of scribes, not from the mouth of books." Written composition cannot convey as full expression as speech does by these movements. However, to fill this deficit in written composition came the accents, with their melodies and rules which give understanding to hidden things. The accents also serve in place of the actions that occur during speech.

There are two types of melodies. The first is the melody constructed on the words, with a view toward their meaning.[1] For a change in the sound distinguishes between a break and a connection, speeding up and slowing down, joy and sadness, surprise and dread, and so forth. This is the most praiseworthy melody in music, for it is designed not only to give pleasure to the ear, but also to give spirit and animation to the words pronounced. This is the type that the Levites used, for without it they would not have been able to arrange musical accompaniments. And it is the appropriate one for the composing of songs in our holy tongue. The second type is the popular melody on which the words of the song are constructed. Its purpose is only appeal to the ear. As a result, many songs whose meanings are far removed—as far as east is from west—may all share the same popular melody if they have the same meter and rhyme.

Now listen to the words of the Kuzari:[2] "Wherein is the superiority of the holy tongue, seeing that other languages have the advantage of having composed poems (meaning metered and rhymed) constructed on melodies?" (In other words, [poems] that relate from the outset, in their meters and rhymes, to known melodies which had been composed for other words with the same meter. These are of the second type of which we spoke. In terms of the perfection of our holy tongue, this is appropriate; it lacks nothing, this type being not as perfect as the first.) Since the Kuzari assumes that all melodies were necessitated by the meter and the rhyme, the Advocate responded that "it has become clear to me that the melodies are not necessitated by the meter of the speech, that, whether [metrically] empty or full, one can play 'Praise the Lord for he is good' [Ps 136:1] to the same melody as 'Who alone works great marvels' [Ps136:4]." (That is, one can play a metrically empty [line] such as "Praise the Lord for he is good," which does not have syllables of equal length, to the same melody as a metrically full [line] such as "Who alone works great marvels," in which every word has three syllables.) He continued: "This is in the melodies which are active [*ba'alê ma'asim*]" (in other words, which have the power to give accent [or: meaning; Hebrew: *ṭa'am*] to the words and to make them enter the soul of the listeners, like the actions of the gestures and winks which we mentioned). "But for poems called *'anshadia*,[3] rhymed utterances (constructed on melodies, these being of the second type mentioned), in which the [metrical] composition is becoming (that is, in these rhymed verses the composition, based on one melody for all [poems] of the same meter, without concern for providing understanding of their meanings, is becoming), they (the authors of the holy tongue) had no feeling, because of the greater superiority of the accents," as he goes on to explain. Finally the Advocate admits that we sinned, transgressed, and erred by bringing the rival of the Hebrew language into her house, by employing the meters of popular secular poetry. . . .

Archivolti goes on to condemn the spread of popular melodies to liturgical poetry, since one should distinguish the holy from the profane.

CHAPTER 32. THE WAYS OF POETRY. I open my lips with forthrightness to know and inform that we do not intend to speak here about the poetry which is [defined as] "Its best is its falseness," about which the Philosopher [Aristotle] wrote the Book of Poetics. Also, not about the poetry which the Caesarean [Eusebius] wrote about in his book *Praeparatio Evangelica* XII, 16: "Plato said that it is proper that songs recited to honor God should be metrical and euphonious. Now this is the lesson that we learn from him through words. The Hebrews show us through deeds, for hymns and metrical poetry for divine worship were not customary among them, except those composed by the prophets through the Holy Spirit." We will not discuss this here because its ways are high-flown, in order to cause wonder, and who can reach its heights except if the spirit of the Lord causes miracles in him. However, we will engage in a discussion of poems composed by the ancient poets, some of the ways of biblical poetry.

We begin with [the observation that] there are four types of discourse: simple [i.e., ordinary] discourse, rhetorical discourse, enigmatic discourse,[4] poetic discourse. Simple discourse follows only the rules of grammar, when one person speaks to another.

Rhetorical discourse is not satisfied only with the rules of grammar, but chooses the best of euphonious words, those which appeal to the listener, to bring him close and persuade him of all that the speaker wishes. This discourse gives glory to kings, and God, may he be blessed, desires it like a burnt offering, as in "take words with you" [Hos 14:3]; for one should not elicit words for him haphazardly, as it says: "Let not your heart hasten to elicit a word before God" [Ecc 5:1]. They said [that this means] "A person should always arrange his prayer, and afterward pray," for prayer is a substitute for sacrifice, as it says: "Instead of bulls, we will pay [the offerings of] our lips" [Hos 14:3]. Is it not the rule to guard against linguistic pitfalls which the grammarians and rhetoricians opposed strongly, lest it be like sacrificing a defective animal, or at least like being suspected of not having sacrificed the firstborn of the flock?

Enigmatic discourse observes the aforementioned points and hides in it something in succinct, unexpected words which lead to the desire to solve the difficult matter. And from this, the one who understands derives pleasure, when he puts twists in the straightforward. [Archivolti provides a biblical example, explained as a riddle.] Riddle [*ḥida*] and *mašal* are related, almost synonyms, in that both are, in their intent, like layers of clothing to the wearer; but riddle is the covering and hiding of a revealed thing, and *măsal* is a way of making the understanding of a hidden thing easier by comparing it to a similar thing. . . .

Poetic discourse is not only mindful of grammar, rhetoric, and succinct wording, but also observes meter and rhyme. Meter is the regulating of the number of syllables in one half [of the line] to the number of syllables in the other half, as we will explain. And rhyme [*yaḥas*] is the observance of rhyme at the ends of lines, as we will explain. All of these were composed in order to make the discourse fit to match the melodies of the accents, so that the aural effect of the written word would be the same as that of the spoken word, to reproduce in the hearts [of the listeners] the intent [of the speaker], as we mentioned. With these will we deal.

However, it is proper to take care that poetry not lead you to accent the penultimate instead of the ultimate, or vice versa; and also not to make a quiescent *shwa* into a mobile *shwa;* also not to divide words in half. Every verb that you wish to employ in your poetry, see if it occurs in that form [*binyan*] in the Bible, for the rhythmic requirement of poetry does not permit you to depart from accepted linguistic usage. . . .

Archivolti defines poetic terminology, explains the rules of meter, and discusses various types of poems. He notes different types of rhyme: cases in which only the last consonants rhyme, cases in which the last two consonants rhyme, and cases in which the last three consonants rhyme.

In order to show you that rhyme had its conception and birth in the Holy [Scriptures], I present the following verses for you here:

Deut 32:6—[the rhyme is *-neka*]

הלוא הוא אביך קנך / הוא עשך ויכננך

halo' hu' 'abika qaneka / hu' 'aseka wayekoneneka.

Jud 14:18—[the rhyme is *-ti*]

לולא חרשתם בעגלתי / לא מצאתם חידתי

lule' ḥaraštem be'eglati / lo' meṣa'tem ḥidati.

Ps 115:8—[the rhyme is *-hem*]

כמוהם יהיו עשיהם / כל אשר בטח בהם

kemohem yihyu 'osêhem / kol 'aser boṭeaḥ bahem.

Prov 31:18—[the rhyme is *-rah*]

טעמה כי טוב סחרה / לא יכבה בליל נרה

ṭa'ama ki ṭob saḥrah / lo' yikbeh balayla nerah.

Prov 5:15—[the rhyme is *-reka*]

שתה מים מבורך / ונוזלים מתוך בארך

šete mayim miboreka / wenozlim mitok be'ereka.

Ps 2:3—[the rhyme is *-temo*]

ננתקה את מוסרותימו / ונשליכה ממנו עבתימו

nenatqa 'et mosrotêmo / wenašlika mimmenu 'abotêmo.

and many like these. But be careful not to rhyme *suka* with *ṣuqa* . . . or *masa* with *maṣa*. . . .

Know now that poetry comes in many types [of meter]. The first type has its origin in the "holy mountains" [the Bible]; its proceeds with four cords without a peg, that is, four [cords in a foot], which is eight [cords] in the *delet* and the same in the *soger*. It is composed in various ways. There are cases in which there is no rhyme except in the *soger*, as you see in the following [he quotes two lines of a medieval poem; the second line is Prov 10:5.]: There are cases which have one rhyme at the end of the *delet* and another rhyme at the end of the *soger*. [He quotes two lines of a poem with this rhyme scheme; the second line is the first half of Prov 8:34.]

It was not uncommon to insert a biblical verse into a medieval poem. Since all or most of a biblical verse fits into a metered poem, this verse must have been metered to begin with, thus "proving" that the Bible contains metrical verses. Cf. Moshe ibn Ezra, Kitāb al-Muḥāḍara, *end of chapter 8.*

NOTES

1. That is, the words are primary, and the melody is arranged to fit the words. The second type is the opposite: the melody is primary, and words are composed to fit the melody.

2. *Kuzari* 2.69 and following. Archivolti gives a combination of quotations from ibn Tibbon's Hebrew translation with his own interspersed explanations (indicated by parentheses).

3. The Amsterdam, 1730, edition and Buxtorf read *'ansharia*.

4. Lit.: "discourse by means of riddles." The word *ḥida* is sometimes used as a close associate of *mašal*. See Archivolti's discussion below.

ABRAHAM PORTALEONE

Abraham ben David Portaleone (1542–1612) was a noted Italian physician, from a family in Mantua which had produced numerous such physicians. In addition, he was well educated in philosophy and knew ten languages, both ancient and modern. His most famous work is Šilṭê Haggibborim *[Shields of Heroes, from Song 4:4], composed in his old age, after he had suffered a stroke which partially disabled him. It was written for his children and was to serve as a kind of penance for his having neglected the study of Torah.* Šilṭê Haggibborim, *the first Hebrew book employing European punctuation, addresses itself to all of the details of the Temple: its service, architecture, personnel, and so forth. Although it has technical sections, it is extremely discursive, drawing on all of the known sciences of the time. Chapter 4, from which our excerpt is taken, discusses the songs of the Levites and their musical instruments.*[1] *This leads to a general discourse on the history and theory of music, citing Plato by way of Marsilio Ficino, and then touches on the related issue of poetry. Portaleone reiterates the commonly accepted notion that the authors of the Bible knew all of the rules of music; indeed, they were the first to use them. But he does not find rhyme and meter in biblical poetry, for the most part, as befits true poetry according to classical and medieval definitions. He recognizes poetry in the Bible by its euphony but is at a loss to explain the scribal conventions in writing it. He does find some instances of rhyme, although these are not always true rhyme; and even more forced are his examples of meter, which he finds in what most would consider a prose passage. The meter which he finds here is syllabic, as it was in Italian poetry and then in Italian Hebrew poetry, not quantitative (cords and pegs) as it was in Spanish Hebrew poetry.*

Editions and Translations: Šilṭê Haggibborim *(Mantua, 1612); Sha'ul Shepher,* Haššir Šebammiqdaš *(Jerusalem, 1965); Daniel Sandler, "The Music Chapters of 'Shiltey ha-Giborim' by Avraham Portaleone" (Dissertation, Tel Aviv University, 1980). A Latin translation of a small section is contained in the appendix of J. Buxtorf's* Liber Cosri.

Šilṭê Haggibborim

In order to rid you of this faulty opinion, which in former days those fools continually instilled in the ears of perfectly God-fearing people like us, I have decided to write down for you briefly the rules of composed song and its characteristics, and to show you in this chapter that our holy fathers, of blessed memory, knew all its conventions and observed all its particulars exactly without deviation.

I respond by saying that rational song is a science which teaches the sensible man the modulation and harmony of many various tones which intertwine and ascend one after another, in both proper gradation and permissible combination, in order to provide the ear with a fine, clear tune with good and euphonious melody.

According to Plato in his dialogue entitled *De Justo* [= *De Republica*],[2] the parts of composed song are three: the narration, which this philosopher called *orazione* [*oratione*]; the order, or the rule for measuring time, either in silence or rest, or in quick and frequent succession in the sounds of the tune, called *ritmo* [*rhythme*]; and the arrangement of the notes suitable for song, called *armonia* [*harmoniae*].

The *orazione* is of two types: the simple, called *prosa*, and the poetic, called *verso*. The simple is direct and straightforward speech, with wisdom and understanding, expressing without any rhetorical conventions that which is enclosed and kept in the recesses of the heart alone. But the poetic is rhymed expression, with connected parts, making known the intention of the speaker with terse, arranged, and metered words. However, this definition fits only poetic narration according to the rules of poetry which our later sages invented.

As for the poems in the Torah, Prophets, and Writings, I have not come upon [those with] meter or the necessary conventions, for I do not find in them the required pegs and cords, or an equal [number of syllables] in the first and second lines of the verse [*bayit*]. I do not know why and wherefore some are written either log over brick and brick over log—like the Song of the Sea [Exodus 15] and the Song of David on the Day That the Lord Saved Him [2 Samuel 22] and the Song of Deborah [Judges 5]—or log over log and brick over brick—like the Ha'azinu Song [Deuteronomy 32] and the "Song" [i.e., the list] of the Sons of Haman [Esth 9:7–9], while others are written in a continuous [block of text] in the manner of prose narrative—like the Song of the Well [Num 21:27–29] and the whole Book of Psalms and Song of Songs and the like.

It being the case that the ancient poems are recognizable to the ear simply by virtue of the pleasantness of reciting them, even when there is no difference in the way they are written, as I have said, nevertheless I cannot hide the fact that in some of the ancient *mešalim* which resemble poems I have found rhymes at the end of verses [*batim*]. However, the number of syllables is usually not the same, as, for instance [Num 21:27–29], "*Bo'u ḥešbon*," which has four syllables, with the rhyme "*tibbaneh wetikonen 'ir siḥon*," which has ten syllables with a rhyme almost the same as the first.[3] "*Ki 'eš yaṣe'a meḥešbon*" has eight syllables with a true rhyme identical to the rhyme in the first *bayit* having four syllables.[4] "*Lehaba miqiryat siḥon*" also has eight syllables with a true rhyme, the same as the rhyme in the *bayit* of ten syllables.[5] "*'akela 'ir mo'ab*" has six syllables without a rhyme. "*Ba'alê bamot 'arnon*" has six syllables also, if you elide the *'ayin* of *ba'alê*. This line has a quasi-rhyme; I know that *'arnon* is not a true rhyme with *siḥon*, but it is almost identical and should therefore be called a *šir 'ober*.[6]

I have also found poems without rhyme but with an equal number of syllables in the verses [*batim*], for instance [Num 21:17–20]:[7] "*'ali be'er 'enu lah*" has eight syllables, if the *he* of *lah* is pronounced. "*Be'er ḥaparuha sarim*" also has eight syllables. "*Karuha nedibê ha'am*" also has eight. "*Bimḥoqeq bemiš'anotam*" likewise has eight. "*Umimmidbar mattana*" has eight if you read the *dalet* of *umimmidbar* [as a separate syllable], instead of eliding it as grammar requires.[8] Likewise, "*umimmattana naḥali'el*," if *naḥali'el* is read as if written without a *yod*, you read with elision *naḥale'l*, also eight syllables. "*Uminnaḥali'el bamot*," if *naḥali'el* is read as written, has eight. "*Umibbamot haggay*" has six syllables. "*'ašer bisde mo'ab*" also has six syllables. "*Ro'š happisga weniš qa-*" has seven syllables;[9] "*-pa 'al penê hayšimon*" has seven syllables.

NOTES

1. At the end of the chapter, Portaleone acknowledges the influence of his teacher Judah Moscato, whose *Nepuṣot Yehuda* also contains a discussion of music.
2. It is called *De Justo* in the Latin translation of Marsilio Ficino. For more details see Sandler, "The Musical Chapters," 168, notes 3–5.
3. *Ḥešbon* and *Siḥon* is not quite an acceptable rhyme, because only the last consonant is the same, not the last two consonants.
4. It is a true rhyme because the last two consonants are the same. In this case the words are the same: *ḥešbon* and *meḥešbon*, a "good" rhyme to the medieval ear. But, as Portaleone notes, the number of syllables in these rhyming lines is not the same.
5. That is, *siḥon* rhymes with *siḥon*.
6. A poem with vowel-consonant rhyme, not consonant-vowel-consonant rhyme. See Sandler, "The Musical Chapters," 170, note 2.
7. Portaleone has to work hard to make the number of syllables in each *bayit* agree.
8. Portaleone wants to consider the *shwa* under the *dalet* mobile instead of quiescent in order to get eight syllables.
9. He gets this count by dividing the word *nišqapa* between two parts of the *bayit*. This was permissible in medieval Hebrew poetry.

IMMANUEL FRANCES

Immanuel ben David Frances (1618–ca. 1710) was born in Leghorn (Livorno), Italy. He was a poet and an antimessianic activist, opposed to supporters of the Kabbalah and false messianic movements. In these endeavors he was in close accord with his poet brother, Jacob Frances. During the last part of his life, which was beset by the tragic deaths of family members, he served as rabbi in Florence. He authored love poems, satirical debates on women and rabbis, and religious poems. He employed the meters of the Spanish-Arabic school but also introduced the terza rima *and the* ottava rima *of the Italian poets into his poetry.*

Meteq Sepatayim *[Sweetness of Lips, from Prov 16:21] was written in 1677 during a sojourn in Algiers. It is in the form of a dialogue between a teacher and his student, Jachin and Boaz (these are the names of two pillars in Solomon's Temple; cf. 1 Kgs 7:21), and so recalls a number of other works of this type, an example from our corpus being* The Kuzari. *Its concern, like that of Moshe ibn Ezra's* Kitāb al-Muḥāḍara wa-'l-Mudhākara, *is with contemporary Hebrew poetry, but it opens with a discussion of biblical poetry, citing various earlier authorities such as Judah Halevi, Don Isaac Abravanel, and Moshe ibn Ḥabib.*[1] *The style is often flowery, full of biblical and rabbinic allusions, yet clarity is not sacrificed.*

Frances divides biblical discourse into three types: prose, (prophetic) rhetoric, and poetry. He rejects the idea that biblical poetry had rhyme and meter, objecting to Abravanel's attempt to find meter in the Song of the Sea. He prefers the conclusions of Judah Halevi's Advocate that biblical poetry, lacking meter, is for that reason superior in that it does not require linguistic manipulations metri causa. *Yet he sees the origin of metrical poetry in the biblical period, following ibn Ḥabib, and not a later borrowing from the Arabs. He must, then, like others who hold this view, posit the existence of nonmetrical poetry in the Bible and metrical poetry from the same period in nonscriptural contexts.*

In his criteria for the identification of poetry, Frances is somewhat innovative. He does not refer to the stichographic scribal practice or to the term šir. *Instead he identifies poetry by its use of parallelism ("the doubling of language in different words") and by the tendency of the poet to speak of himself in the third person. The first criterion appears quite modern, while the second is based on what moderns would consider a naive view of authorship. Another modern touch, which foreshadows a Form Critical approach, is Frances's typology of biblical poetry.*

He finds, based on their contents, that biblical poems can be divided into twelve types, among them praise, thanksgiving, petition, and so forth. He notes that most poems contain a combination of types.

Like a number of others, Frances discusses the term mašal. *He is not totally successful in distinguishing the various uses of this term but is rather good in his explanation of certain metaphorical or allegorical passages.*

Edition: H. Brody, Meteq Sepatayim [Hebräische Prosodie von Immanuel Frances] *(Cracow, 1892; reprint, Israel, 1969). For a discussion of the work see M. Hartmann,* Die hebräische verskunst nach dem Metek Sefatajim des Immanuel Fransis und anderen Werken judischer Metriker *(Berlin, 1894).*

Meteq Sepatayim

JACHIN: Why have you hastened to come?

BOAZ: To please my lord, the Strong Hammer, the Right Column, for you are rich in all wisdom, especially in the art of poetry, and I am weak and poor in all science and wisdom. And you said, "I will surely do well by you. I will lead you in the straight path, in the choicest art of poetry, in pure language." And you, my lord, Bundle of Myrrh, keep your promise. For you are bound to finish the work [which you began].

JACHIN: I am prepared to satisfy your desire, only do not forsake the study of the Gemara, for it is your mainstay. The art of poetry is the dessert, for honor and glory; but talmudic study is grain and bread and food for a hungry soul in the days of famine and scarcity. For the sages have already said: "Everyone needs an expert in rabbinic learning [lit.: a master of wheat]" [*b. Berakot* 64a].

BOAZ: I accept your words, my lord. They are refined like silver, sweeter than the honeycomb, they adorn my neck like necklaces; but let my lord keep his promise.

JACHIN: Before I educate you in the ways of metrical poetry in which you will go, I deem it proper to inform you a bit about the paths of rhetoric and poetry, whose origin is in the holy mountains—the twenty-four [books of the Bible]. Indeed, as high as the sky is over the land, so are their ways higher than ours. They should be for you a restorer of life to sustain your songs judiciously and to proceed to the art of poetry that is before us.

Know that all manner of speech written in the Holy Scriptures is of three types. The first is prose, that is, the common language understood by man, woman, and child. Of this type are the Pentateuch, Joshua, Judges, Samuel, Kings, Jonah, Chronicles, Ruth, Esther. Since we do not need this for our purpose, we will not discuss it. The second [type] is rhetoric, including Isaiah, Jeremiah, Ezekiel, and most of the Twelve [Minor Prophets].[2] The third [type] is poetry, the Song of the Sea, Ha'azinu, the Song of Deborah, Psalms, and the like. Although the rhetorical and the poetic are related, the poetic is purer and more polished. And although we do not find in [biblical] poems meter or rhyme, nevertheless there is a caesura in every line. It is possible that it is based on a melody unknown to us. Don Isaac Abravanel, in his commentary on the Torah, tried to find meter in the Song of the Sea, but it was in vain, and his words on this matter are incorrect. After his praise of the art of poetry he wrote that for the sake of the meter letters were contracted, and they added two *yods* and a *waw* in the word *yekasyumu* [Exod 15:5], and a *yod* in *ne'dari* [15:6], and a *waw* in *tebi'emo* and *wetiṭṭa'emo* [15:17], *tibla'emo* [15:12]. They omitted [the word] "the heart of" in "all the inhabitants of Canaan melted" [15:15].[3] I am amazed that from his [Abravanel's] holy mouth such a thing could come—that the greatest of prophets [Moses] would have to constrict his discourse and pervert the meaning for the sake of the melody. For it is known that it is considered a disparagement to say of a poet that he constricts his words for the sake of the meter. Therefore, my son, do not endorse him and do not heed his words on this matter.

[Instead,] set before you the Advocate in *The Kuzari,* 2.72 and 78, who correctly proved the vast superiority of scriptural poems over metrical ones, in that for the sake of the meter the latter sometimes require a quiescent *shwa* where they should have a mobile *shwa* and a mobile *shwa* where they should have a quiescent *shwa,*[4] and connect what should be separated and separate what should be connected. Scriptural poems are not so, for they do not have to add or subtract anything.

BOAZ: Truly, in my eyes this is the right way; I will not stray right or left from it. But tell me, who was the first inventor of poems?

JACHIN: Our rabbis of blessed memory attributed the invention of poems to Adam. They said that since the Sabbath Day became an advocate before the Holy One Blessed Be He, he [Adam] opened with the Psalm for the Sabbath Day [Ps 92].[5] However, from the biblical text it seems that Lamech was the first [to invent poetry], when he said "Hear my voice, wives of Lamech" [Gen 4:23].

BOAZ: And how do we know that these words of his are poetic?

JACHIN: From the doubling of language in different words, and from the fact that he said "wives of Lamech" and not "my wives"; for it is the way of poets to speak of themselves in the third person [lit.: as if they were someone else]. For instance, "Assemble and harken, sons of Jacob" [Gen 49:2]; "the speech of Balaam, son of Beor" [Num 24:3]; "Arise, arise, Deborah" [Jud 5:12]; "Get up, Barak" [Jud 5:12], and others like these. The reason is that from so much solitude the intellect reaches a higher level, and the body remains as if without a soul; and it seems to them [the poets] that they are other persons. Thus did Samuel say to Saul: "you will prophesy and you will become another man" [1 Sam 10:6]. You will see also that the poets sometimes, when they are composing their poems, become seized with wonder and do not feel anything from so much solitude. And it appears, as Nachmanides said in his commentary on the Torah, that Lamech was a great savant in intellectual skills, and taught his sons. To the oldest he taught the art of shepherding—the making of tents and [tending of] flocks [cf. Gen 4:20]. To the second he taught the art of music—lyre and pipe [cf. Gen 4:21]. And to the third the art of the smith—to forge copper and iron [cf. Gen 4:22]. His wives rebelled against him, either because he killed Cain and Tubal-cain, as Josippon[6] wrote, or because they did not want to mate with him, as our rabbis said, since they knew that a flood would come over the earth to destroy all flesh.[7] Lamech reproved them in rhetorical and poetic discourse so that his words would enter their heart.

It is possible that Lamech's contemporaries deified him and his sons, for it is their foolish way to deify all inventors of an art; they would call each the god of the art he invented. In the books of the ancient heathen they wrote that the god of shepherding is called Pan, the name of the god of music is Apollo, the god of the smith is Vulcan. All were the sons of Jupiter, and their sister was Venus, the wife of Vulcan. She was the goddess of lovemaking, because she was the first to become licentious. Perhaps Lamech and his two [*sic*] sons were gods to their contemporaries, for Vulcan is close to the name Tubal-cain, and the names of the others became corrupted by the passage of time and the confusion of tongues [Genesis 11]. The name Na'amah comes from the word *ne'imot,* "pleasures," for lovemaking. The text informs us that these were descendants of the cursed Cain, and so are not gods. The word *father* in the expression "Father of those who dwell in tents and among herds" [Gen 4:20] is a reference to idolatry, just as in "They say to wood, you are my father" [Jer 2:26].

BOAZ: I have heard that a certain philosopher named Pythagoras, when he heard the sounds of a smith's hammer, measured each sound and found that since some were heavy and some light, the sound of their utterance was a pleasant sound called consonance, and from that he discovered the science of music.

JACHIN: And I have heard that it was not Pythagoras but Yubal, when he heard the sound of his brother Tubal-cain's hammer. It also says in the Midrash that Na'amah was beautiful, and that the angels strayed because of her, and someone said that she was the wife of Shamdon and the mother of Ashmodai, king of the demons.[8] But we have dwelt on this too long; let us return to our topic.

BOAZ: I have seen different names for poems, and so I am dying to know if they have meanings.

JACHIN: *Šir, mašal, zimra, maskil, lamenaṣṣeaḥ,* and *miktam* are names of the poems. The first three are synonyms and include all types of songs and poems. The last three are specific types. [*He goes on to give fanciful etymologies for these terms.*]

BOAZ: If poetry in the holy tongue [i.e., biblical poetry] did not have rhyme and meter, who, then, invented rhyme and meter?

JACHIN: In the opinion of the Advocate in *The Kuzari* [2.78], and also in the opinion of Judah al-Ḥarizi [*Taḥkemoni,* 18], the Jews learned it from the Arabs. But the author of *Darkê No'am* [Moshe ibn Ḥabib] testifies that when he was in the city of Murviedro, in the kingdom of Valencia, which in earlier times was a great city, [now] called Sagunto,[9] the people of the community told him that at the top of a mountain there was the grave of an army officer of Amaziah, king of Judah. He went up there to see it; there was on it a gravestone with an epitaph inscribed thereon, of which, after much effort, he read a verse: "*se'u*[10] *qina beqol mara / lesar gadol leqaḥo yah //.* He was not able to read any more except that in the second verse[11] there was written "to Amaziah." Therefore I say that in my opinion prophecy and poetry spoken in the Holy Spirit [i.e., biblical poetry] did not have rhyme and meter, for the reasons given by the Advocate, as I have told you, but other poems did have meter and rhyme. When the exile began, this [rhyme and meter] began to spread throughout the lands, and the other nations learned the art of poetry from them [i.e., the Jews]. But the Jews, because of many troubles and wanderings, forgot it, and it became loathsome to them, until close to the year 4700 [i.e., the tenth century C.E.] God enlightened the hearts of the ancient poets, and they restored the crown of poetry to its former self; but the taste of the poetry was the taste of mallow juice.[12] After them arose famous poets and rhetoricians in every generation: among them R. Isaac Khalfun,[13] and the great poet R. Solomon ibn Gabirol, around the year 4800 [= 1040 C.E.], and after them R. Isaac ibn Ghiyyat, and his student R. Joseph Hadayyan, and after them R. Abraham ibn Ezra and R. Moshe ibn Ezra, R. Judah Halevi, and R. Judah al-Ḥarizi. And afterward arose R. Immanuel ben Solomon of La Marca [Immanuel of Rome], who wrote many poems but became corrupted with lewd poems that one is forbidden to listen to.[14] May God grant atonement to him and to those who publish everything: there are still thorns among the vines—among his colleagues who have many respectable poems.

BOAZ: You said that *mašal* is a general term [for poetry], but are there not cases in which it means simply "comparison"?

JACHIN: You have spoken well. Poems are termed *mašal* because in poetry and elegant prose one finds many [comparisons]: "Like palm-groves that stretch out, Like gardens beside a river" [Num 24:6]; "Like aloes planted by the Lord" [Num 24:6]; "Like an eagle who rouses his nestlings" [Deut 32:11]; "As one asleep, the Lord, as a warrior . . ." [Ps 78:65], and many more.

BOAZ: I see in Psalm 49:5 that it says "I will turn my ear to *mašal;* I will open my riddle with the lyre." This [use of *mašal*] seems to refer to the doubling of meaning in different words [i.e., parallelism, a sign of poetry]. I do not understand this [sense of the word] in relation to that [sense of the word].[15]

JACHIN: The commentators have already explained that both are closed matters, understood only by men of intellect. Let us return to our subject. I have said that scriptural poems have neither rhyme nor meter. They are of twelve types: (1) praise of the Lord, like Psalm 90 and Psalm 8, and others; (2) thanks to Him for a particular deliverance or favor, like the Song of the Sea [Exodus 15], the Song of the Well [Num 21:18], the Song of Deborah [Judges 5], and the like; (3) prayers, petitions, and confessions of sins, like Psalm 22, Psalm 57, Psalm 51, and many others; (4) prophecies and promises, like the Blessing of Jacob [Genesis 49] and the prophecy of Balaam [Numbers 23]; (5) praise of the righteous, like Psalm 112, and the acrostic of the Woman of Valor [Proverbs 31], according to its literal interpretation; (6) condemnation of the wicked, like Psalm 14, Psalm 52, and others; (7) happy occasions, like Psalm 45, according to its literal interpretation; (8) words of chastisement and reproof, like the Ha'azinu Song, the Book of Proverbs, and the like; (9) justification of complaints, like Psalm 7 and most of the dialogues of Job; (10) love poetry in the form of allegory, like Song of Songs; (11) lamentations over the destruction of the Temple, like the Scroll of Lamentations, or on the death of the righteous, like the Lament of David over Saul and Jonathan [2 Samuel 1], and Abner [2 Sam 3:33]; (12) lamentations over the fall of the enemies of Israel in the form of mockery, like the Lament over Tyre and its prince [Ezekiel 27–28], and over Pharaoh [Ezekiel 29 and 32]. Most poems are composed of different types.

And now I will present to you, from the limited knowledge that I have acquired, a little of the manner of poetry and elegant prose of the Bible. Know that the purpose of the poet is to convey his meaning to others. And since the love of sweetness and usefulness are two bands that tug on the hearts of men, drawing them on so that by means of them [sweetness and usefulness] they will reach the love of goodness in and of itself,[16] they [the poets] seek to accomplish this by the development of poems with exaggerations, as in the Ha'azinu poem, "Give ear, heavens, and let me speak; And listen, earth, to the words of my mouth" [Deut 32:1]. And so Isaiah, "Listen, heavens and give ear, earth" [Isa 1:2]. And the sons of Korah, "Listen to this, all the peoples" [Ps 49:2].

It being human nature to give ear and listen to great and famous men, they portrayed themselves as wise and virtuous, albeit it is not right for a person to praise himself, as a wise man said, "Let another praise you, not your own mouth" [Ps 27:2]. Don't you see that even the greatest of prophets [Moses], who was very modest, portrayed himself with the term *king*, as it is written "When there was a king in Jeshurun" [Deut 32:5]. And King David said in his last words "The utterance of David, son of Jesse, The utterance of the man set on high, The anointed of the God of Jacob, And the sweet singer of Israel" [2 Sam 23:1]. For the familial aspect he said "son of Jesse," since he used to go out among a great populace, as our sages said [*b. Berakot* 58a]; and for the heroic aspect by which he was characterized he said "utterance of the man set on high"; and for the aspect of greatness and honor he said "anointed of the God of Jacob"; and for the aspect of wisdom he said "sweet singer of Israel." Wise men also praised their compositions when they announced the benefits that derive from them. Thus King Solomon said at the beginning of the Book of Proverbs "To know wisdom and discipline," which is useful; "to understand *mašal* and *meliṣa*," about sweetness; and afterward he said "the beginning of wisdom is the fear of the Lord," which is goodness in and of itself. In Psalm 49 it says "my mouth will speak wisdom" about the useful; "I will turn my ear to *mašal*" on the sweetness, and afterward "why should I fear days of evil." From this later sages learned to praise their compositions.

[*He goes on to give examples from medieval writings.*]

Boaz asks about the identification of a certain payyṭan. *Jachin clarifies this and then returns to the subject of biblical poetry.*

We have said that poetry is full of *mešalim*. In the Bible there are poems which are entirely *mašal*, the *nimšal* being presented only in the allegorical interpretation, such as Song of Songs. The *mašal* is the love of a king for a young beautiful girl, and the *nimšal* is the love of God for the congregation of Israel. [God's] blessed name is present only in the allegorical allusion of "Solomon" which, as our sages explained, [stands for] "the King of whom peace is His" [i.e., God].[17] Likewise it says "I adjure you, daughters of Jerusalem, by gazelles and hinds of the field." "Gazelles" [*ṣeba'ot*] alludes to the Holy Name [*YHWH ṣeba'ot*, "Lord of Hosts"]. And "hinds" [*'ayyalot*] is from the same word as "my strength [*'eyaluti*] [i.e., God] hasten to my aid" [Ps 22:20]. Likewise "A woman of valor" until the end of the acrostic is a *mašal,* and in the opinion of some exegetes [it is an allegory of] the Holy Torah or of the pure soul.

There are [on the other hand] *mešalim* after which the *nimšal* is made explicit: the parable of Oholah and Oholibah [Ezekiel 23], the parable of Tyre [Ezekiel 27]. Now, my son, attend to these *mešalim* and you will find that they all have some relationship to the *nimšal.* Ezekiel compared Tyre to a beautiful ship full of merchandise and precious stones with masts of Lebanon cedar, oars of Bashan oak, and a crew of valiant men, bearers of shields. This is because Tyre is a great city, full of good things, located on the coast; and merchants from all lands would come to trade there. And he compared [Ezekiel 28] its prince to a covering[18] cherub in the Garden of Eden because of his great wisdom, as is known, and he said that his covering was every precious stone—carnelian, topaz, diamond, etc.—which is a *mašal* for his great wealth. And he compared Pharaoh, king of Egypt, to a great sea serpent lying in the midst of a canal [Ezekiel 29], because the land of Egypt is full of canals branching off of the Nile River,[19] and there you will find the sea serpents called crocodiles. Isaiah, whose words are clear and who provides us with brilliant discourse, compared God in his revenging Edom to a treader [of grapes] in a winepress, clothed in red [Isaiah 63]. This is because the word *Bozrah* [*boṣra*], their capital, and *vintage* [*baṣir*] are from the same root, and the wine, which is red, and which is called "the blood of the grape,"[20] suggests blood [*dam*] and also the name of the nation, Edom. Job also said [Job 7:6]: "My days go more swiftly than a weaver's shuttle, they are spent without *tiqwa* ["hope/thread"]. There *tiqwa* means both "hope" and "thread." [The meaning "hope" is proved from] "Perhaps there is hope [*tiqwa*] [Lam 3:29], and [the meaning "thread" is proved from] "thread [*tiqwat*] of scarlet yarn" [Josh 2:18]. He compared his days to the shuttle, the implement with which one moves [the thread of] the woof through [the threads of] the warp, back and forth. The word *tiqwa* serves as a *mašal,* "thread," and as a *nimšal,* "hope." Likewise Eliphaz said: "Just as I have seen, the plowers [*ḥoršê*] of iniquity and the sowers of trouble will reap the same" [Job 4:8]. For the word *ḥoršê* has a double meaning, relating to thought, as in "He seeks a cunning workman [*ḥaraš*]" [Isa 40:20], and to plowing, as in "Do not plow [*taḥroš*] with an ox and an ass" [Deut 22:10]. He [Eliphaz] used *ḥoršê* as a *mašal,* and added "sowers of trouble" [which brings out the sense of "plowing"], and also used it as a *nimšal,* in the sense of "those who plan."

Isaiah also used names with double entendres, one a proper noun and one an adjective, when he said: "You will not be called Azubah [forsaken], neither will your land be called Shemamah [desolate], but you will be called Hephzibah [my delight is in her] and your land, Beulah [possessed]" [Isa 62:4].[21] Azubah and Hephzibah are two queen mothers, the first the mother of Jehoshaphat[22] and the second the mother of Manasseh,[23] the daughter of the prophet himself. It is possible that Shemamah and Beulah were female names familiar to him.

BOAZ: Is it possible that a woman would be called Shemamah [desolate]?

JACHIN: It is entirely possible. We find in Chronicles names stranger than this: Helah [sickness] [1 Chr 4:5], Mirmah [deceit] [1 Chr 8:10], Amal [trouble] [1 Chr 7:35]. He [Isaiah] used proper nouns which double as verbs when he said: "Sons I raised and reared up [*giddalti weromamti*]" [Isa 1:2], for these are people's names, the sons of Heman, the heads of watches [1 Chr 25:4].

They would often repeat for emphasis,[24] as in "until the people will pass" in Exod 15:16, "If it had not been the Lord who was on our side" in Ps 124:1–2. There is threefold repetition of "the temple of the Lord" in Jer 7:4, and "land" in Jer 22:29. There is fourfold repetition of "arise" in Jud 5:12, and "turn" in Song 7:1. In order that elegant prose and praiseworthy poetry should not be too easily understood, they used unusual and difficult language. This we find especially in the Book of Job.

BOAZ: Why is the discourse of the Book of Job difficult to understand whereas the rest of Scripture is not, especially Song of Songs, which is holy of holies,[25] yet nevertheless it is clear and easy to understand?

JACHIN: The discourses of Job and his friends are closed arguments and deep matters, and therefore they use strange and foreign language which is not understood by the general public. Not so the Song of Songs, which is a *mašal* of a lover speaking gently to a young girl, and she, leaning on her lover, responds to him with words of love and affection. Therefore the words of both of them are in language easy to understand. Sometimes they would employ Aramaisms in elegant prose and biblical poetry, for example, *q-t-l* [Job 13:15; 24:14], *k-p-n* [Job 5:22; 30:3], *d-w-r* [Ps 84:11], *'-r-q* [Job 30:3, 17], *'-t-'* [Isa 21:12; Deut 33:2; and elsewhere], and *ḥ-w-h* [Job 32:6 and elsewhere]. These and the like you will find only in biblical poetry and elegant prose.

The dialogue continues with a discussion of later Hebrew poetry.

NOTES

1. He also makes reference to several Italian Jewish authors, including Immanuel of Rome and Judah Moscato. However, Azariah de' Rossi is not mentioned, perhaps because he was still persona non grata in the Jewish community.

2. Excluding Jonah, which is prose.

3. This is not Abravanel's complete list.

4. Frances discusses this matter at some length later in his book (Brody, 40ff.). Boaz asks: "I have heard that poets are permitted to make a quiescent *shwa* mobile and a mobile *shwa* quiescent, so what is the error of the aforementioned poet?" Jachin responds that as a general rule this is not permitted, only if absolutely necessary.

5. For the rabbinic sources of this legend see Ginzberg, *The Legends of the Jews,* V, 112, note 103.

6. Josippon (also called Pseudo-Josephus) is an anonymous Hebrew historical narrative written in Italy in the tenth century.

7. *Genesis Rabbah* 23:4.

8. Brody's edition reads "šamron" for "šamdon." Cf. Ginzberg, *The Legends of the Jews,* I, 150; V, 147, note 45; V, 171, note 11.

9. The equation of Murviedro with Sagunto, which is correct, is not found in *Darkê No'am* but was added by Frances.

10. Brody: *se'i.*

11. Hebrew: *bayit.* Ibn Ḥabib: *šir.* See the note on Moshe ibn Ḥabib *ad loc.*

12. That is, it was tasteless; cf. Job 6:6.

13. Brody: *dalpun.*

14. Despite this opinion, the work of Immanuel of Rome served as a model for the poetry of Frances's brother, Jacob, and presumably for his own poetry as well.

15. Boaz is asking about the relationship of *mašal* meaning "comparison," which is not limited to poetry, and *mašal* meaning "poem."

16. The poets use aesthetic and practical means to reach their end, which is an appreciation of that which is intrinsically (morally/philosophically) good.

17. *Hammelek šehaššalom šelo.* This is a play on the name of Solomon.

18. The Hebrew in Ezek 28:14 is *sokek,* whose meaning here is uncertain. It plays on the word *miskatek,* "covering, adornment," in 28:13.

19. Cf. Rashi on Gen 41:1.

20. Deut 32:14; Gen 49:11. The expression is common in medieval Hebrew poetry.

21. The verse is cited incorrectly in the text.

22. Cf. 1 Kgs 22:42; 2 Chr 20:31.

23. Cf. 2 Kgs 21:1.

24. The text reads "doubling of a subject in different words," but the editor notes that the better reading is "sometimes to strengthen their discourse with different words."

25. See *m. Yadayim* 3:5.

GLOSSARY

'Arabiyya: the doctrine of the supremacy of the Arabic language and culture.

bayit: a verse of poetry, composed of two hemistiches. Cf. *delet* and *soger*.

brick over brick: See log over log.

cord and peg [*tenu'a* and *yated*]: the constituent parts of a poetic foot. In Hebrew poetry a cord is a syllable containing one vowel. In metrical notation it is designated by -. A peg is a syllable containing a mobile *shwa* (or *ḥatep* or the conjunction *waw* vocalized with a *šuruq*) plus a vowel. E.g., בְּנֵי. In metrical notation it is designated by ˘-.

delet: the first hemistich of a verse (*bayit*).

gemaṭria: the adding up of the numerical equivalent of the letters in a word or phrase.

Ha'azinu: the poem in Deuteronomy 32.

ḥaruz: rhyme. In medieval Hebrew poetry the rhyme occurs at the end of the *soger* and is usually carried throughout the poem. Rhyming syllables have the same final consonant + vowel (+ consonant), as opposed to English rhyme, which requires only the same vowel (+ consonant). Occasionally *ḥaruz* is used to mean "a line of metrical verse."

Holy Spirit: divine inspiration; the creative force through which biblical poetry was composed. This is used to distinguish the inspiration of the authors of the Writings from prophetic inspiration.

i'jāz al-qur'ān: the "wonderful inimitability" of the Qur'an.

log over log, brick over brick: rabbinic terminology for the stichographic writing of certain passages in masoretic Bibles. Log over log, brick over brick forms a pattern of two columns:

Log over brick, brick over log forms a pattern of interwoven lines and spaces:

mašal (plural: *mešalim*): proverb; parable; allegory; metaphorical language; "vehicle."

meliṣa: formal or elegant prose; rhymed prose; poetic form of expression; rhetoric.

mišqal: meter.

nimšal: explanation of a *mašal*; the reality to which the allegory refers.

noṭariqon: interpreting the letters of a word as abbreviations for other words, e.g., as an acronym.

payyṭan: author of a *piyyuṭ*.

peg: See cord and peg.

piyyuṭ: postbiblical liturgical poetry (developed between the second and fifth centuries C.E.). *Piyyuṭim* are rhymed but do not have the quantitative or syllabic meter of later Hebrew poetry. They have rhythm based on the number of words, and a strict strophic structure. The term *piyyuṭ* is sometimes used to mean "rhymed, metrical poetry," as in the work of ibn Parḥon.

qaṣīda: ode; classical form of Arabic poetry; full-fledged poem by Arabic standards.

rajaz: primitive form of poetry; a form short of poetry; rhymed, nonmetered couplet.

ṣaḥot/ṣaḥut: clear language; pure style; linguistic precision.

šir: poem; song (sometimes interchangeable with *šira*).

šira: poem, poetry; song; a passage marked by this term in the Bible.

soger: the second hemistich of a verse.

BIBLIOGRAPHY

Texts and Translations

Abravanel, Don Isaac.
Commentary on the Latter Prophets. Jerusalem, 1955.
Commentary on the Pentateuch. Jerusalem, 1963.

Allemanno, Yoḥanan.
Barukh, J. *Ša 'ar Haḥešeq*. Livorno, 1790; reprint, Halberstadt, 1862. (Introduction to *Ḥešeq Šelomoh*.)

Archivolti, Samuel.
'Arugat Habbosem. Venice, 1602; Amsterdam, 1730.

Aristotle.
Hutton, J. *Aristotle's Poetics*. New York and London, 1982.
Lucas, D. W. *Aristotle's Poetics: Introduction, Commentary, and Appendixes*. Oxford, 1968.

Averroes.
Butterworth, C. *Averroes' Middle Commentary on Aristotle's* Poetics. Princeton, 1986.
Butterworth, C. *Averroes' Three Short Commentaries*. Albany, 1977.

Avicenna.
Dahiyat, I. M. *Avicenna's Commentary on the* Poetics *of Aristotle*. Leiden, 1974.

Buxtorf, Johannes.
Liber Cosri. Basle, 1660; reprint, Gregg International Publishers, 1971.

Duran, Profiat.
Ma'aseh 'Epod. Ed. Y. T. Friedlander and Y. Hacohen. Vienna, 1865; reprint, Jerusalem, 1970.

Eusebius.
Gifford, E. H. *Eusebius: Preparation for the Gospel*. Oxford, 1903.

Falaquera, Shem Tov ibn.
Tama, M. *Seper Hammebaqqeš*. The Hague, 1772; Warsaw, 1924; reprint, Jerusalem, 1970.
Levine, M. H. *Falaquera's Book of the Seeker (Sefer ha-Mebaqqesh)*. New York, 1976.

al-Farabi.
Arberry, A. J. "Farabi's Canons of Poetry." *Rivista degli Studi Orientali* 17 (1938) 266–78.

Frances, Immanuel.
Brody, H. *Meteq Sepatayim* [*Hebräische Prosodie von Immanuel Frances*]. Cracow, 1892; reprint, Israel, 1969.

Halevi, Judah.
Hakkuzari. Beḥamiša Ma'amarim 'im Šenê Habbi'urim. Qol Yehuda We'oṣar Neḥmad. Commentaries by Judah Aryeh Moscato and Israel Zamosc. Hebrew translation by Judah ibn Tibbon. Vilna, 1904.
Baneth, D. H. *Kitāb al-Radd wa-'l-Dalīl fi 'l-Din al-Dhalīl.* Jerusalem, 1977.
Even Shmuel, Y. *Seper Hakkozari Lerabbi Yehuda Hallewi* [The Kosari of R. Yehuda Halevi]. Tel Aviv, 1972.
Hirschfeld, H. *Book of Kuzari by Judah Hallevi.* New York, 1946.
al-Ḥarizi, Judah.
Reichert, V. E. *The Taḥkemoni of Judah al-Ḥarizi: An English Translation.* Jerusalem, 1973.
Toporowsky, Y. *Taḥkemoni.* Tel Aviv, 1952.
Ibn Ezra, Moshe.
Halkin, A. S. *Kitāb al-Muḥāḍara wal-Mudhākara.* Jerusalem, 1975.
Halper, B. *Seper Širat Yisra'el.* Leipzig, 1924.
Ibn Ḥabib, Moshe.
Heidenheim, W. *Darkê No'am 'im Marpe' Lašon.* Rodelheim, 1806.
Ibn Janaḥ, Jonah.
Kitāb al-Luma' (Seper Hariqma). Ed. M. Wilensky. Berlin, 1931; reprint, Jerusalem, 1964.
Sepher Haschoraschim. Wurzelworterbuch der Hebräischen Sprache von Abulwalid Merwan Ibn Ganah (Rabbi Jona). Aus dem Arabischen ins Hebräische ubersetzt von J. Ibn Tibbon. Ed. W. Bacher. Berlin, 1896; reprint, Amsterdam, 1969.
Ibn Kaspi, Joseph.
Last, I. *'Asara Kelê Kesep.* Pressburg, 1903.
Ibn Parḥon Solomon.
Maḥberet He'aruk. Ed. S. G. Stern. Pressburg, 1844; reprint, Jerusalem, 1970.
Ibn Quraysh, Judah.
Becker, D. *The* Risāla *of Judah ben Quraysh.* Tel Aviv, 1984.
Ibn Saruq, Menaḥem.
Stern, S. G. *Tešubot Talmidê Menaḥem ben Ya'aqob 'ibn Saruq.* Vienna, 1870; reprint, Jerusalem, 1968.
Saenz-Badillos, A. *Menaḥem ben Saruq,* Maḥberet, *Edicion critica e introduccion.* Granada, 1986.
Ibn Tibbon, Moshe.
Peruš 'al Šir Hašširim. Lyck, 1874.
Leon, Judah Messer.
Nopet Ṣupim. Photograph of ms. with introduction by R. Bonfil. Jerusalem, 1981.
Jellinek, A. *Nofet Zufim.* Vienna, 1863; reprint, Jerusalem, 1971.
Rabinowitz, I. *The Book of the Honeycomb's Flow: Sepher Nopheth Ṣuphim by Judah Messer Leon.* Ithaca and London, 1983.
Maimonides, Moses.
Pines, S. *The Guide of the Perplexed.* Chicago, 1963.
Mizraḥi, Avshalom bar Moshe.
Carmoli, E. *'Imrê Šeper.* Paris, 1841.
Moscato, Judah.
Nepuṣot Yehuda [Nofuzath Jehuda]. Lemberg, 1859.
Qol Yehuda. Commentary on *The Kuzari.* [See *sub* Halevi.)

Philo.
Colson, F. H. *Philo*. Loeb Classical Library, vol. IX. Cambridge, Mass., 1941.
Portaleone, Abraham.
Šiltê Haggibborim. Mantua, 1612.
Sandler, D. "The Music Chapters of 'Shiltey ha-Giborim' by Avraham Portaleone." Dissertation, Tel Aviv University, 1980.
Shepher, S. *Haššir Šebammiqdaš*. Jerusalem, 5725 [1965].
Qunṭres Bediqduq Sepat 'Eber (Anonymous).
Poznanski, S. *Qunṭres Bediqduq Sepat 'Eber*. Berlin, 1891.
de' Rossi, Azariah.
Cassel, D. *Me'or 'Ênayim*. Vilna, 1866; reprint, Jerusalem, 1970.
Saadia Gaon.
Allony, N. *Ha'egron. Kitāb 'uṣul al-shi'r al-'ibrānī*. Jerusalem, 1969.
Goodman, L. E. *The Book of Theodicy: Translation and Commentary on the Book of Job by Saadiah Ben Joseph Al-Fayyumi*. New Haven and London, 1988.
Rosenblatt, S. *Saadia Gaon: The Book of Beliefs and Opinions*. New Haven, 1948.
Šeqel Haqqodeš (ascribed to Solomon Almoli).
Yalon, H. *Šeqel Haqqodeš. Ma'amar Qaṣar Bimle'ket Haššir*. Jerusalem, 1965.
Yeda'ya Ha-Penini (Bedersi).
Seper Happardes. Constantinople, 1516.
Luzzatto, J. "Seper Happardes." *'Oṣar Hasiprut* 3 (1889–90) 1–18.
Miscellaneous Collections.
Adler, I. *Hebrew Writings concerning Music in Manuscripts and Printed Books from Geonic Times up to 1800*. Munich, 1975.
Migne, J. P. *Patrologiae cursus completus. patrum latinorum. patrum graecorum*. Paris, 1844–46.
Schirmann, H. *Haššira Ha'ibrit Biseparad Ubiprobans*. Jerusalem and Tel Aviv, 1954, 1956.

Secondary Sources

Aguzzi-Barbagli, D.
"Humanism and Poetics." In Rabil, vol. III, 85–170.
Allony, N.
"'Iyyunim Wediyyunim Be*seper Ha'iyyunim Wehaddiyyunim (Kitāb al-Muḥāḍara wa-'l-Mudhākara)* le-R. Moše 'ibn 'Ezra'." *Studia Orientalia. Memoriae D. H. Baneth dedicata*, ed. J. Blau et al. Jerusalem, 1979, 47–71.
———.
"Mi Ḥibber 'et Šeqel Haqqodeš?" [The Authorship of Šeqel Haqqodeš?]. *Kiriat Sepher* 18 (1941–42) 192–98.
———.
Mittorat Hallašon Wehaššira Bimê Habbênayim. Jerusalem, 5704 [1944].
———.
"The Reaction of Moses Ibn Ezra to 'Arabiyya (Arabism)." *Actes du XXIXe Congrès international des orientalistes. Section 3: Études hebraïques*. Paris, 1975, 1–16.

———.
“Tegubat R. Moše ’ibn ‘Ezra’ Le‘arabiyya Beseper Hadiyyunim Wehassiḥot.” *Tarbiz* 42 (5733 [1973]) 97–112.
Alter, R.
The Art of Biblical Poetry. New York, 1985.
Altmann, A.
“*Ars Rhetorica* as Reflected in Some Jewish Figures of the Italian Renaissance.” In Cooperman, 1–22.
Andersen, F. I., and Forbes, A. D.
“‘Prose Particle’ Counts of the Hebrew Bible.” In *The Word of the Lord Shall Go Forth*, ed. C. L. Meyers and M. O’Connor. Winona Lake, Ind., 1983, 165–83.
Apfelbaum, A.
Seper Toldot Hagga’on R. Yehuda Mosqaṭo [Biographie des R. Jehuda Moscato]. Drohobycz, 1900.
apRoberts, R.
“Old Testament Poetry: The Translatable Structure.” *Publications of the Modern Language Association* 92 (1977) 987–1004.
Arberry, A. J.
Arabic Poetry. Cambridge, 1965.
Ashtour, E.
The Jews of Moslem Spain. Philadelphia, 1984.
Bacher, W.
Die hebräische Sprachwissenschaft vom X. bis zum XVI. Jahrhundert. Trier, 1892.
Baer, Y.
A History of the Jews in Christian Spain. Philadelphia, 1961.
Barnett, R. D. (ed.)
The Sephardi Heritage: Essays on the History and Cultural Contribution of the Jews of Spain and Portugal. London, 1971.
Baron, S. W.
History and Jewish Historians. Philadelphia, 1964.
———.
A Social and Religious History of the Jews. Vol. 6, ch. XXIX; vol. 7, ch. XXX, XXXII. Philadelphia, 1958.
Baroway, I.
“The Accentual Theory of Hebrew Prosody.” *English Literary History* 17 (1950) 115–35.
Beeston, A. F. L., et al. (eds.)
The Cambridge History of Arabic Literature: Arabic Literature to the End of the Umayyad Period. Cambridge, 1983.
Berlin, Adele.
The Dynamics of Biblical Parallelism. Bloomington, 1985.
———.
“Poetry, Old Testament.” *Dictionary of Biblical Interpretation*. Nashville, forthcoming.
Berlin, Anne D.
“Shame of the Gentiles of Profiat Duran: A Fourteenth-Century Jewish Polemic against Christianity.” Unpublished B.A. Honors Thesis, Radcliffe College, March 16, 1987.

Bettan, I.
"The Sermons of Juda Muscato." *HUCA* 6 (1929) 297–326.

———.
Studies in Jewish Preaching. Cincinnati, 1939.

Bonebakker, S. A.
"Religious Prejudice against Poetry in Early Islam." *Medievalia et Humanistica* 7 (1976) 77–99.

Bonfil, R.
"Some Reflections on the Place of Azariah de Rossi's Meor Enayim in the Cultural Milieu of the Italian Renaissance." In Cooperman, 23–48.

Brann, R.
"Andalusian Hebrew Poetry and the Hebrew Bible: Cultural Nationalism or Cultural Ambiguity?" *Approaches to Judaism in Medieval Times*, vol. III, ed. D. Blumenthal. Atlanta, 1988, 101–31.

———.
The Compunctious Poet: Cultural Ambiguity and Hebrew Poetry in Muslim Spain. Baltimore, 1991.

———.
"Dana's *Poetics of Moshe ibn Ezra*." *JQR* 76 (1986) 373–74.

———.
"The 'Dissembling Poet' in Medieval Hebrew Literature: The Dimensions of a Literary Topos." *JAOS* 107 (1987) 39–54.

———.
"Judah Halevi: The Compunctious Poet." *Prooftexts* 7 (1987) 123–43.

Cantarino, V.
Arabic Poetics in the Golden Age. Leiden, 1975.

———.
"Averroes on Poetry." *Islam and Its Cultural Divergence*, ed. G. L. Tikku. Urbana, 1971, 10–26.

Cantera y Burgos, F.
"España Medieval: Arqueologia." In Barnett, 29–68.

Cantera Burgos, F., and Millas, J. M.
Las Inscripciones hebraicas de España. Madrid, 1956.

Carmi, T.
The Penguin Book of Hebrew Verse. New York, 1981.

Cheyne, T. K.
Founders of Old Testament Criticism. London, 1893.

Cohen, G. D.
The Book of Tradition (Sefer Ha-Qabbalah) by Abraham ibn Daud. Philadelphia, 1967.

Cooper, A. M.
"Biblical Poetics: A Linguistic Approach." Dissertation, Yale University, 1976.

Cooperman, B. D. (ed.)
Jewish Thought in the Sixteenth Century. Cambridge, Mass. 1983.

Cripps, R. S.
"Two British Interpreters of the Old Testament: Robert Lowth (1710–1787) and Samuel Lee (1783–1852)." *Bulletin of the John Rylands Library, Manchester* XXXV (March 1953) 385–404.

Dana, J.
Happo'etiqa šel Haššira Ha'ibrit Biseparad Bimê Habbênayim 'al pi R. Moše 'ibn 'Ezra' Umeqoroteha [Poetics of Medieval Hebrew Literature According to Moshe ibn Ezra]. Jerusalem, 1982.

———.
"Miqra' Weqor'an Betorat Haššir šel R. Moše ibn 'Ezra'." *Beth Mikra* 24/1 [76] (5739 [1979]) 89–93.

Davidson, I.
"The Study of Medieval Hebrew Poetry in the XIX Century." *Proceedings of the American Academy for Jewish Research* 1 (1928) 33–48.

de Moor, J. C.
"The Art of Versification in Ugarit and Israel, I: The Rhythmical Structure." *Studies in Bible and the Ancient Near East Presented to Samuel E. Loewenstamm.* Jerusalem, 1978, 119–39.

Diez Macho, A.
Mose Ibn 'Ezra como poeta y preceptista. Madrid-Barcelona, 1953.

Dukes, L.
Zur Kentniss der neuhebräischen religiosen Poesie. Frankfurt-am-Main, 1842.

———.
Naḥal Qedumim. Hanover, 1853; reprint, Israel, 1969.

Farmer, H. G.
A History of Arabian Music to the XIIIth Century. London, 1929.

———.
Sa'adyah Gaon on the Influence of Music. London, 1943.

Fenton, P.
"Gleanings from Moseh Ibn 'Ezra's Maqalat Al-Hadiqa." *Sefarad* 36 (1976) 285–98.

Fishbane, M.
Biblical Interpretation in Ancient Israel. Oxford, 1985.

Fleischer, E.
Širat Haqqodeš Ha'ibrit Bimê Habbenayim [Hebrew Liturgical Poetry in the Middle Ages]. Jerusalem, 1975.

Gabrieli, F.
"Estetica e poesia araba nell' interpretazione della Poetica aristotelica presso Avicenna e Averroe." *Rivista degli Studia Orientali* 12 (1929–30) 291–331.

Genot-Bismuth, J.
"Contribution a une recherche sur l'elaboration d'un metalangage de la poétique dans la pratique hebraïque medievale: l'exploitation du terme meliza." *Sefarad* 41 (1981) 231–71.

Gibb, H. A. R.
Arabic Literature. Oxford, 1963.

Ginsburg, C. D.
The Song of Songs and Coheleth. New York, 1970 (orig. pub. 1857 and 1861).

Ginzberg, L.
The Legends of the Jews. Philadelphia, 1961 (orig. pub. 1909).

Gitay, Y.
"Review of *The Book of the Honeycomb's Flow* by Judah Messer Leon. Translated by I. Rabinowitz." *Quarterly Journal of Speech* (Aug. 1985) 379–83.

Goitein, S. D.
"Ha'im Higia' R. Yehuda Hallewi 'el Ḥop 'Ereṣ Yisra'el" [Did Judah Halevi Reach the Shores of the Land of Israel?] *Tarbiz* 46 (1977) 245–50.
Goldenberg, E.
"Hebrew Language, Medieval." *EJ* 16:1607–42.
Goldin, J.
The Song of the Sea. New Haven and London, 1971.
Goldstein, D.
The Jewish Poets of Spain. New York, 1965.
Goldziher, I.
History of Classical Arabic Poetry. Hildesheim, 1966.
Gray, G. B.
The Forms of Hebrew Poetry. New York, 1972 (orig. pub. London, 1915).
Greenberg, M.
"Jewish Conceptions of the Human Factor in Biblical Prophecy." *Justice and the Holy: Essays in Honor of Walter Harrelson,* ed. D. A. Knight and P. J. Paris. Atlanta, 1989, 145–62.
Greenberg, M. (ed.)
Paršanut Hammiqra' Hayyehudit [Jewish Bible Exegesis: An Introduction]. Jerusalem, 1983.
Greenfield, C. C.
Humanist and Scholastic Poetics, 1250–1500. Lewisburg, 1981.
von Grunebaum, G. E. (ed.)
Arabic Poetry: Theory and Development. Wiesbaden, 1973.
Habermann, A. M.
"Poetry, Italy." *EJ* 13:681–93.
Halkin, A. S.
"Judeo-Arabic Literature." *The Jews,* ed. L. Finkelstein. Philadelphia, 1960, 1116–48.
———.
"The Judeo-Islamic Age." *Great Ages and Ideas of the Jewish People,* ed. L. W. Schwarz. New York, 1956, 215–63.
———.
"The Medieval Jewish Attitude toward Hebrew." *Biblical and Other Studies,* ed. A. Altmann. Cambridge, Mass. 1963, 233–48.
———.
"Yedaiah Bedershi's Apology." *Jewish Medieval and Renaissance Studies,* ed. A. Altmann. Cambridge, Mass. 1967, 165–84.
Hamori, A.
On the Art of Medieval Arabic Literature. Princeton, 1974.
Hartmann, M.
Die hebräische verskunst nach dem Metek Sefatajim des Immanuel Fransis und anderen Werken judischer Metriker. Berlin, 1894.
Harvey, S.
Falaquera's Epistle of the Debate: *An Introduction to Jewish Philosophy.* Cambridge, Mass. 1987.
Hazan, E.
"Meḥazara We'ad Ṣimud." *Jerusalem Studies in Hebrew Literature* 1 (1981) 182–95.

———.
Torat Haššir Bepiyyuṭ Haseparadi [The Poetics of the Sephardi Piyut]. Jerusalem, 1986.
Herder, J. G.
Vom Geist der ebräischen Poesie. Leipzig, 1824 (orig. pub. 1782).
Herrick, M.
"Rhetoric and Poetics." In Preminger, 702–705.
Heschel, A. J.
The Prophets. Philadelphia, 1962.
Hirschfeld, H.
Literary History of Hebrew Grammarians and Lexicographers. Oxford, 1926.
Hrushovski, B.
"Notes on the Systems of Hebrew Versification." In Carmi, 57–72.
———.
"Haššiṭot Hara'šiyyot šel Heḥaruz Ha'ibri min Hapiyyuṭ We'ad Yamênu, Masa 'al Musagê Hayyesod." *Hasifrut* 4 (1971) 721–49.
———.
"Prosody, Hebrew." *EJ* 13:1195–1240.
Idel, M., and Lesley, A.
A Renaissance Kabbalist and Humanist: Yohanan Alemanno. New Haven, forthcoming.
Jospe, R.
Torah and Sophia: The Life and Thought of Shem Tov ibn Falaqera. Cincinnati, 1987.
Kamin, S.
"Rashbam's Conception of the Creation in Light of the Intellectual Currents of His Time." *Studies in Bible, 1986*, ed. S. Japhet. *Scripta Hierosolymitana* 31 (1986) 91–132.
Katzew, J. D.
"Moses ibn Ezra and Judah Halevi: Their Philosophies in Response to Exile." *HUCA* 55 (1984) 179–95.
Korpel, M. C. A., and de Moor, J. C.
"Fundamentals of Ugaritic and Hebrew Poetry." *UF* 18 (1986) 173–212.
Kugel, J. L.
The Idea of Biblical Poetry: Parallelism and Its History. New Haven, 1981.
———.
"The Influence of Moses ibn Ḥabib's *Darkhei No'am*." In Cooperman, 308–25.
———.
"Is There but One Song." *Biblica* 63 (1982) 329–49.
———.
"Some Medieval and Renaissance Ideas about Biblical Poetry." *Studies in Medieval Jewish History and Literature*, ed. I. Twersky. Cambridge, Mass., 1979, 57–81 (= *The Idea of Biblical Poetry*, 181–203).
Kurylowicz, J.
Metrik und Sprachgeschichte. Wroclaw, 1975.
———.
Studies in Semitic Grammar and Metrics. Wroclaw, 1972.
Lesley, A.
"Hebrew Humanism in Italy: The Case of Biography." *Prooftexts* 2 (1982) 163–78.

———.
"Jewish Adaption of Humanist Concepts in Fifteenth- and Sixteenth-Century Italy." *Renaissance Rereadings: Intertext and Context*, ed. M. C. Horowitz, A. J. Cruz, and W. A. Furman. Urbana and Chicago, 1988, 51–66.

———.
"Sixteenth-Century Italian Jewish Analysis of Biblical Poetics." Paper read at the Colloque Poésie et Religion, McGill University, Montreal, Quebec, April 19, 1985.

———.
"A Survey of Medieval Hebrew Rhetoric." *Approaches to Judaism in Medieval Times*, ed. D. R. Blumenthal. Chico, 1984, 107–33.

Lowth, R.
Isaiah: A New Translation with a Preliminary Dissertation and Notes. London, 1848 (orig. pub. 1778).

———.
Lectures on the Sacred Poetry of the Hebrews. London, 1835 (orig. pub. 1753).

Makdisi, G.
"Scholasticism and Humanism in Classical Islam and the Christian West." *JAOS* 109 (1989) 175–82.

Marcus, R.
"A Sixteenth Century Hebrew Critique of Philo." *HUCA* 21 (1948) 29–71.

Mashiah, Y.
"The Terminology of Hebrew Prosody and Rhetoric with Special Reference to Arabic Origins." Dissertation, Columbia University, 1972.

Mirsky, A.
"'Erkê Haššira Ha'ibrit Biseparad." In Barnett, 186–274.

———.
"Koaḥ Hammiqra' Bešir Separad." *Sinai* 73 (1973) 19–23.

Monfasani, J.
"Humanism and Rhetoric." In Rabil, vol. III, 171–235.

Morais, S.
Italian Hebrew Literature. New York, 1926; reprint, 1970.

Navarro Peira, A., and Vegas Montaner, L.
"'La Poesia hebrea': Capitulo XVIII del Tahkemoni de al-Harizi." *Sefarad* 42 (1982) 140–71.

———.
"'Los poetas hebreos de sefarad': Capitulo III del Tahkemoni de al-Harizi." *Sefarad* 41 (1981) 321–38.

Netanyahu, B.
Don Isaac Abravanel. Philadelphia, 1968.

Neubauer, A.
Mele'ket Haššir. Frankfurt am Main, 1865.

Nicholson, R. A.
A Literary History of the Arabs. London, 1930.

O'Connor, M.
Hebrew Verse Structure. Winona Lake, Ind., 1980.

Pagis, D.
"Hamṣa'at Ha'iambus Ha'ibri Utemurot Bameṭriqa Ha'ibrit Be'iṭalia." *Hasifrut* 4 (1973) 651–712.

———.
Ḥidduš Umasoret Beširat Haḥol Ha'ibrit: Separad We'italia [Change and Tradition: Hebrew Secular Poetry in Spain and Italy]. Jerusalem, 1976.

———.
Širat Haḥol Wetorat Haššir Lemoše 'ibn 'Ezra' Ubenê Doro [Secular Poetry and Poetic Theory: Moses ibn Ezra and His Contemporaries]. Jerusalem, 1970.

———.
"Parallel Theories of Poetry in Medieval Hebrew Criticism." *Association for Jewish Studies Newsletter* 17 (July 1976) 5–10.

———.
"Poetry, Medieval Hebrew Secular." *EJ* 13:681–90.

Peters, F. E.
Aristotle and the Arabs. New York, 1968.

Preminger, A. (ed.)
Encyclopedia of Poetry and Poetics. Princeton, 1965.

Preminger, A., and Greenstein, E. L. (eds.)
The Hebrew Bible in Literary Criticism. New York, 1986.

Rabil, A. (ed.)
Renaissance Humanism: Foundations, Forms, and Legacy. Philadelphia, 1988.

Reines, A.
Maimonides and Abravanel on Prophecy. Cincinnati, 1970.

Renan, E.
Les écrivains juifs français du XIVe siècle. Paris, 1893.

Rosenthal, E. I. J.
"The Study of the Bible in Medieval Judaism." *Cambridge History of the Bible*, vol. II. Cambridge, 1969, 252–79.

Roth, C.
The Jews in the Renaissance. Philadelphia, 1959.

Roth, N.
"Jewish Reactions to *'Arabiyya* and the Renaissance of Hebrew in Spain." *Journal of Semitic Studies* 28 (1983) 63–84.

———.
"Maimonides on Hebrew Language and Poetry." *Hebrew Studies* XXVI/1 (1985) 93–101.

Ruderman, D.
"The Italian Renaissance and Jewish Thought." In Rabil, vol. I, 382–433.

Ruiz, G.
"Las introducciones y cuestiones de don Isaac Abrabanel." *Simposio Biblico Español, Salamanca, 1982*. Madrid, 1984, 707–22.

Salfeld, S.
Das Hohelied Salomo's bei den judischen Erklarern des Mittelalters. Berlin, 1879.

Sarna, N.
"Hebrew and Bible Studies in Medieval Spain." In Barnett, 323–66.

Scheindlin, R.
"The Influence of Muslim Arabic Cultural Elements on the Literature of the Hebrew Golden Age." *Conservative Judaism* (Summer 1982) 63–72.

———.
"Rabbi Moshe ibn Ezra on the Legitimacy of Poetry." *Medievalia et Humanistica* 7 (1976) 101–15.

———.
Wine, Women, and Death. Philadelphia, 1986.

Schirmann, H.
"The Function of the Hebrew Poet in Medieval Spain." *Jewish Social Studies* XVI (1954) 235–52.

———.
"La metrique quantitative dans la poésie hebraïque du Moyen-Age." *Sefarad* 8 (1948) 323–32.

Schreiner, M.
"Le Kitab al Mouhadara wa-l-Moudhakara de Moise b. Ezra et ses sources." *Revue des Etudes Juives* 21 (1890) 98–117; 22 (1891) 62–81, 236–49.

Segal, L. A.
Historical Consciousness and Religious Tradition in Azariah de' Rossi's Me'or 'Einayim. Philadelphia, 1989.

Shepard, S.
Shem Tov: His World and His Words. Miami, 1978.

Shulvass, M. A.
The Jews in the World of the Renaissance. Leiden, 1973.

Simon, U.
'Arba' Gišot Leseper Tehillim [Four Approaches to the Book of Psalms]. Ramat Gan, 1982.

Simonsohn, S.
History of the Jews in the Duchy of Mantua. Jerusalem, 1977 (orig. pub. in Hebrew, 1962–64).

Sirat, C.
A History of Jewish Philosophy in the Middle Ages. Cambridge, 1985.

Smith, G. A.
The Early Poetry of the Hebrews in Its Physical and Social Origins. The Schweich Lectures, 1910. London, 1912.

Spiegel, S.
"On Medieval Hebrew Poetry." *The Jews*, ed. L. Finkelstein. Philadelphia, 1960, 854–92.

Springarn, J.
Literary Criticism in the Renaissance. New York, 1899; reprint, 1963.

Steinschneider, M.
Bibliographisches Handbuch über die theoretische und praktische Literatur für hebräische Sprachkunde. Jerusalem, 1937.

———.
Die hebräischen Ubersetzungen des mittelalters und die Juden als Dolmetscher. Graz, 1956 (orig. pub. 1893).

———.
Jewish Literature from the Eighth to the Eighteenth Century. New York, 1970 (orig. pub. London, 1857).

Stern, S. M.
Hispano-Arabic Strophic Poetry. Oxford, 1974.

Talmage, F. E.
David Kimhi: The Man and the Commentaries. Cambridge, Mass., 1975.

Tene, D.
“Linguistic Literature, Hebrew.” *EJ* 16:1352–90.
Tobi, Y.
“Saadia’s Biblical Exegesis and His Poetic Practice.” *Hebrew Annual Review* 8 (1984) 241–57.
———.
“Torat Haššir šel RaSaG—Yayin Yašan Beqanqan Ḥadaš.” *Dappim Lemeḥqar Besiprut* 1 (1984) 51–78.
Twersky, I.
“Joseph ibn Kaspi: Portrait of a Medieval Jewish Intellectual.” *Studies in Medieval Jewish History and Literature*, ed. I. Twersky. Cambridge, Mass., 1979, 231–57.
Waltke, B. K., and O’Connor, M.
An Introduction to Biblical Hebrew Syntax. Winona Lake, Ind., 1990.
Waxman, M.
A History of Jewish Literature from the Close of the Bible to Our Own Days. New York, 1939–41.
Weinberg, B.
A History of Literary Criticism in the Italian Renaissance. Chicago, 1961.
Weinberg, J.
“Azariah de’ Rossi and Septuagint Traditions.” *Italia* V/1–2 (1985) 7–35.
———.
“Azariah de’ Rossi: Towards a Reappraisal of the Last Years of His Life.” *Annali della scuola normale superiore di Pisa* 8, 2 (1978) 493–511.
Werner, E., and Sonne, I.
“The Philosophy and Theory of Music in Judeo-Arabic Literature.” *HUCA* 16 (1941) 251–319; 17 (1942–43) 511–73.
Yahalom, J.
“Re’šitah šel Haššeqila Hammeduyyeqet Bešira Ha‘ibrit.” *Lešonenu* 47/1 (1982–83) 25–61.
———.
Sepat Haššir šel Happiyyuṭ Ha’ereṣ Yisra’eli Haqqadum [Poetic Language in the Early Piyyuṭ]. Jerusalem, 1985.
Yellin, D.
Torat Haššira Hasseparadit [Introduction to the Hebrew Poetry of the Spanish Period]. Jerusalem. 1978.
Zafrani, H.
Poésie juive en Occident Musulman. Paris, 1977.
Zinberg, I.
A History of Jewish Literature. Vol. I, Philadelphia, 1972; vol. IV, Cincinnati and New York, 1974.
Zohari, M.
“R. Moše ’ibn ‘Ezra’ Keḥoqer Hammiqra’.” In *Bikkurê ‘Eṭ*. Jerusalem, 1975, part 1: 135–40. (A slightly different version was published in *Beth Mikra* 6 [1961] 32–38.)
Zucker, M.
“Fragments of the *Kitāb Taḥṣīl al-Sharā’i‘ al-Samā‘iyah*.” *Tarbiz* 41 (1971–72) 373–410.

GENERAL INDEX

Abraham, as preserver of Hebrew language, 22
Abravanel, Don Isaac, 4, 10, 34, 100*n*3, 119–133, 165; connection between prophecy and poetry in, 49; definition of *šir* according to, 45; distinctions of *mašal* according to, 34–35; position of on figurative language as poetry, 49; types of poems according to, 45, 145
Accents, 155, 156; masoretic, 9
Accentual meter, 11, 14
Acquisition of human perfection, 154
Active melodies, 155–156
Adam, as inventor of poetry, 165
Adjectives, use of with and without nouns, 24
Advocate, in *The Kuzari*, 61, 62–66, 165
'Al Tehi Ka'aboteka, 108
'Al tiqre, 114*n*2
Al-Andalus, 10, 20; discussion of Hebrew language in, 21
Al-Farabi, 26
Al-Ḥariri, 18, 19
Al-Ḥarizi, Judah, 18, 39; discussion of poetry by , 38
Al-Jurjani, 27
Al-Mansuj al-mushajjar, 37
Allegorical discourse, 32, 89
Allegorical intepretation, 6, 34; of Song of Songs, 47
Allegorical method of poetic interpretation, 9
Allegory, 7, 137; philosophical, 5; use of, 120
Allemanno, Yoḥanan, 139–40; and definitions of *šir*, 34
Allusion, biblical, 23, 24, 118*n*8
Alter, Robert, criticism of Lowth's categories by, 14
Amaziah, tombstone of, 117, 167
Anaphora, 78–79
Andalusian influence on biblical poetry, 11
Antithesis (*Muṭābaqa*), 76–77
Antithetic parallelism, 14
Arab supremacy, doctrine of, 17
Arabic: connection of to Hebrew, 21–22; Hebrew, and Aramaic, connections between, 59–60; influence of in Christian Spain, 20; as less favorable than Hebrew, 20; medieval, 3; speakers of, 22. See also *'Arabiyya*
Arabic culture, 26
Arabic language, ambivalence toward, 20
Arabic literary theory, 30; Greek influence on, 53*n*1
Arabic meter in Hebrew poetry, 26, 114*n*3
Arabic metrical system, 66*n*5
Arabic models of rhetoric, 25
Arabic poetic style, 10
Arabic poetic theory, influence of, 10
Arabic poetics, 67–68
Arabic poetry, as best poetry, 17
Arabic rhetoric, 15, 19
Arabic rhetorical style, in Bible, 52*n*23
Arabic-style poetry, 33
'Arabiyya, 17, 21, 22, 173; effect of on Jewish intellectual development, 23
Aramaic, Arabic, and Hebrew: connections between, 59–60; knowledge of, 21, 22; rationale for use of, 110; as spoken by exiles from Babylonia, 70
Aramaisms, 171
Arameans (speakers of Aramaic), 22
Archivolti, Samuel, 31, 32, 39, 42, 154–159; four discourses of, 32–33
Aristotelian formulation, 26
Aristotle: essence of poetry for, 124; last letters of poems discussed by, 94*n*10
Armonia (*harmoniae*), 161
Arrangement of notes, 161
'Arugat Habbosem (The Bed of Spices), 67, 154–159
'Ašer (relative pronoun), 15
Ashkenaz communities, Hebrew in, 20–21
Assonance, 15
'Atbaš, 95, 96*n*6
Augustine, 9

INDEX TO BIBLICAL AND RABBINIC PASSAGES

ADELE BERLIN is Professor of Hebrew and Director of the Meyerhoff Center for Jewish Studies at the University of Maryland, College Park. Her specialty is biblical literature, and she has written extensively on the use of literary theory in interpreting the Bible.